THE TWEED RING

William the Conqueror Seizing the Reins of Power; To the Victors Belong the Spoils; caricature by Frank Bellew of Boss Tweed; courtesy of the New-York Historical Society, New York City

THE TWEED RING

ALEXANDER B. CALLOW, Jr.

OXFORD UNIVERSITY PRESS

LONDON OXFORD NEW YORK

OXFORD UNIVERSITY PRESS

London Oxford New York
Glasgow Toronto Melbourne Wellington
Cape Town Ibadan Nairobi Dar es Salaam Lusaka Addis Ababa
Delhi Bombay Calcutta Madras Karachi Lahore Dacca
Kuala Lumpur Singapore Hong Kong Tokyo

Library of Congress Catalogue Card Number: 66-24440
First published by Oxford University Press, New York, 1966
First issued as an Oxford University Press paperback, 1969
This reprint, 1975
Printed in the United States of America

TO LAWRENCE KINNAIRD

Historian, Teacher, Friend

PREFACE

The Tweed Ring, a political phenomenon of its time, made its appearance after the Civil War. From 1866 to 1871, it plundered the City of New York with such precision that it has received the singular distinction of being labeled the model of civic corruption in American municipal history. William Marcy Tweed and his colleagues, Peter Barr Sweeny, A. Oakey Hall, and Richard Connolly, built and masterminded a political organization which dominated both city and state politics. And yet, surprisingly, the Tweed Ring has never been the subject of a serious work. When it has received attention in the Sunday supplements and magazine articles, or in a chapter or two from biographers, political scientists, and historians dealing with other topics, the more sensational aspects of its history have been emphasized. The purpose of this work is to deal with the history of the Ring in a more comprehensive fashion. It is, then, a study of a political machine—the story of how the Tweed Ring with its control of Tammany Hall, patronage, the State legislature, the immigrant, the courts, the police, and organized crime, created the first modern city machine in New York City, the model for later city bosses of New York.

No history of the Tweed Ring could be written without the use of the materials located in the libraries of New York City. I wish to thank the staff of Special Collections, Columbia University Library, for their assistance in helping me to use the Edwin P. Kilroe Tammaniana Collection, a massive collection of nearly 60,000 items, indispensable to any study on New York politics. Thanks are due to the librarians of the Manuscript Room in New York Public Library, and particularly to the Local History Room of the same library, for their helpful guidance in making available their knowledge of the library's extensive pamphlet collection. I am also indebted to the librarians of the New-York Historical Society, one of the most gracious libraries in the land.

For permission to include portions of this book which first appeared as articles, I would like to thank *American Heritage*, the *New-York Historical Society Quarterly*, and the *New York Times Magazine*.

To Sheldon Meyer of Oxford University Press, I owe immeasurable gratitude for his patience, understanding, and good judgment. To my wife, Marie Eleanor Callow, I owe everything: time, patience, love, and understanding, all of which only deepens my awe of the female who can endure the disagreeable male when he is involved in that most difficult of indoor sports, writing a book. And, finally, I would like to acknowledge my two sons, Scott Alexander and Sean Michael, without whose delightful distractions this book would have been finished six months earlier.

A. B. C.

Santa Barbara
May 1966

CONTENTS

LIST OF ILLUSTRATIONS

PART ONE

THE COMING OF THE RING

1

"THAT IMPUDENT AUTOCRAT"

Skilled to pull wires, he baffles Nature's hope,
Who sure intended him to stretch a rope.

James Russell Lowell, "The Boss"

Americans may disagree over politics and foreign policy, but on one subject there may be consensus. If those who are knowledgeable about the American past were asked to name the most infamous city political machine in our history, it would be a safe bet that most, perhaps all, would cite the Tweed Ring of New York City—William Marcy Tweed, the "Elegant" Oakey Hall, Peter "Brains" Sweeny, and Richard "Slippery Dick" Connolly—who dominated New York politics from 1866 to 1871.

There have been many corrupt city machines more successful and certainly more ruthless than the Tweed Ring, yet to the American imagination, the Tweed Ring is still the most audacious and notorious of them all; indeed, the classic example of municipal fraud. The significance of the Ring, however, was neither in its reputation nor in the grandeur of its larcenies, but in its creation—a big-city political organization. The Tweed Ring produced the first real "city boss" in the United States.[1] Boss Tweed and his three indispensable colleagues became the architects of the first modern city machine in New York and one of the first in the country. The Tweed Ring, then, constituted both a critical episode in the history of a great city and an important chapter in the history of American urban politics. To see how the Ring operated, how it gained and sustained power, how its impact reflected the public's attitudes toward corruption, reform, and urban institutions, should illuminate to some degree those fascinating and gaudy years of post-Civil War America.

The Tweed Ring, like other big city political machines, was a distinct, peculiar American institution, created by clever men out of conditions indigenous not only to the city and state but to the nation as well. From the 1850's through the Civil War the momentum of economic, political, and social change generated problems that baffled and overwhelmed New Yorkers and set the stage for machine rule. In this period, old civic problems were magnified and new ones were created. Housing, employment, welfare services, sanitation, health, and law enforcement demanded responsible government from the city and the state. But expansion was so rapid in economic activity, population, and size that the city outgrew its government, leaving an obsolete city government hopelessly inadequate to cope with the problems of a modern urban-industrial society.

A rurally dominated State legislature either ignored the city's problems or met them only halfway, partly because it was jealous of its power and was reluctant to give the city the necessary authority to deal meaningfully with its growing pains, and partly because it was consumed with an anti-urban bias. Like many State legislatures in America, it was often blind to the creative potentiality of a great city. Instead, it tended to see New York City as a threat to agrarian values, the cesspool of vice, crime, disease, and filth, a refuge for moral cripples, shady politicians, and the irresponsible poor—foreign and domestic.

Well-meaning reformers further compounded the problems of responsible government. Dismayed and distrustful of rapid urbanization, many turned to history and learned the wrong lesson. They tried to mold government to accord with an ideal that typified an older, simpler, and less urban America. Their panacea called for a small, inexpensive, intensely economy-minded government, based on the proposition that the best government was the government that governed least and taxed less. To them responsible government existed when politics was replaced by the standards of business efficiency, when, as it were, politics was taken out of politics. Good government could be managed only by "good" people, the middle and upper classes—the affluent, the well-educated, the virtuous. This urge to escape the often harsh and brutal realities of mid-century America and to recapture the great days of Jeffersonian Arcadia, complicated the task of city government. The ideals of the past were irrelevant to the problems created by the burgeoning growth of the city. Above all, these ideals ignored a profound political, economic, and social change that was creating a new political elite and certainly a different political style that could adapt a political organization to meet at least some of the needs and provide some of the services that city government would and could not.

In effect, the era of the Tweed Ring reflected a transition phase of New York politics that spelled the end to the long rule of the middle and upper classes. The old ruling elite of the "best" people was gradually being evicted from power by a three-pronged attack: by the entrepreneur, demanding favors and a special license for his commercial and industrial interests; by the immigrant, who was seeking a firmer economic and political stake in American life; and by the professional politician, adept in trading jobs for the immigrant vote and special favors for the businessman's bribes.

In this struggle for power, the old middle and upper classes never really presented any formidable competition, primarily because they could not adjust to the political and social changes that were creating for them a new, strange urban world. Seeing themselves as the guardians of Protestant, Anglo-Saxon standards, they regarded the immigrant as a threat to the purity of the Anglo-Saxon stock, its religion, its values of self-reliance and independence. Thus the immigrant was alienated and made more accessible to the professional Tammany politician who understood some of his problems. The old elite's genteel tradition in manners, education, and culture, gave it a marked distaste for personal contact with the masses. Its conception of the proper politician as a gentleman devoted to disinterested public service, made for a disdain that underestimated the wit and ability of a son of a saloonkeeper or livery stable owner turned politician. The middle- and upper-class view of politics as a means to moralize society committed them to the tactics of moral exhortation, and obscured the practical, concrete aspects of organized politics.

Thus the professional politician of humble origin was given greater rein to do the things he knew the best. Steeped in the logistics of grass-roots practical politics, he organized the bleak, sprawling areas of the poor into political strongholds, and devoted himself to the mundane business of building and entrenching a political organization. In one sense, the old ruling classes beat themselves. In another sense, professional politicians, like Messrs. Tweed, Sweeny, Hall, and Connolly, outmaneuvered the old elite by exploiting the growing complexities of urban life.

Another phenomenon that helped make the Tweed Ring possible was a decay in business and political standards. The triumph of big business and the emergence of an age of enterprise coming in the aftermath of the Civil War, produced powerful industrialists like the oil, steel, railroad, traction, and utility kings, unprincipled speculators like Jim Fiske and Jay Gould, who made corrupt alliances with politicians to protect and enlarge their economic stake. Corruption became a national infection in the big cities, the State legislatures, the reconstruction governments in the South, and in the federal government itself, with the scandals of the Grant administration.

Along with this, there was a kind of moral twilight: Americans were tired of great causes. The crusade against slavery before the war, the crusade to maintain the Union during the war, and now the crusade to reconstruct North and South, was almost more than one could bear. Moreover, crusades breed cynicism. Bounty jumpers escaped the army, wartime contractors became millionaires, and now a few city politicians were taking their pickings.

Finally, there was the impact of the big city upon the public's interest in municipal politics. A big city like New York encouraged what could be called aggressive apathy toward city government. Who understood the intricacies, the enormous complications of municipal politics? City government seemed coldly impersonal, remote, a dull business, run by third-raters who could not make a living in a respectable profession. What really counted was not the shabby game of city politics but getting ahead. As the man said right after the Civil War, "You can see it in people's faces, you can feel it in the air, everybody and everything's goin' places." [2]

Out of all these developments emerged a man who by experience and ability was best able to manipulate them to his advantage. William Marcy Tweed had many of the attributes celebrated in post-Civil War America—energy, enterprise, enthusiasm for his work. If we forget for a moment his powers for mischief, we could liken him to a successful businessman of the era. The august *Journal of Commerce* admitted that his executive capacity was extraordinary. George Alfred Townsend said, "But for all, he is a powerful business man, always at work, never wearied out . . . stirring from morn till midnight, doing a great part of this work himself . . . and has gone on from grade to grade until he rules New York." [3] Of all his attributes, however, it was his talent for political organization that was the most outstanding.

William Tweed was a first-rate political manager, an intuitive leader of men, and in some ways, a consummate professional politician. It was his mastery of urban politics, abetted by the political astuteness of the other members of the Ring, that consolidated, centralized, and modernized politics in a way never seen before their time. Contrary to popular opinion, Tammany had never dominated New York politics *before* the Civil War. The Whigs and the Know-Nothings were fierce competition; in the nine years between 1834 and 1843 the Democrats and Whigs were equally balanced in political strength. If the Democrats managed to gain power from 1843 to the war, power was precariously held, always vulnerable to the enemies, Whig, Know-Nothing, and Republican.[4] But with the coming of the Tweed Ring the political face of New

York was changed. From the era of the Tweed Ring onward, the Democrats monopolized New York City politics. The Republican party, except for brief moments of glory—and then bolstered by dissident Democrats—was never a serious threat to the warriors of Tammany Hall. A good deal of the credit for this goes to the Tweed Ring who fashioned the classic architecture of Tammany. The Ring eventually fell, but its creation, a modernized city machine, has come down to our own day.

The Tweed Ring built its machine by capturing the four fortresses of power: Tammany Hall, City Hall, the Hall of Justice, and the state capitol. To the victors belonged the spoils—control of the Democratic party and city offices. An empire of patronage was created when 12,000 Tammany followers, who called themselves the Shiny Hat Brigade, were placed in every branch of city government.[5] The police, election officials, and criminals abided by the Ring's whims. Continuing the Tammany tactic of the 1840's, the immigrant was effectively wooed to the Tammany banner. Key executive posts were controlled: John Hoffman was Governor; Oakey Hall was Mayor; Richard Connolly, who manipulated city finances with the finesse of a shell-game shark, was Comptroller; and Tweed himself assumed several public and private positions in order to strengthen the Ring's influence in both politics and the business community. He maintained a firm hand over the city legislature as President of the Board of Supervisors; he controlled a rich source of patronage as Deputy Street Commissioner and as Commissioner of Public Works; he held executive positions in banks, railroads, gas, printing, and insurance companies, and was the third largest owner of real estate in New York. With the 1867 elections, he enlarged the power of the machine in the State legislature by becoming a State Senator, where he became a powerful influence over financial and legislative policy as chairman of the important State Finance Committee, and the leader of the so-called Black Horse Cavalry, a group of politicians of both parties who sold their votes for a price.

And climaxing it all, on election day the Ring mustered an

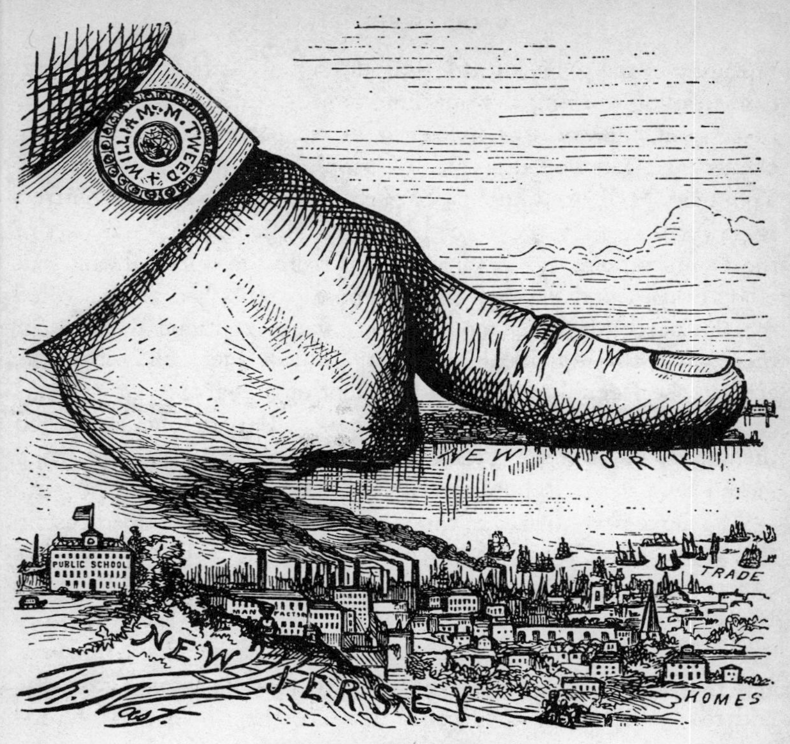

UNDER THE THUMB.

THE BOSS. "Well, what are you going to do about it?"

Cartoon by Thomas Nast; courtesy of the New-York Historical Society, New York City

army of renegades—barroom brawlers, thugs, ex-convicts, devoted followers, corrupt election officials—who voted early and often, stuffed ballot boxes, intimidated voters, and miscounted the votes. Masterminding the operation was the Boss himself, who enhanced his reputation by a simple question: "Well," he challenged the reformers, "what are you going to do about it?" [6]

The astonishing thing was that the Tweed Ring was successful despite the fact that at no time did it control a majority of all the voters in the city.[7] Part of its success came from intimidation and repeating at the polls, but the Ring did not always have to cheat. It is misleading to think that machine politics rested entirely on election fraud. For all the efficiency of its organization, the Ring needed and received the votes of people who were not a part of Tammany Hall. And here party partisanship was a staunch buttress to power. After all, the Tweed Ring's Tammany Hall was part of the Democratic party, and it got votes from those local Democrats who always voted for their party, whose parents had always voted for the party; local Democrats who would continue to vote for their party through ideals, habit, apathy, or the feeling that the enemy, the Republicans, should be kept out regardless of machine corruption. In the same era, Republicans in Philadelphia supported their party for the same reasons, even though the city was being sacked by a venal Republican city machine.

The fierce partisanship of the New York press also helped sustain the Ring. Until almost the very end, most of the Democratic papers minimized the corruption of the Ring, just as most of the Republican press underplayed the scandals of the Grant administration. In addition, small shopkeepers, big businessmen, lawyers, and judges, some of whom had no particular love for Tammany, realized nevertheless they could advance their own self-interests by exploiting the favors of Tammany; and others, in the same group, hated Tammany but were terrified of its power of punishment and did not dare vote against it.

One force, which added the final cohesive element to the Ring's organization, was the character of the Boss himself. Tweed brought a personal touch to the cold, steely world of urban politics, that matched his gifts as a political organizer. The Boss had charm, a personal magnetism that made many men admit, although reluctantly, that he was an immensely likable man. Although capable of erupting into violent outbursts, he was gay and congenial. He had a booming hearty personality that befitted his physique. For William Marcy Tweed looked like something that God hacked out with a dull axe. A craggy hulk of a man, he was nearly six feet tall and weighed almost 300 pounds. Everything about him was big; fists, shoulders, head (which sprouted receding reddish-brown hair, like weeds growing from a rock, carved into a mustache and closely cropped chin whiskers); eyes, blue and friendly; the diamond, which "glittered like a planet on his shirt front"; and his nose, a particularly rocky pinnacle. "His nose is half-Brougham, half-Roman," said one observer, "and a man with a nose of that sort is not a man to be trifled with." [8]

Tweed's sheer physical bulk awed most men into respect. His gift for making friends seemed to go beyond the politician's contrived approach and won the loyalty of some and suspended the suspicion of others. His crudeness and bluster were attractive to roughnecks of the political back alleys of New York, but he could also be suave. Years of being an inveterate clubman—at the rather plush Manhattan, the Americus, the Blossom, the Oriental—social contacts made in holding city offices, had polished him. In the Blossom Club, said a historian of New York clubs, "You will meet Tweed, with his large, grand, good-humored phiz and physique; but here, again, the will of a Roman slumbers under the suavity of a Parisian—for no man so well illustrates the Latin phrase, *Suaviter in modo, fortiter in re.*" [9]

Despite his reputation for vulgarity, he numbered friends in every walk of life. He knew Astor, Vanderbilt, and Stewart, Raymond of the *Times*, Bennett of the *Herald*, and Oswald Ottendorfer, an immensely influential German newspaperman. There were tales of drunken orgies on Sunday. If true, it could only suggest that he kept bad company, for Tweed neither drank nor smoked. Like many great scoundrels, he was a good family man, a dutiful husband, a devoted father, although the reformers complained that he carried devotion too far in providing his sons with important city jobs. His charities were legion—to the poor, the hospitals, the schools, the churches, the infirm. This is not to suggest that the proper image of Tweed should be that of a misunderstood Robin Hood, but rather that Tweed was more than the one-dimensional picture of pure evil painted by his critics. He was a rogue, to be sure, but a jolly one at least and a refreshing interlude before his solemn successors—the Kellys, the Crockers, the Murphys, the grim, silent ones.

His talents as an organizer, his gruff charm, his knack of making friends, had a personal rather than a mass appeal. Although accused of being a demagogue, Boss Tweed was not a Huey Long, mesmerizing the rank and file from the public platform. On the many occasions he had to speak—before a torchlight parade in Tweed Plaza, in the State Senate, or at a Tammany Hall Fourth of July celebration—there was no blazing eye or electrifying voice, only a painfully uneasy man whose sputtering delivery made him at times incoherent.

Lack of talent to bewitch the crowd was more than compensated for by one enduring quality, a particular kind of honesty. As Tweed himself identified it: "I challenge any politician in New York to point out one instance where I have broken my word." [10] Unlike his colleague, Slippery Dick Connolly, the Boss could be counted on; a promise was a bond. If, for example, he cut a contractor in on thousands of dollars of graft, the contractor knew Tweed would see to it that he got his money. In his own way, Boss Tweed was honorable. The *New York Telegram*, pondering this strange integrity of the political underworld, guessed that this was the "secret cause" of his great strength.[11] On the day of Tweed's death his secretary tried to sum up, not altogether successfully, this quality in Tweed's character by comparing him to the new leader of Tammany, "Honest" John Kelly. "Tweed was not an honest politician, but a level one," he said. "Kelly is honest but not level." [12]

In the beginning, at least, Tweed did not fit the usual stereotype of a Tammany politician—he was neither Irish, Catholic, nor a ragged slum boy. He was born on April 3, 1823, from a Protestant, third-generation Scottish family. His home at No. 1 Cherry Hill, midway between the East River and City Hall, was a quiet, respectable middle-class neighborhood. His father, "a clever, decent old gentleman," was a solid middle-class manufacturer of chairs, who also had an interest in a brushmaking firm. His mother adored her little boy, and, it was said, spoiled him.[13]

At first Tweed seemed destined for a successful career in business. He studied bookkeeping and joined the brushmaking concern in which his father owned stock. A remarkable executive and organizing ability soon became evident, and within two years he was made a member of the company. He was just nineteen, a strapping young man with fine dark hair and clear blue eyes, almost good-looking. Already he had developed those traits that would be so valuable in later years: amiability, the big smile, an extraordinary memory for faces and names, and financial acumen. But apparently he found the business world too bland.

For every red-blooded young man of Tweed's day who longed for excitement that would relieve the long, boring hours spent as a bookkeeper, clerk, or factory-hand, membership in the New York volunteer firemen offered fun, companionship, danger, and—for those with a taste for it—politics. In 1848 Tweed joined John J. Reilly, a State Assemblyman, and his friends who were organizing a fire company. It was Tweed who suggested the name of the company: the Americus Engine Company, Number 6. It was Tweed who gave it its symbol—a snarling red tiger—a symbol that Thomas Nast, the cartoonist, was later to attach to Tammany Hall. It was Tweed who, as foreman in 1849, became a dashing hero with his brilliant red flannel shirt and white firecoat, and made No. 6, now called the Big Six, into one of the famous fire companies of the day, rivaling other such proud names as the White Ghost, Dry Bones, and Old Junk. And it was the Big Six that gave Tweed his stepping-stone into politics.

New York fire companies, equalitarian, clannish, intensely loyal, were social as well as political organizations. Tweed led an unusually cohesive company of seventy-five men, who could be counted on to vote the Tweed scriptures on issues and candidates, and lend a bully's hand on election day. Each of the partisan seventy-five could himself influence the votes of his family or friends. More were forthcoming from his fame as a fireman. All this, plus Tweed's extensive knowledge of his neighborhood and the people in it, made him important to the politicians of the Seventh Ward. Virtue was rewarded. In 1850 he ran as Democratic candidate for assistant Alderman and was beaten by only a slim margin. In the following year he was nominated for Alderman and won.

As the Honorable William Tweed, he began to learn his trade, for the chambers of the Aldermen was an excellent school in practical politics. Armed with powers over patronage, the city purse, and city improvements, Tweed could consolidate and build a following in the Seventh Ward, perform favors for businessmen and politicians alike, and generally extend his position in the Democratic party. For example, the Alderman appointed the police of his ward, from patrolman to precinct commander. He granted licenses to saloons and franchises to streetcar lines and ferries, and had the power to override the Mayor's veto if he disapproved. He sat as a Justice in the Mayor's Court which tried all prisoners accused of violations at the polls, and some of the accused might include some overenthusiastic voters from his own ward or the ward of a friend.

If the Board of Aldermen gave an ambitious politician an opportunity to learn some of the fundamentals of urban politics, it also provided basic training in the arts of graft. The Aldermen had a long history of corruption in New York, or as Tweed once described it, "There never was a time when you couldn't buy the Board of Aldermen." [14] Tweed saw his opportunities and took them. He joined a band of political buccaneers whose wholesale corruption earned them the title of the Forty Thieves. His experience with the Forty Thieves was a portent of things to come, for it was as an Alderman that Tweed learned some of the techniques of corruption that would be used in even a grander fashion when the Tweed Ring was formed thirteen years later.

The Aldermen had the power to grant franchises that yielded the greatest amount of graft. The method was simply to sell them to the highest bidder. Schemes involving franchises for the Third Avenue Railroad, the Gansevoort Market property, and the Broadway streetcar line brought in thousands of dollars in graft.[15]

Also profitable were city improvements. For example, contracts were given to businessmen for the paving, widening, or extending of city streets, or for building or repairing public offices. The contractors presented padded bills, a percentage of which was split among the Aldermen. A technique of legislative extortion known as "strike" legislation, or "cinch" bills was an added source of income. Legislation was proposed that caused severe hardship to merchants, bankers, insurance companies. To protect their interests, businessmen bribed the Aldermen to kill the legislation. For example, Tweed's colleague, the Honorable Wesley Smith, presented a bill that would save the city money by lowering the fees of the Coroner. Then, in a procedure known as "ringing the bell," Smith called on the Coroner and was reported to have said, "Give me $250 and I'll kill the resolution in committee." The bribe was paid and, as one writer put it, "The bell no longer rang—for the Coroner." [16]

As an Alderman, Tweed served his apprenticeship in politics. He had made money and important friends, but not enough; he had built a local following, but not strong enough to buttress a play for higher stakes. To get what he wanted, he needed more gilt on his political credentials. He decided to run for Congress in 1852, while still serving his term as Alderman.

Tweed spent two unhappy, singularly undistinguished years in the House of Representatives. He disliked the formal nature of Washington, particularly the tradition of merely tolerating first-term Congressmen. In Washington he was nothing. He was assigned to only one committee, the rather unprestigious Committee on Invalid Pensions. He never engaged in Congressional debates. He made only one speech. It was an elegant piece of "platitudes in stained glass attitudes" in favor of the Kansas and Nebraska bill and was intended for home consumption. Nor did he have any ambitions to go on to the United States Senate. He once told a reporter, "If I wanted to go to the Senate, I'd go; but what for? I can't talk, and I know it. As to spending my time in hearing a lot of snoozers discuss the tariff and the particulars of a contract to carry the mails from Paducah to Schoharie, I don't think I'm doing that just now." [17]

At the conclusion of the Thirty-third Congress he did not want to succeed himself in Congress. Disgusted with life in Washington, he decided to resume his promising career in New York. Instead, he found that his luck, his fortune, and New York had changed. He had lived too well in Washington and was almost penniless. His Congressional career, for what it was, had not advanced his reputation, only buried it—New York had forgotten him. He had lost touch with New York politics and, worst of all, New York politicians had lost interest in him. Moreover, Tammany Hall was in unfriendly hands as the city was suffering the painful spasm of the nativistic movement.

Tweed ran again for Alderman, only to be beaten by the Know-Nothings, the anti-Catholic, anti-immigrant nativist party which was then at the peak of its power. He fought them so well, however, that he became known as the champion of the foreign element, which helped him later, but not in the mid-'fifties. In desperation he accepted an appointment as School Commissioner in 1855, for there were still enough friends and unpaid political debts to muster a dole for the ex-Congressman. But this was offset by a disaster that seemed to signal the end of his political career. He lost control of his own Seventh Ward, a profound humiliation for a professional politician like William Tweed. Alone and deserted, this thirty-one-year-old political hack had come home to New York and failure.

2

THE TRIUMPH OF TWEED

His pockets make a jingling sound,
It is his bunch of "private" keys
That fit the Public Treasuries.

Oliver Herford, "The Boss's Keys"

In Tammany Hall, there have been at least two classic ways to rise to political power. One is through attrition, patience, and some ability: long, steady service to the Hall, dedication to party loyalty, bone-hard work on the many and often dreary details of party work, an ability for leadership, and especially the knack to harness hostile spirits to the cause and to cajole laggards to greater devotion. The other way is through aggression, precise timing, and some luck. Here the potential chieftain gains power by destroying the existing leader. But this takes preparation and sure political instinct. The new leader must first make the "right" friends. He must gain a power position through his ward or through a strong political office, or both. He must exploit the political and economic issues that can enhance his bid for power. Then at the right moment he must toss his political career into the breach. He must fight. He must not only rise up and smite the leader but he must be canny enough, lucky enough, to seize the spoils of victory and consolidate his power in the Hall. This is the road William Marcy Tweed traveled. It was a rocky, dangerous road because his opponent, Fernando Wood, the leading figure in Tammany Hall, was one of the most adept political operators of the day.

Elected Mayor of New York three times, 1854, 1856, and 1859, Wood was one of the most powerful politicians in New York. Tall and slender, he was a man of immense charm, with an array of friends ranging from business executives to day laborers. John Bigelow called him the handsomest and most brilliant man he had ever met, and the most corrupt man who ever sat in the Mayor's chair.[1]

What Bigelow might have added was that Fernando Wood and his organization were the precursors of the Tweed Ring, that Wood was, in a very real sense, Tweed's mentor, although they disliked each other intensely. E. L. Godkin astutely saw this when he said that Wood was the Tweed Ring's Julius Caesar and Tweed its Augustus.[2] Indeed, it has been said that "it was in Wood's school that most of the Tammany leaders of the next generation learned their politics."[3] Wood demonstrated how power could be centralized. As the model of craftiness in government, he was a masterful exponent of applying corrupt practices. His methods were observed by Tweed and he used them later with even more success. Sometimes Tweed learned his lessons the hard way. "I never yet went to get a corner lot," he said, "that I didn't find Wood had got in ahead of me."[4]

There was much to be learned from Wood's techniques in building an organization. His position as Mayor was an excellent position to build patronage and instill party discipline. He consolidated his organization by making the Police Department his creature and, at the same time, forming a close relationship with the underworld. He sold public offices, franchises, and city contracts to the highest bidder. To enlarge the immigrant vote, Wood established a naturalization mill for newly arrived aliens. At election time, he was an expert in strategically placing "repeaters" in the closely contested election districts.

If Wood had one capital virtue as a political thief it was duplicity. He excelled as the pirate posing as the Puritan, a technique, incidentally, Tweed never learned. He began his first administration as a supposed reformer, and many New Yorkers believed his extravagant promises to cleanse municipal politics. To camouflage his adventures in graft and his co-operation with the criminal world, he won the support and gratitude of the respectable gentry by backing important civic projects, a tactic that Tweed did borrow. Who but a high-minded man would recommend the establishment of a municipal university and a free academy for young women? Wood ingratiated himself further by using his influence to help create Central Park.[5] Later, when charges of corruption were made, he reacted with wide-eyed innocence, and allayed the suspicions of many by pointing to his support for the university and Central Park as the proof of his honesty and civic benevolence. The politician Charles Halpine summed it up in a verse:

> The royal prince who reigns in hell
> Has been maligned in various matters,
> And now would have the people tell
> How silly they regard such clatters.
> He asks your votes; 'tis not for pelf,
> But to rebuke all saints and sages
> Who say the archangels and himself
> Have not been cronies through all ages.[6]

Fernando Wood rather than Tweed might have become the first city boss in New York, but he failed in what Tweed eventually accomplished, unifying the party and dominating Tammany Hall. Throughout most of the violent decade of the 1850's, Tammany was in a turmoil of bitter factional fights. The slavery issue split and severely weakened the party. The City Reform party and the Know-Nothing party cut into party ranks, and siphoned off dissident Democrats. Political blood was shed in a party war between the Hardshells and Softshells, as they fought over power, patronage, and the control of the meeting place itself.

Disunity was the bane of Wood's ambitions, but it was a boon for Tweed. A fractured party diffused authority and opened up an avenue to power for an aspiring politician skillful enough to exploit the situation. Factionalism weakened the hold of the old Democratic mighties and ripened Tammany Hall for dominance by a single man and his machine. It was Tweed's great opportunity. The man who could heal the party's wounds and dispose of Fernando Wood stood a very good chance of emerging as its undisputed boss.

Tweed's success began, ironically, with his rival's genius for duplicity. Unlike Tweed, Wood never inspired complete trust and loyalty in his followers, and for good reason: he exacted high fees for offices sold to his supporters, and then proceeded to swindle them, leaving behind a hard core of Wood-haters Tweed could use later.[7] It was in Wood's relations with the immigrants and Know-Nothings, however, that deceit proved to be Wood's downfall and Tweed's triumph.

Like any good Tammany politician, Wood tried vigorously to win the immigrant vote, the bedrock of Tammany support. But the 1850's were troubled times, especially for the Catholic-Irish immigrant, who was disorganized, bewildered, and frustrated politically by the bigotry of the Know-Nothing nativist movement. His chances of finding a job diminished; he became an object of derision; his character and religion were assailed by the nativist Know-Nothing party's vicious hate campaign. If the immigrant vote was important, Fernando Wood reasoned that so indeed was the support of the Know-Nothings. Wood tried a finesse: he joined the anti-immigrant Know-Nothing party.[8] It was a capital error in judgment. When Wood's relation with the nativists became publicized, the immigrants were appalled and Tammany was in danger of losing its traditional support by the newcomer. For Tweed it was a stroke of good luck, for it opened a path to political power. But the time was not yet ripe. He needed power and a continuing base for that power which could sustain his drive to win not only the battle but the war itself. Tweed threw himself back into Seventh Ward politics, exercised his gruff, easy charm, and made friends. His chance came in 1857.

Once again, Wood provided a helping hand. During his second administration, beginning in 1856, Wood became bolder in his operations, especially in his manipulation of the police force. Up came the cry for reform. The Republican-controlled State legislature responded with vigor. It shortened Wood's term by half, created the metropolitan police force under a state board, and transferred numerous municipal functions to other authorities. Ironically, the legislature made it easier for Tweed.

Even more important, 1857 was the year William Tweed became a member of the Board of Supervisors. At the time, few would guess that this was a major elevation, because up to 1857 the position of Supervisor was of relatively minor importance. It was Tweed's good luck that the State legislature, obsessed by the spirit of reform (and not unmindful of how reform could enhance Republicans in a Democratic-dominated city), decided to make the Board bipartisan. In 1857 the State legislature increased the power, the independence, and the membership of the Supervisors to make it the legislative organization for the county. The Mayor and Recorder were no longer to sit as members as they had since 1787, when the Board was first created. The Board itself was enlarged to twelve men—six Democrats and six Republicans. This change to a bipartisan board was hailed as a great reform measure. It was thought that six Republicans could surely stifle any scheme of the infamous city Democrats. It turned out to be a crushing irony, for what the reformers did was to "reform" the Board of Supervisors into what one man called "a city politician's paradise."

In the first place, it did not fundamentally handicap the Democratic party in New York. The party could still carefully select its candidates for the Board *before* presenting them to the public. Moreover, it tended to choose men who were little known outside their own wards, but who were loyal party hacks who would do as they were told. In the second place, by enlarging the Board's power it also enlarged its opportunity for corruption, for the Supervisors would now audit county expenditures, appoint Inspectors of Elections, and supervise public improvements, taxation, and various city departments. More important, with such critical powers over appointments of Election Inspectors and expenditure of city money, one weak link in the Republican chain of six could make reform a mockery.

It was a situation ready-made for a man with the talents of Tweed. He simply made the Supervisors his own creature, a many-headed creature, which at once allowed him to plunder, to build a political fortress from which he could strike at Fernando Wood, and to muster a following by dispensing the "right" favors to the "right" people. For the next thirteen years, from 1857 to 1870, Tweed was a Supervisor and four times the Board's president, which gave him further "opportunities," for it meant he sat on committees handling annual taxes and planning, a new courthouse and civil courts, and later he also served as chairman of the committee on county officers. As a Supervisor he was able to hold the Board under his control most of the time and have it go along with his schemes.[9] Meetings were held at irregular hours, often in private, to keep the public ignorant of the Board's proceedings. A Republican Supervisor could always be reached by bribery; first it was Peter P. Voorhis, a coal dealer and a scamp; later it was Henry Smith, the personification of a "Tammany Republican." On the few occasions when a maverick or an honest Supervisor tried to make trouble, Tweed had devices to deal with him. On one such occasion, Supervisor Smith Ely, Jr., later Mayor of New York, had been talking to the newspapers and the reform-minded Citizens' Association about possible transactions in graft among the Supervisors. The day of an important meeting arrived, but Ely was told by the clerk that no meeting was to be held. He went home. At four o'clock that afternoon Tweed, with the troublesome Ely safely out of the way, held the meeting which passed some expensive appropriations and a tax-levy involving several millions of dollars.[10] And that was that.

Tweed created the machinery for graft almost immediately by forming a Supervisor's ring, one of several profitable combines that preceded the forming of the notorious Tweed Ring itself. Nobody can explain the operation better than the Boss himself, as he did years after his downfall to an investigating committee from the Board of Aldermen.

> Mr. John Briggs, Mr. Walter Roche and myself used to meet together nearly every day, at my office in 95 Duane Street; . . . we were all members of the various committees before which bills were brought and all knew the bills before the different committees, and we agreed what bill we would go for; there was hardly a time when our three votes wouldn't carry most anything. . . . We passed bills excessive in amount. . . . Pretty nearly every person who had business with the Board of Supervisors, or furnished the county with supplies, had a friend in the Board of Supervisors, and generally some one member of that Ring; and through that one they were talked to; and the result was their bills were sent in and passed, and the percentages were paid on the bills, sometimes to one man, sometimes to another.[11]

Thus Tweed and friends began a systematic course of lobbying before the Supervisors, demanding of claimants a 15 per cent tribute.[12] Totally lacking the sophistication of later-day graft, it was simple, it was blatant—above all, it worked. Membership in the Ring changed through the years. In 1864, the Republican Henry Smith was added; in 1865, John Fox; in 1866, James Hayes; in 1869, Andrew J. Bleakley and Isaac J. Oliver; although, Tweed said, "They didn't know all that was going on. . . . They didn't know what bills were being passed and what were not; they only knew they got their percentages once in a while." [13]

If there was one scheme that best reflected the operations of the Supervisors' Ring, it was when Tweed capitalized on the conversion of Harlem Hall into a church. Using his position as a member of the Supervisors' Committee on Armories, he bought 300 of the Hall's benches for five dollars each, seventeen of which he sold at cost to a friend. The trick came with the remaining benches. They were sold to furnish the county armories not at even double or triple their price, but for $600 apiece! The Supervisors approved the sale, of course. It was all in a day's work. It cost the taxpayers of New York $169,800.[14]

When right-minded citizens began to feel there was something terribly wrong with the Board of Supervisors and suggested an investigation, Tweed was hurt, and answered indignantly, "We are not answerable for the conduct of those who, either from malice or because they are irretrievably bad, or because they desire to occupy the offices which we now hold, circulate stories calculated to injure those among us who are known to be among the best and firmest of our citizens." [15]

If profitable action began in 1857, so did Tweed's increased political power. In the roll of the Union Democratic Republican General Committee, Tweed's name was last on the list of leaders of the Seventh Ward in 1857; it was first in 1858. Tweed had toppled the prominent "shoulder-hitter" Isaiah Rynders from leadership.[16] More important, he was laying the foundation of the future Ring by promoting friends to office: by 1858 George Barnard was Recorder; Peter "Brains" Sweeny was District Attorney; and Richard "Slippery Dick" Connolly was County Clerk. Unlike Wood, Tweed was building his following not by exacting fees for political promotion, but by friendship, the firm cement of the personal favor; slowly and cautiously Tweed was winning over the most potent powers of Tammany, the ward leaders: Peter Sweeny of the Twentieth, John Roche of the Sixth, Matthew Brennan of the Fourth, and Richard Connolly, who was on the executive committee of the Twenty-first. Their political help would prove most important in the coming showdown with Wood and his powerful Mozart Hall.

Eighteen fifty-nine was a treacherous year for a showdown. While Wood had failed to dominate the city Democrats, he was still strong enough to defy Tammany, bolt the Hall, and create a rival Democratic organization called the Mozart Hall Democracy. In ordinary times, this might have been the moment for Tweed to make his bid for power. But the city seethed with the troubles that were bringing the country to the brink of civil war. Tammany Hall was badly split. The issue was forced, however, when Mozart Hall nominated Wood for Mayor. There was one tactic Tweed could use to attack Wood: the authority of the Supervisors to appoint Election Inspectors. Before the Supervisors met, Tweed and the Democrats on the Board conferred at the home of one of their colleagues, John R. Briggs. Isaac Fowler, a Supervisor and a powerful Tammany brave, arrived in top hat and carriage, took Tweed aside, whispered to him, and departed. Tweed informed the others that Fowler had given him $2500 to persuade Peter P. Voorhis, a Republican Supervisor, to be absent when the Supervisors appointed the election officials.

The scheme worked. Voorhis lived up to the bargain, and Tweed was able to draw up a list from which 609 officials were chosen. Not surprisingly, nearly 550 were Democrats. Not surprisingly either, gamblers, saloon-keepers, and thugs were among those appointed election officials. But astonishingly, Fernando Wood won the election. The Tammanyites were still divided, and Wood with his elegant ways was able to get the support of most of the middle class and gentry, and his old alliance with the underworld provided repeaters and intimidation at the polls. It was slavery, however, the crucial issue of the period, that carried the day for Wood. He won most of the Southern sympathizers, from commercial men to workingmen.

Eighteen years later, Tweed gave a somewhat different version of the motives that led to the bribing of that unreliable Republican, Peter Voorhis. It gave him a chance to be a political philosopher.

Q. Why was it so important that the appointment of the Inspectors of Election should be in the hands of one political party? . . .

A. So as the other side shouldn't cheat us. . . .

Q. Do I understand you to say that this combination was made to appoint the Inspectors with a view of controlling the elections?

A. Oh, no, sir; with a view to have justice done on our side of the question.

Q. Then why the bribing? Why the manipulation in the selection of the Inspectors?

Said Tweed after some evasion: "They were to be our friends; to see that our men were allowed to vote, and see that everything was done fair, so far as we were concerned."

Q. Did it occur to you at that time, that the six supervisors who were paying $2,500, or who were cognizant of $2,500 being paid—that they possibly might not be safe parties to select Inspectors of Election?
A. Oh, no; I don't think men are governed in those matters by correct ideas of what should be between man and man; I have never known a party man that wouldn't take advantage of such a circumstance.[17]

Eighteen sixty-one was the year to beat Wood. The first task was to cleanse the Hall's reputation for bigotry, given it by Wood's dealings with the Know-Nothing party. The opportunity to do so was presented by Isaac Fowler, Grand Sachem of Tammany as well as Postmaster, who had stolen $150,000 worth of postal receipts. Fowler had served the party well and Tammany looked after its own. A United States Marshal, Isaiah Rynders, Tammany Hall to the bone and a former thug, went to Fowler's hotel to arrest him, but stopped first at the bar, drank several whiskies, announced often and loudly what his mission was. By the time he reached the Postmaster's room, Fowler had vanished. With Fowler gone, Tweed made his move. Exerting all his influence, he was successful in making James Conner the next Grand Sachem. By Tammany standards, Conner was eminently respectable: he was Irish, Catholic, and well-liked. Thus the Hall was back into safe hands, and Tweed could emerge as the champion of Tammany's honor, by organizing efforts to rally and win back the disillusioned Catholics and immigrants.

The second problem was to beat Wood himself. Recognizing the rising power of Tweed, Wood slyly came forward with a compromise proposal couched in the persuasive terms of party harmony. Mozart would call off the war with Tammany, if Tammany in turn would give its backing to Wood for Mayor. It was an adroit tactic: Tweed's acceptance would have actually signaled his surrender, for if Wood regained the mayor's office, he would be in a formidable position to destroy Tweed politically. While Tweed refused, he did make a sensible compromise regarding candidates for the State legislature and some unimportant city offices. He agreed that both Tammany and Mozart would share in offering candidates for these offices. Compromise on this level was realistic and necessary, because Wood's Mozart Hall was powerful enough in 1861 to challenge Tammany. The crux of the fight, however, lay in who would win the city- and county-wide offices. Here Tweed prepared for an all-out battle. He was "determined that Wood should be destroyed, even if it meant the sacrifice of every man on the regular Democratic city and county tickets. . . ." [18]

To help the cause, Tweed decided to run himself. In the light of Tweed's success with the Forty Thieves and his manipulation of the Supervisors, it is ironic, perhaps, that he ran for Sheriff. The contest was the closest in any three-corner race in the history of New York City up to that time. George Opdyke nosed out the Tammany nominee, C. Godfrey Gunther, and James Lynch beat Tweed for Sheriff. Despite his own defeat, it was a resounding victory for William Marcy Tweed, because the ultimate goal was achieved. Fernando Wood was beaten at the polls.

Though Tweed had managed to eliminate his chief rival to power, the full measure of his victory lay in patching the broken Tammany. The break between Tammany and Mozart continued; but Tweed, and especially his colleague, Peter Sweeny, applied political first aid. Astutely they wooed Wood supporters away with promises of patronage. Anti-Wood followers were likewise rewarded. The former antagonisms began to die. The party started to heal.

Elijah F. Purdy, a banker of considerable wealth, represented the kind of political friend who could advance Tweed's interests. In 1861, when Wood lay politically wounded, Purdy, a veteran of many a Tammany war, used his influence to help secure the election of Tweed as chairman of the New York County Democratic

Central Committee. If election to the Supervisors was a step toward power, this was a giant stride. It put Tweed on the way to the capture of the biggest and last obstacle to dominance of New York City politics, Tammany Hall itself. On the surface, however, this was not apparent in 1861. The chairman of the New York County Democratic Central Committee had seldom held a key place in the leadership of the Hall; usually he was the figurehead for stronger, more important forces. But Tweed smashed precedent. He dominated the Central Committee. He made the chairmanship into what it had not been before—a dynamic political power.

From 1861 to 1863 it became evident to Democratic leaders that Tweed had a great flair for leadership and executive ability, although his methods were not always subtle or gentle. His tactics of getting a motion carried were devastatingly simple. He would declare the measure passed without asking for any negative votes, "with a significantly admonishing glance at the opposing side." [19] On another occasion, he demonstrated the vigor of his leadership at a Tammany nominating convention, when he ruled that a friend had been nominated unanimously for judge, although the hall echoed with the enraged "Noes" of some thirty delegates. When the dissenters tried to nominate another man, Tweed struck back with a tactic Tammany had used thirty years before against the rebellious "Loco-Focos." He had the lights turned out.[20] Only this time it worked.

By 1863 Fernando Wood, faced with a much more united Tammany, could not run for Mayor, and wisely accepted a compromise to run for Congress. When Wood later tried to make a comeback, thanks to Tweed he no longer had the strength. There is no better testimony to Tweed's final triumph over Fernando Wood than the fact that in 1867 when Bagley, Wood's candidate, opposed Tweed for the State Senate, he received exactly nine votes![21] Thus for a while quiet was restored in the ranks of the Democrats. But it was not a peaceful quiet. Said one writer, "It resembled too closely that which in a menagerie follows the hour of feeding. . . . The hungry politicians, instead of clutching at each other's throats, now crunched and munched their spoils with greedy relish . . . their appetite for plunder soon revived, and, to satisfy it, their leaders were forced to make new drains upon the public purse."[22] Hungriest of all was William Marcy Tweed.

Tweed consolidated his position on January 1, 1863, when he was made chairman of the General Committee of Tammany Hall. This was achieved largely through the efforts of Sweeny, who managed to pack the committee with the faithful. The committee still was ornamented with a few "respectable" men—like John T. Hoffman, James T. Brady, Edward Cooper, and John Clancy—an old Tammany custom; but the majority was made up of Tweed and his henchmen: Sweeny, Terrence Farley, Matt Brennan, "Mike" and Richard B. Connolly, "Captain" Isaiah Rynders, and others of the same stamp. January 1 was also the day the Proclamation of Emancipation was to take effect. It had a somewhat similar meaning for a group of Tammany braves who wished to liberate themselves from their old chieftains and create a new dynasty of sachems. The Tweed followers—young, restless, ambitious—who had constituted the war parties which had long hunted Wood's scalp, demanded more power, more shares in the spoils of the war. The Tammany weekly, the *Leader*, supported them by suggesting that the old chiefs were no longer competent to rule the tribe. Accordingly, new sachems were chosen on April 21, 1863. The biggest warrior to fall from power was the Grand Sachem himself, Nelson J. Waterbury, who had broken with the Tweed faction. As the *Leader* put it, he was "invited to retire"[23] and Elijah Purdy, a Tweed stalwart, was elected to wear the blankets of the Grand Sachem. Three months later Purdy resigned and his great friend William Marcy Tweed became Grand Sachem of Tammany Hall. At no time in Tammany history had one man been both chairman of the General Committee and Grand Sachem. Tweed had captured Tammany Hall.

Tweed now had a machine in the making, but its parts were not finally assembled. His chief collaborator, Peter Sweeny, was

Cartoon by Thomas Nast suggesting the cabinet posts members of the Tweed Ring would occupy if Tweed became President in 1872; courtesy of the New-York Historical Society, New York City

on the scene, but neither Hall nor Connolly had assumed their roles. Tweed still needed money, tighter control of the peripheries of New York politics, and key men in key offices.

In the years he was gaining political power, Tweed was also enlarging his personal fortune by engaging in various business ventures. On January 29, 1861, in a meeting of the Supervisors, he refused a bill of Edmund Jones and Company, a printing house favored by Wood, which was profiting from excessive charges made for stationery and other supplies delivered to the city. The printer was sent for and a corrupt alliance was made between Jones and Tweed that was to profit them for three years, until he pushed Jones aside. Always taking the long view, Tweed himself went into the printing business. In 1864 he bought the controlling interest in the New York Printing Company, and it was no coincidence that thereafter this company and not Jones's did all the city's printing. All railroads, ferries, and insurance companies were forced to patronize it if they wished to stay in business. He also organized a marble company and bought a quarry in Massachusetts, from which the stone for the new County Courthouse was bought at excessive prices. Even before this, in the autumn of 1860, Tweed found another source of profit. After a meager reading of the law, Judge George Barnard, a good friend, admitted Tweed to the bar. If Tweed's knowledge of the law was scanty, his fees were enormous. The Erie Railroad alone paid him over $100,000, not for his legal ability, but for his political influence.

While these excursions allowed him to move his family to a swank Murray Hill residence just off Fifth Avenue, the most important advance he made, aside from leadership of Tammany Hall, was his appointment (by another great and good friend, Charles G. Cornell) as Deputy Street Commissioner. It was as if he had been presented with an army. The department, employing thousands of laborers, was a post unmatched for patronage. Tweed used it as a tactical position from which to build a political machine. Aldermen, ward leaders, and "distinguished" city statesmen of all kinds had to apply to him for jobs for their ward supporters. They all had to truck and crawl to Tweed, for without jobs to give their following would disappear. Here, too, was an army to be used in manipulating ward primaries when ward leaders showed a spirit of revolt. In a period of rapid city growth, the department supervised the building of scores of new streets and sewers, and repaired wharves and piers, roads, and public buildings. It gave Tweed an opportunity to influence and make more new friends—especially contractors.

Tweed was Deputy Street Commissioner from 1863 to 1870; the title "Deputy" was in fact a misnomer; it was he, not the Commissioner, be it Charles Cornell or Charles MacLean, who really controlled and ran the department. At the end of 1863, just before Tweed assumed office, the total expenditure of the department was $650,000. Under the administration of Tweed this figure increased fourfold within four years.[24] So, too, did the department's payroll, and interesting new city offices appeared. In 1864, for example, there were twelve Manure Inspectors, twenty-two Distributors of Corporation Ordinances; the work of twelve Deputy Tax Commissioners was eased by having seventeen clerks to help them. Sinecure positions such as these involved not work but a political obligation.

Thus, by 1866, the year the Tweed Ring began operation, Tweed stood at the threshold of power never before realized in New York City politics. He had money; he had Tammany; he had tightened his control to the very outskirts of the city. The *Springfield Republican*, looking back at the rise of the Boss, thought him a kind of apparition and was puzzled. Most persons, it said, would have a vague notion that in order to become a professional politician one must study the science of representative government, finance, political economy, and other abstruse subjects, such as are dealt with in the works of Mill, Bentham, and Adam Smith, "but not so with Tweed."[25] Indeed, not so Tweed, who had risen by a science more earthy but perhaps in its way as abstruse as those dealt with by the political philosophers.

3

"THOSE BEASTLY RASCALS"

When I was young, a long frock coat
And soft hat caught the people's vote.
Now folks is never satisfied,
They wants to see a MAN inside.

Oliver Herford, "The Statesman"

JIMMY WALKER, the last of the dandies to serve as Mayor, appeared at City Hall one day in a new suit, with a dapper twist—slanted pockets in the jacket. He dismissed the compliments of the reporters by saying, "I don't even compare to the way the Elegant Oakey used to dress."[1]

Abraham Oakey Hall—"The Elegant Oakey," as he was called—was the most resplendent of all New York's Mayors, and one of the most colorful. He was Mayor of New York—or more precisely, Tweed's Mayor—from 1868 to 1872. For Tweed's time or any time, Abraham Oakey Hall was a preposterous fellow in New York City politics. At once the buffoon and the scholar, this nervous, witty, sparkling little man delighted New York with his rhetoric of inanities and his absurd pince-nez. He charmed the public with his bad puns, his calculated irreverences, his gaudy elegance. Oakey Hall was the blithe spirit of the Tweed gang. He was a showman for whom politics was a stage, and he brought to that stage an extraordinary versatility of roles—strutting, prancing, and wisecracking throughout the stormy years of the Tweed era. But Hall was not only a politician; his repertoire included the roles of playwright, lecturer, poet, journalist, lawyer, clubman, humorist, and not least, humbug. And New York was charmed. "I've been called the King of the Bohemians," he boasted, "and I'm jolly proud of the title." [2] It took some time, however, for New Yorkers to realize that he was Tweed's left-hand man as well.

Oakey Hall, a slim, agile, little man, with the air of a pixie, had a shock of wavy black hair, and a heavy black mustache which merged with a stylish General Grant beard. His motto was inscribed on his stationery: *Fortuna Juvat Audentes* (Fortune favors the bold). Hall's impact on New York was such that James Gordon Bennett, publisher of the powerful *New York Herald*, called him "the Admirable Crichton of our city politicians." Soon after Hall's election as Mayor, Bennett wrote this remarkable eulogy:

> It will be a refreshing novelty to have for Mayor of New York a strictly upright, honorable, capable man, and at the same time one who writes a drama or a farce with equal success, acts a part as well as most professionals on the stage, conducts the most difficult cases on the calendar, sings a good song, composes a toast with remarkable eloquence and taste, mixes a lobster salad as well as Delmonico's head cook, smokes the best cigar in New York, respects old age, and admires youth, as poets and orators invariably do.[3]

But Bennett had barely touched upon the astonishing versatility of Abraham Oakey Hall. The Mayor had changed his religion almost as often as he had changed his politics. He had been Presbyterian and Swedenborgian, and at his death was Roman Catholic. A political chameleon with a keen eye for survival, he had been, with almost dazzling speed, a Whig, Know-Nothing, Republican, Mozart Democrat, and Tammany Democrat. And when he changed his clothes, he attracted the same newspaper attention as would a regular news event. It was not a mere cliché to say he "dressed for the occasion"; he did so literally. A newspaper carried this item on Hall's appearance in a patriotic parade. "Oakey Hall's get-up at the parade yesterday was gorgeous. His blue suit represented the cause of the Union; his gray overcoat that of the Rebs; his be-e-eautiful necktie the bright Heavens above us, and his polished boots the culture so pre-eminently his own." [4]

The Elegant Oakey Hall politicked with his clothes. The man who wore a different neckie and sleeve buttons every day made his elegance a political weapon. A veteran newspaperman remembered how Hall delighted the Irish on St. Patricks Day. "In 1870, when the great day came, there was a terrible snow storm. It was an Irish snow storm, flakes as big as your fist. Well, the elegant Oakey stood on the reviewing stand dressed in a green suit, a green hat, a green tie, everything green, even green spats. He stayed all through the parade despite the inclement weather. Naturally, it made a great hit with the Irish . . . after that people took to calling him Mayor O'Hall." [5] When he appeared at German celebrations dressed in the colors of the fatherland, the *New York Sun* named him the Honorable Abraham Von O'Hall.

Once at the Annual Ball of the Americus Club, the social club for the hierarchy of the Tweed organization—politicians, judges, lawyers, policemen, saloonkeepers—Hall was again gorgeous. His biographer, Croswell Bowen, cited this newspaper report. Hall "was faultlessly attired in a bottle-green fly-tail coat, with half sovereigns of pure guinea gold for buttons and a green velvet collar and lapels, a waistcoat and a light unwhisperable of the same material and color and a new satin necktie of large dimensions. His kids were also green; his shirt front was embroidered with shamrocks in green floss silk, and immense emeralds winked in his button holes. He wore a pair of eye glasses with rims of Irish bog-oak and attached to a green silk cord." [6]

As a man of letters, he wrote books, pamphlets, magazine and newspaper articles, ranging from short stories and children's stories to satire and literary criticism. His prose was stuffed with erudite Latin quotations and references to the classics and Shakespeare. So overwhelmed was the *New York World* that it declared:

"As long as he will stand by Shakespeare—the World will stand by him." [7] One pamphlet concerned his pet peeve, entitled "Horace Greeley Decently Dissected"; another, a Christmas story with a new twist: a lobbyist appeared as the main character. He received some prominence as drama critic and literary editor of the *Leader*, a Tammany journal. Hall used it for more than dissecting the aesthetics of the arts; it became the mouthpiece of the Tweed Ring, tirelessly cataloguing the virtues of the Boss, Tammany Hall, and Oakey Hall.

He wrote and acted in some of his own plays. The Olympic Theatre in 1869 produced an extravaganza entitled, *Loyalina, Brigadier General Fortunio and His Seven Gifted Aides-de-Camp*, which was apparently enjoyed by New York theater-goers despite its title. The talented Mayor went on to greater accomplishments: a burletta called *Humpty Dumpty*, *Fernande* (not too well received); and *Let Me Kiss Him for His Mother*. When his political career came to an end with the downfall of the Tweed Ring, the Mayor wrote and acted in *The Crucible*, an artfully contrived drama with a simple plot: Abraham Oakey Hall did not at any time conspire with the Tweed Ring. It was not meant to be a comedy.

As the most sought-after public speaker in the city, his repertoire was as extensive as his wardrobe. He lectured knowledgeably about politics, New York history, literature, drama, divorce, and the favorite topic of all, "A Night in Crimeland," a lecture culled from the city's best collection of books on crime—his own. When he talked, pacing nervously, gesturing like an actor, his eyes sparkling, his words—as rich as his clothes—tumbling out rapidly but gracefully, Oakey Hall was playing one of his finest roles. For it was difficult for a listener to believe that he was not hearing a witty and learned college professor rather than a professional Tammany politician, and a sachem at that.

As the man who often signed his official papers "O.K." his "Hall-mark" was the terrible pun. Discussing the "Chinese question" before a large group, he said, "If this was a question one would feel disposed to joke about, we could very well say to-night —on this hot night of June, that the coolie question was a very good one to talk about." [8]

Hall's value to the Ring amounted to more than being an elegant, clowning punster, who diverted attention from the Ring's systematic plundering of the city treasury. He brought a sorely needed respectability to the Tweed Ring. For here was no stereotype of the Tammany politician—Irish, crude, educated in the corner saloon, born in Cockroach Row, or one who had clawed his way out of Hester Street. He was a kind of freak among those in the Ring's inner circle, utterly different in background and manners. Born of a solid English ancestry on his father's side, aristocratic French on his mother's side, he had a B.A. from New York University, several months at Harvard Law School, and legal training in the New Orleans firm of John Slidell, a diplomat under Polk who achieved even greater fame in the Civil War in the noted "Trent Affair."

Oakey Hall, then, was a solid citizen, one of the "better people," who could lay claim to respectability and membership in New York's gentry. His manners were exquisite. He had married well, a socialite, the former Katherine Louise Barnes who, throughout her husband's long association with Big Bill Tweed and his cronies, had refused to have any of "those Tammany politicians" in her home.[9] Indeed, one of Hall's most important roles was to act as liaison man between the Ring and New York society. It was as the inveterate clubman that Hall crashed this rarefied world.

For years the Elegant Oakey was a familiar figure in New York's finest social bastions. He was a member of nine clubs, including the most prestigious, the Union Club. As Hall the clubman, he succeeded in winning over many of the gentry, soothing their apprehensions about Hall the politician and the forces rumored behind him. In the plush dining rooms and dignified libraries he played the part of the well-bred and accomplished gentleman-scholar, the responsible Mayor representing a responsible Democratic party.

If Hall tickled the masses and impressed the gentry, not everyone was won over. The *New York Times*, a Republican paper which found it difficult to admire *any* Democrat, described him as the Honorable Oakum Hall. The *New York Telegram* said he had only one defect, "a lack of ability." Nor was the cartoonist, Thomas Nast, deceived. Like the boy in the fable, he could not see the emperor's clothes. When Hall attacked Nast as the "Nast-y artist of Harper's Hell Weekly—a Journal of Devilization," Nast counterpunned with a demolishing two-word portrait: "Mayor Haul." Even Tweed himself had his doubts. "Hall's all right," he is reported to have said, "all he needs is ballast. If Oakey had had ballast enough to hold him down in the District Attorney's chair, he would have become a great man in time. Now he won't. Politics are too deep for him. They are for me and I can wade long after Oakey has to float." And then as an afterthought, "He's lightheaded." [10]

Lightheaded? Perhaps. Driving this seemingly superficial, gaily bedecked butterfly was an insatiable ambition, matched by a political acuity that even Boss Tweed may have underestimated. Hall's ambition, unlike that of the other Ring members, was not simply to achieve power and use it as an instrument of profit, for his law practice gave him more than an adequate living. Hall reached for power because power was the spotlight that brought attention and approval. Public office represented for him the stage that promised the best audience, where he could flash his dazzling showmanship and capture the attention of thousands. His desire for approval (to use Croswell Bowen's phrase) was as inordinate as Tweed's desire for money. His career would show that if he had to be a capital rogue to be a good showman, so be it.

In 1848, at the age of twenty-two, Hall came to New York and soon did well. He formed a law partnership with Augustus L. Brown and Aaron J. Vanderpoel, and the firm prospered as counsel to city officials, railroads, and speculators like Jay Gould. Hall's value to the firm rested more on his ability to make important friends and smooth negotiations than on any great knowledge of the law. He was especially adroit as a lobbyist at the state capitol in Albany, where he met his later colleague, Peter Barr Sweeny.

Politics and all the opportunities to bemuse the public were now possible. Changing sprightly with the political wind from Whig, to Know-Nothing, to Republican, he went from Assistant District Attorney in 1851 to District Attorney from 1855 to 1858. In 1861 his political career was resumed with gusto. With the backing of Fernando Wood and his anti-Tammany, anti-Tweed Mozart Hall, he managed to defeat for District Attorney the Tammany candidate, Nelson J. Waterbury, and the respected reformer, Abraham R. Lawrence. Three years later it was time for another change. He sensed a turning point in New York politics—the rise of William Marcy Tweed. Accordingly, on February 1, 1864, he signed his name in the book that registers each new member of the Tammany Society.

In 1866, now as a Tammany Democrat, with the powerful support of Boss Tweed, he was handily re-elected District Attorney and was admitted to the inner circle of the Tweed Ring, as Tweed recognized the many talents of Oakey Hall. His many years in the District Attorney's office alone could be invaluable in the operation of the Ring. As the city prosecutor, Hall had become intimately acquainted with Crimeland, as he liked to call it. He had prosecuted over 12,000 cases, although it was said that he had pigeonholed another 10,000. Thus he was regarded with affection by the storm troopers of the Ring's army, the thugs and leaders of the lower wards. This of course suggested a pun. "Few persons," Hall said, "have so many *tried* friends as I have, and tried friends are always magnanimous." [11] He had gained immense favor with the Irish by not prosecuting—by his own admission—some 10,000 liquor dealers who had evaded the excise tax on whiskey.[12] With the police he made contacts that were to prove invaluable to the Ring. He brought to the Ring the services of a skilled and eminently respectable law firm. The firm in turn benefited. It was estimated that in 1870 alone it received $204,500 in fees from the city.[13]

By 1868 the dazzling little man with the pince-nez was on the threshold of political success. In a sweeping victory the Elegant Oakey Hall became Mayor. Everything he wanted seemed to be his. Even Charles A. Dana of the *Sun*, who detested him, was forced to admit that nothing seemed to stem Hall's popularity. Indeed, Dana ruefully admitted, it was predicted by friends and enemies alike that Hall might some day become Governor of New York and even President of the United States.[14]

In sharp contrast to Tweed's crudeness and Hall's glitter, Peter Barr Sweeny was subtle, crafty; he had the guile of the artful dodger; he had a flair for the cunning, the sly. As such he made a chilling impact upon the imagination of New Yorkers. He was regarded as a dark, brooding, mysterious Machiavellian—the man with the black brains. Friends and enemies alike respected his intelligence and especially his cunning, and his reputation won him many names: Brains Sweeny, the Sly Sweeny, the Great Democratic Warwick, Spider Sweeny, and Peter the Paragon. His friends called him Squire.

Sweeny looked sinister. A short, solidly built, ugly man, he had a large head covered with a mass of thick, black hair; his walrus mustache was jet black; he always wore black clothes and a high-crowned black silk hat; and his eyes shone "like little dollars in the night." His voice was deep and his manners quiet, undemonstrative—catlike.

Sweeny served as Tweed's right-hand man, although the Boss found him personally distasteful. "Sweeny is a hard, overbearing, revengeful man. He wants his way. He treasures up his wrath. He has considerable ability of a kind. . . . We were so opposite and unalike that we never got along very well."[15] Like him or not, Sweeny was indispensable to Tweed. He essayed the "grand, gloomy, and peculiar": his work was done in the caucuses, private offices, hotel rooms, the corridors, the corners of lobbies. Sweeny was the political manager, the manipulator, the inventor of ingenious schemes. A kind of politician's politician, he had gained a vast knowledge of city affairs during long years in the tough and ruthless world of ward politics. "What Peter B. Sweeny doesn't know isn't worth knowing. He is a walking encyclopedia of useful political information; but, unlike other encyclopedias, he keeps all his knowledge to himself. . . . Just leave him alone and he'll come home bringing his party behind him." [16] He was particularly valuable as the compromiser, the healer of bruised egos, the peacemaker who prevented Tammany warriors from scalping each other. He operated "like oil on troubled waters. He is a sort of mollifying oil—a peaceful, heavenly spirit." [17]

Sweeny always served as the manager—backstage. While he held several public and private offices—District Attorney, City Chamberlain, president of the Central Park Commission—he preferred to work more in the shadows, or as a director in the Ninth National Bank, Mutual Gas Company, Brooklyn Banks, Dry Dock and Erie Railroads, plotting the mischief George Washington Plunkitt quaintly called "honest graft." Sweeny had few personal friends. He had the political manager's morbid fear of publicity. In dealing with individuals, he could be aggressive, domineering; but in public he was painfully shy. Elected District Attorney in 1857, his shyness was such that he could not finish his first speech to a jury; ashamed, he resigned his office and fled to Europe to recover. There was a story that Richard Connolly tried to pump some political warmth into him by spending an evening making him talk and smile while he pounded Sweeny on the back and shook his hand. "Now," Connolly is supposed to have said, "if you'll only do that when you go out among the lads you'll be a grand success. You can talk, but unless you smile, even when you're condemning your bitterest opponent, it will not have all the effect it should have." [18] Sweeny knew his limitations and talents as well as anyone. As he summed himself up:

> I am not, and never claimed to be, a leader. If there is any one entitled to that designation among the Democracy of our city, it is Senator Tweed. . . . He has remarkable executive ability, and is a recognized leader. Mayor Hall, Comptroller Connolly, and others I might name, are more leaders than I am. I am a

> sort of adviser. I try to harmonize the interests of the party, and endeavor to secure good nominations and sound principles, as I understand them. But I do not aspire to the position of a leader. I am simply a passenger in the ship, with the privilege of going ashore if I do not like its management or its course.[19]

On another occasion he was careful to add, with equal candor, "Everyone . . . who knows me, knows that I have never had anything but the public welfare and the prosperity of my friends at heart."[20]

Peter Barr Sweeny was of more humble origin than any other member of the Ring. He was born in 1824 in New York City, a year after Tweed, of poor Irish parents. His family's only claim to respectability was the rumor that Catholic priests years before had been a part of the family. For a while his mother ran a saloon in the Sixth Ward; later his father opened a saloon in Jersey City, where young Peter worked as a waiter. Like Tweed, Sweeny began his political education as a volunteer fireman. He spent some time at St. Peter's Roman Catholic parochial school. He was a devout Catholic all his life, a familiar figure every Sunday at St. Xavier's Church on Sixteenth Street. He went to Columbia College but was not graduated. For a while he ran a corner saloon in the Sixth Ward, which also offered entertainment—admission, ten cents; whisky, three cents a glass. It was a place shunned by all decent citizens; but it was also a place to build a political following.

Sweeny read law in the offices of James T. Brady, a leading, colorful attorney later to become a famous New York judge. It was an excellent beginning for a political career. Sweeny became a rising figure in Tammany politics; he was a member of the Tammany General Committee in 1852, and ward boss of the powerful Twentieth by 1855. In 1854 he had an opportunity particularly suited to developing his talents. In that year, his uncle, Thomas J. Barr, was elected to the State Senate; he took Sweeny with him. There Sweeny went to work as a lobbyist for railroads, gas companies, stage lines. In Albany he was nicknamed "the Nephew of my Uncle." He gained an awesome reputation as a lobbyist, and it was soon discovered, as one writer said, that Sweeny "had brains but he lacked a heart." [21] He competed with his Republican counterpart, Abraham Oakey Hall, but admired his style, and was helpful later in bringing him into the Tweed Ring. His acquaintance with Tweed began when as a lobbyist Sweeny tried to push through the famous Broadway Railroad scheme that Tweed had helped to create as a member of the Forty Thieves.

By 1860 he was a member of the State Central Committee, giving battle as a "Cowhide" to August Belmont's New York Hotel crowd, known as the "Silk Stockings." He was strong enough to get the attention and support of the mighty Dean Richmond. By the late 'fifties Sweeny had become a power as a ward boss and Tammany leader. He was important enough to be elected a delegate to the ill-fated Democratic convention in 1860; he figured prominently in the anti-Wood faction, and by virtue of his control in the Tammany General Committee helped to steer Tweed into his prominence in the wigwam. From approximately 1864 on he served the Boss as a powerful ally, and together they relentlessly sought city patronage, adding office after office, until they reorganized Tammany Hall and built the city's first modern political machine. He was appointed City Chamberlain in 1866. "I heard he paid $60,000 for the confirmation," Tweed testified years later.[22] Sweeny, the man who could never excite the masses, who withered under the bright glare of publicity, scored his one and only popular triumph.

The City Chamberlain, or county treasurer, deposited public monies received from taxation and other sources. An antiquated law allowed the Chamberlain to pocket as fees the interest earned on this money. Sweeny's predecessors had taken good advantage of this boon, worth approximately $100,000. By Sweeny's time the interest money had swollen to $209,401. Sweeny with a grand gesture refused to take the money and turned it over to the city! "I am not willing," he said, "to receive a great or any sum of money against the public sense of right, however legally justifiable." [23]

The city was astounded and overwhelmed by Sweeny's apparent honesty. What many New Yorkers had forgotten was that the law allowing the Chamberlain to collect interest fees was already under attack. The estate of the late Daniel Devlin, Sweeny's immediate predecessor, was being sued to recover for the city the interest money he had collected. Sweeny simply gave to the city what was the city's own and made a virtue of a necessity.

Thus Peter Barr Sweeny came to power by a brilliant move, throwing dust in the eyes of the public and making himself and the Democrats popular. The *Herald* enhanced his reputation with extravagant praise that ended on a note that was perhaps more prophetic than the newspaper realized. "We have heretofore spoken of him as Peter Blatherskite Sweeny; we henceforth distinguish him as Peter Bismarck Sweeny.... It marks the commencement of a new era in politics."[24]

The fourth member of the firm, without the leadership of a Tweed, the showmanship of a Hall, or the intelligence of a Sweeny, still brought certain talents and advantages to the Ring. First, he was the leader of a particularly powerful ward, the Twenty-first. Second, he was a sachem in Tammany Hall. Third, he was beloved and heartily supported by the Irish. And last but by no means least, he was Comptroller of the City of New York. He was called the "Big Judge" by his cronies, "slimy" by the reformers. To students of the robust history of New York graft, he will always be known as "Slippery Dick" Connolly.

When the Tweed Ring was at its peak, a newspaperman from the *New York Star* was assigned to interview Richard Connolly and give his impressions of the City Comptroller. Although the paper was friendly to the reigning Democrats, the reporter found his patience stretched. He had to wait a long time to see the Comptroller. He had to wade through a host of visiting politicians who, it seemed to him, were as permanent as the office furniture. Finally the reporter got close enough to the door to overhear a conversation. A man was asking Comptroller Connolly who owned the board fence around the Register's Office. His astounding answer suggested that Connolly's conversation was as slippery as his politics.

Connolly: "Shortly after the Mexican War an aged soldier, with a mahogany nose, cork eyebrow, a Spanish shilling and a dime novel, stepped up to a butcher. 'Butcher,' said the patriot, 'what's the price of beef?' 'Twenty-five cents a pound, sir.' 'Twenty-five cents a pound, great heavens, have you the pluck?' 'I have, sir.' 'So I supposed, you need it.' And so it is with me. I have the pluck and need it; that fence belongs to the Register."

The reporter was now next to the door and heard Connolly say to his secretary: "Give her $10, and be d—d to her. It's all right, charity never hurt anyone yet."

The reporter finally entered the office. The interview was short. Did the Comptroller think John Hoffman, the Democratic Governor of New York, who was backed by Tweed, would make a good President of the United States?

Connolly: "He certainly has a very large moustache."

The Comptroller knew Matthew Brennan, the Sheriff of the City of New York?

Connolly: "Knew him! I should say so. He was a good fellow—rough but fair. He meant well, but didn't know much. Well, we must all die sometimes, and poor Matt, how thunderin' dead he is, to be sure. Permit me to weep."

The reporter decided to leave.[25] Poor Matt Brennan was still very much alive.

James Bryce, the famed English political scientist, thought Connolly the least attractive of all the Ring. Croswell Bowen called him "an unctuous, Uriah Heep type bookkeeper."[26] A contemporary provided the most scathing portrait, one that many persons thought was accurate.

> He was cold, crafty, and cowardly, with a smooth, oily, insinuating manner. . . . His manners were good, though somewhat elaborate, with a decided tinge of obsequiousness to superiors and arrogance to inferiors. . . . He had not an honest instinct in his nature. He lacked courage to carry through great frauds, but he

> was ready enough to follow the lead of bolder rogues. He was an uncertain friend and a treacherous ally. No man gave promises or broke them with less compunction. His strong affection for his wife and children seems to have been his sole redeeming trait, and with this exception his innate portrait is all shadow.[27]

Tweed, a neighbor and a good friend, gave a different and more succinct point of view. "He was a powerful man in his ward and district. We could not get along without him, and annexed him for the vote he controlled." [28]

Slippery Dick Connolly was a big man, whose height was exaggerated by the tall stovepipe hat he habitually wore. His gold-rimmed spectacles, stately nose, clean-shaved face, and gently plump belly gave him an almost distinguished appearance. A skillful professional politician, he won his nickname "Slippery Dick" partly by an amiable but artfully feigned innocence that would have others believe he was an innocent child in politics. In 1857 he earned an annual salary of $3600. In 1871 he was worth $6,000,000.

The only immigrant in the hierarchy of the Ring, Connolly was born in Banta, Ireland, the son of an Irish schoolmaster. After receiving a good education, Connolly migrated to Philadelphia and soon thereafter, went to New York. There he began a grass-roots political career by becoming a regular attendant at every ward meeting and so demonstrative a partisan that he was classed as one of the "Hooray Boys." He became secretary for the Seventh Ward Central Committee, where "his neat penmanship was admired, he could not be trusted even to count votes after a ballot." [29] His hard work and loyalty were rewarded. An appointment in the Custom House was followed by his election as County Clerk in 1851, and his re-election three years later. By 1859 he had risen high enough in Tammany to win election as State Senator. At the end of his term he retired from active political office, though he remained a power in Tammany. He became cashier and general manager in the Central National Bank until 1868, when Tweed made him Comptroller.

His value to Tweed became evident in the late 'fifties. Connolly was a specialist in leading the Irish, a potent factor in the later power of the Ring. Though Fernando Wood sharply challenged Connolly in 1856 on his hold over the Irish, Connolly made a vigorous effort, and his leadership of the Irish was a contributing factor in Wood's defeat in 1859. From then on Connolly worked quietly but effectively in building Irish support, so effectively, indeed, that a remark made about Fernando Wood could as well describe Connolly. "To hear [his supporters], one would think [he] was just biding his time to lead a military expedition to free Ireland." [30] Moreover, as Comptroller, he had another asset—a perverse mathematical ability that confirmed the old adage that figures never lie, but figurers do.

Throughout American urban history one of the most persistent analyses of corruption made by reformers has been a simple, and, indeed, naïve moral argument: the cause of corruption is evil men; the solution to corruption lies in routing the rascals. The character of the Tweed Ring suggests that this is partially true. They were a gallery of rogues. But the view, so prevalent in the Tweed period, that the troubles of New York were almost solely attributable to its bad men was myopic. It obscured other circumstances, infinitely complex and not always sharply related to bad men, that made the Tweed Ring possible. Granted, the *first* cause of corruption was corrupt men, but there were other causes as well.

In effect, the phenomenon of the Tweed Ring also grew out of the thorny political, social, and economic conditions of New York City—its obsolete government, its rapid growth, its decline in moral standards after the Civil War, its leadership, its apathy, its hordes of immigrants, and its Tammany Hall—the most efficient, powerful, and corrupt political machine in America at that time. The story of the Tweed Ring is not just the tale of wicked men and the grandeur of their larcenies; it is also the story of Tweed's town, the city itself, "a ragged purple dream," wrote O. Henry, "the wonderful cruel, enchanting, bewildering, fatal, great city."

4

TWEED'S TOWN

Lobsters! Rarebits! plenty of Pilsener beer!
Plenty of girls to help you drink the best of cheer;
Dark girls, blonde girls, and never a one that's true
You get them all in the Tenderloin when the clock strikes two.

Anon.
O'Conner, *Hell's Kitchen*

WILLIAM MARCY TWEED might well have repeated after St. Paul: "I am the citizen of no mean city." Boss Tweed's New York was a city of contrasts: a bustling metropolis of strangers, a collection of sharply divergent neighborhoods, utter loneliness for some and for others the companionship of chowder and bicycling clubs and Sunday picnics. It was a city whose magnificent hotels like the Astor, Metropolitan, and St. Nicholas, and the elegant restaurants —Delmonico's and Hoffman House—clashed sharply with the wretched poverty of Rag Pickers' Row or the violence of Hell's Kitchen. "Nowhere else," said a contemporary, "does the carriage of the millionaire spatter the gaunt beggar at every hour on every crosswalk. No other human hive can show the counterparts of Fifth Avenue and Baxter Street. . . . The raggedness of our water fronts implies that we are poor indeed, and the massive grandeur of our central plateaus declares that we are rich beyond computation." [1]

In the period after the Civil War, New York, an area now known as Manhattan and the Bronx, was an emerging urban giant which, unlike Philadelphia or Boston, was living for the future, not the past. New York would not reach maturity until Brooklyn, Queens, and Richmond were added in 1898. In 1868, during the days of the Tweed Ring, the city was extending its streets, shops, and brownstone houses uptown and to the east and west, with a long way to go. The Sixth Avenue horsecar line stopped at Forty-Fourth Street; the Eighth Avenue line bumped its way as far as Forty-ninth Street—only the Seventh Avenue car went as far as Central Park. The fare was ten cents in a day when eggs sold for fifteen cents a dozen. If one were affluent and venturesome, he could hire a four-wheel hansom with a cabby in a top hat and go as far as Sixty-first Street for $2 or to High Bridge (or Harlem) for $5.

In 1868 as now, New York was an exciting town, attracting hordes of wide-eyed tourists. If the visitor arrived via ferry across the Hudson River, the landmarks would be Castle Garden and Governor's Island with its fort. (The Statue of Liberty had not yet been built.) If he came by rail and wanted to see the Battery at the lower edge of town, he would stop at Fourth Avenue and Twenty-seventh Street and remain aboard for an exasperating length of time while the locomotive was exchanged for a team of six or more horses. The horses would then puff their way down to Chambers Street, led by a man on horseback waving a flag to warn unwary pedestrians.

After checking into his hotel, the tourist would find an infinite number of things to do. He would go to a baseball game, and top the day off with a show at night at one of the seventeen theaters, most of which were bunched along Fourteenth Street and Broadway. In the spring of 1868, for example, the "first grand baseball match of the season" was played at the new Union Grounds between the Mutual Club and the Eckfords, before a record crowd of 2000 fans; Blind Tom, the noted Negro pianist, was at Lyric Hall; and *Humpty Dumpty*, a play by the distinguished dramatist Abraham Oakey Hall, was appearing at the Olympic.[2] Or the visitor could wander through the financial district whose main street was the short and crooked Wall Street, "though immensely straighter than many who spend their time on it." [3] He could shop for jewelry on Maiden Lane and for clothes at Lord and Taylor, where young boys graciously opened and closed the doors for customers. He might gawk at the city's tallest structure, the 284-foot tower of Trinity Church, or visit the Fifth Avenue Hotel which featured the talk of the town, a "perpendicular railway intersecting each story"—the city's first public elevator. If he was curious about the little round building in City Hall Park with an eagle on top, he would discover it was the city's only public lavatory.

As for the streets of New York, they were covered with cobblestones, horsecars, stages, carriages, wagons, and people, periodically snarled in a series of gigantic traffic jams. The men of the city usually dressed in heavy black suits, derbies, white shirts with paper collars, while the women wore rib-crushing corsets, drab dark dresses, a virtual host of petticoats, and black shoes—shined with Bixby's Blacking—that reached far above the ankles. It was a man's world in which loose talk about women's rights was only painfully tolerated, and where the symbol of vulgarity was not an exotic bathing suit, but a woman smoking a cigarette.

If one went uptown on a Sixth Avenue horsecar, or around the perilous Dead Man's Curve at Fourteenth Street and Broadway, he could see billboards picturing the fads of the day: the marvelous hair tonic of the Seven Sutherland Sisters, Pears's soap, and Fletcher's Castoria. Everybody was curing everything by swallowing Grandreth's Pills, which were not sugar-coated but "little brown, dusty things, and how bitter!" [4] And there was the famous tobacco advertisement showing a horsecar driver smoking his pipe, as a passenger next to him sniffed and said, "If that's Honest Long Cut, blow the smoke this way!"

At night the city was quiet and dimly lit by gaslight; the first electric sign (Manhattan Beach Swept by Ocean Breezes) was not erected until 1881. In the daytime it was a noisy and bustling town. Swarms of people rushed by with such speed that one contemporary complained that one found himself in the same dilemma as the country boy in Horace, who stood waiting on the bank for the river to run by. He went on to say, "We live in a fast age, and New Yorkers are a fast people; hence it seemed intolerable to some that the law regulating driving at the Park should restrict every man to six miles an hour, and arrest summarily every blood who dared to disregard the rule." [5]

The speed and gusto of New York's daily life was matched with equal vigor in its commercial and financial life.[6] Between 1820 and 1870, New York's economic supremacy was so established it could truly call itself the Empire City. With the completion of the Erie Canal in 1825, New York outmaneuvered her rivals, Boston, Philadelphia, and Baltimore, by piercing the hinterland barrier and gaining access to Western markets. Manufacturing and banking boomed. Warehouses were stuffed with goods. Savings bank deposits sky-rocketed. By the Civil War New York was the leading import-export center of the country. Almost three-quarters of the nation's imports passed through her harbor.[7] Her economic prosperity was buttressed by a spectacular increase in population. In 1820, the population of New York was 123,706; by 1870, the heyday of the Tweed Ring, it had leaped to 942,292.[8]

If there was an irony to New York's massive expansion, it was in the building of City Hall. Begun in 1803, the building was constructed of marble with one exception, its rear. The city fathers, not having the foresight, felt that the city would never grow beyond Chambers Street, therefore the back side of the building was made of a very crude sandstone. After all, who would see it? It was not until 1890 that its ugly rump was painted, finally ending a "permanent standing joke." [9]

On the surface it seemed that the city's growth was something unique in itself and in many ways independent of politics. Yet it played a critical part in making the Tweed Ring possible. Growth poured money into the coffers of the business community, which in turn engaged in feverous speculation, especially in real estate. Since he had an inside view of real estate operations, it was no coincidence that Tweed became the city's third largest holder of real estate. Growth brought at once complacency and an itch for large enterprises. Competition for franchises, contracts, the chance to improve Ann Street or to widen Broadway, seemed more worthwhile than competing for public office.

Along with economic expansion and its implications, political apathy was another phenomenon which allowed the Ring to thrive as long as it did. The constant barrage of elections helped to create political disinterest. There were not only the congressional and presidential elections, but also the alternating two-year-term city, county, and state elections. Every year there were some kind of election, many lacking any really genuine issues. With the predominance of the Democratic party in the city, most of the contests for local offices as well as some for the legislature, were settled in the primaries. For the most part, primaries are the most uninteresting of American elections, but for a political machine they can be crucial. Moreover, politics seemed tame after the great issues of the Civil War, especially city politics. The complications of city government, the intricacies of finance and city improvements, were either beyond the interest or knowledge of the average citizen. Many acted accordingly and simply did not vote.

New York had another side, the "dark, nether side," as middle-class reformers breathlessly called it. As the westward movement in America had left pockets of human waste—barren refuges for the poor, lazy, and unlucky—so with the expansion of New York was there an urban equivalent. Middle- and upper-class residents of old New York, the lower area of the city, left their own native poor behind, and fled before the invasion of Irish and German immigrants. There was an exodus uptown to Greenwich Village in the 1840's and then on to Bloomingdale and Manhattanville at 125th Street, and across the rivers. By the early 1870's, some 200,000 New Yorkers lived in the suburbs.[10]

Sleepy, well-groomed, genteel neighborhoods, like the Chelsea district of Tweed's youth, decayed into a ganglia of rotting tenements, foul slaughterhouses, and a Mulligan-stew of nationalities. As one contemporary recalled:

> There was one peculiarity about Chelsea which did not, I think, exist in any other part of the city. Certain blocks seemed to be reserved for certain nationalities. Thus there was Scotch Row for the 'ladies from hell'; London Row for the barsted Britisher; and Yankee Row for the native Americans who had the hardihood to intrude themselves among these foreigners. And oh! I forgot the Irish.[11]

The Bowery, once a respectable section of New York, gave way to the tinkle of pianos in the bordellos, the tough Bowery Boy, and cheap dance halls were "a bloated wench displays her ugly face as if she imagined it as full of attractions as it is of hideous sores and blotches."[12] As the *New York Times* said on September 14, 1924, "Oh the Bowery, where for two centuries everything happened, and now nothing happens."

The melancholy area between Eighth Avenue and the Hudson River was home for prostitutes, pimps, criminals, and, above all, the poor. Legend has it that it got its name as a result of a conversation between two policemen. "This place is hell itself," one is supposed to have said. "Hell's a mild climate," said the other. "This is Hell's Kitchen, no less."[13]

East of Hell's Kitchen's ragged streets, bounded roughly by Fifth and Seventh Avenues and by Twenty-third and Thirtieth Streets, lay Satan's Circus, later called the Tenderloin. Here was a jungle of bawdy houses, saloons, and cheap boarding houses. Sixth Avenue was its Broadway and the wicked Haymarket saloon was its City Hall. When Police Captain "Clubber" Williams, known for the justice he carried at the end of his nightstick, was transferred to the Twenty-ninth Precinct in 1876, he added another saying to New York folklore. "Well," said Williams, "I've been transferred. I've had nothing but chuck steak for a long time, and now I'm going to get a little of the tenderloin."[14] From the days of the Tweed Ring well into the twentieth century, this area was prime tenderloin for police and politicians, many of whom became rich by protecting its vice and crime.

Thus the Empire City, the economic colossus, the clearing

house of ideas, the heart of culture, music, art, the theater, had its creative juices soured by the emergence of one of the worst slums in the country. The spidery streets of the lower part of the city, choked with garbage and the poor, twisted their way through Hell's Kitchen, Satan's Circus, and the Bowery; they passed Rag Pickers' Row, Cat Alley, Rotten Row, the Great Eastern, Sebastopol, Bummers' Retreat, Mulligan Alley, Cockroach Row, and the Five Points; they shaped what could be properly called Tweed's Town. The Reverend De Witt Talmage explored these dark places, "in order that I might take straighter aim at iniquity," and concluded, "Cain was the founder of the first city.... May the eternal God have mercy on our cities." [15]

A writer of the period sought to capture some of the essential elements of Tweed's Town by asking what would the Mayor see if he made a trip to the lower depths of the city.

> ... He found the streets ... ill-paved, broken by carts and omnibuses into ruts and perilous gullies, obstructed by boxes and signboards, impassable by reason of thronging vehicles, and filled with filth and garbage, which was left where it had been thrown, to rot and send out its pestiferous fumes, breeding fever and cholera, and a host of diseases all over the city. He found hacks, carts, and omnibuses choking the thoroughfares, their Jehu drivers dashing through the crowd furiously, reckless of life; women and children were knocked down and trampled on, and the ruffians drove on uncaught; hackmen overcharged and were insolent to their passengers; baggage-smashers haunted the docks, tearing one's baggage about, stealing it sometimes, and demanding from timid women and stranger men unnumbered fees for doing mischief, or for doing nothing; emigrant runners, half-bulldog and half-leech, burst in crowds upon the decks of arriving ships, carried off the poor foreign people, fleeced them, and set them adrift upon the town; rowdyism seemed to rule the city; it was at the risk of your life that you walked the streets late at night; the club, the knife, the slung-shot, the revolver were in constant activity ... low dram-shops polluted the Sabbath air ... and night sent forth their crowds of wretches infuriate with bad liquor, to howl out

blasphemies, to fight, or to lie prone, swine-like, on the sidewalks and in the gutters. Prostitution, grown bold by impunity, polluted the public highway, brazenly insolent to modesty and common decency; and idle policemen, undistinguished from other citizens, lounged about, gaped, gossipped, drank, and smoked, inactively useless upon street corners and porter-houses.[16]

Here was a tenement population of half a million; 18,000 more of whom lived in cellars, seldom penetrated by sunlight.[17] Here some 15,000 beggars and 30,000 children roamed the streets, and old hags begged with babies—rented babies—pinching them to make them cry when they entered a saloon.[18] On Thirty-ninth Street between Ninth and Tenth Avenues, thirteen five-story tenements held 1000 tenants. "Cattle were better housed than human beings in Hell's Kitchen," reported a State legislative committee.[19]

There were several places in the lower depths of town that served as rendezvous, for business and pleasure, of the Ring and the multitude of lesser chiefs like the ward leaders, judges, and city officials. At the corner of Prince and Wooster streets stood the St. Bernard Hotel, often used as headquarters for the Ring on election days because of its convenient location. Mercer, Green, Houston, Wooster, Leonard, and Crosby streets, and the infamous Arch Block, among others, offered "gilded misery." A writer of the period portrayed the girls in the bordellos in these words:

Reader! know you the history of those beings whom we find collected together in this state of degradation? Look at the wretched rooms, where like hopeless galley-slaves they are enchained. Crime and vice and the despair of too late repentance crowd upon them! Look at the miserable creatures as they stand on the very edge of the abyss without the power to move one step backward! Vapid impudence and physical and moral corruption speak out from faces in which not one atom of womanhood can be detected! You turn with loathing from them . . . whose appearance today fills you with disgust . . . in the brilliant parlors of prostitution. . . . They were arrayed in gold and silks, they were spoiled pets of rich sensualists, and never dreamt that the gilded sin was a stone around their necks which would at last drag them down to so terrible a depth![20]

If the politician were thirsty, he had many places to go: the Broadway Gardens ("for Quakers and pacifists to avoid"),[21] the Stag Cafe (operated by Dan the Dude), Paddy the Pig's, McElroy's Pig's Head, the Burnt Rag, Charlie Ackron's Tivoli (which featured short-change artists), or the Star and Garter. ("Gentlemen are requested not to smoke when dancing with the ladies.") [22] At the height of the crusade against the Tweed Ring, a reporter visited the lower part of town, or what the *Times* called "Tweed's Principality." The next day these headlines appeared:

Total Depravity in New York
Scenes Inside a Notorious
Resort
Near Murderers' Block
A Queer Bar-Room, A Wretched Show Above-Stairs,
A Stupid Dance
Hideous Music—The Character of the "Guests"—Men
Of Respectability Among Pugilists, Thieves, Gamblers, etc.
A Wretched Spectacle.[23]

The favorite place for politicians, sporting men, and "others," was Harry Hill's dance hall. There gathered such prominent thieves as Dutch Heinrich, Sheeny Mike, "Big Nose Bunker," Dublin George, and "The Doctor"; fighters and gamblers like John Morrissey, Yankee Sullivan, "Dutch Charlie," and Tom Hyer; prostitutes, like Sadie the Goat; well-known politicians, lawyers, physicians, members of the legislature, Aldermen, Congressmen, and the more daring members of the financial and commercial community from banker to clerk. "Here youthful levity takes the first steps on the slippery road of sin, and first inhales its poisonous atmosphere." [24] While Tweed and Hall preferred the atmosphere of Delmonico's and the more somber bar of the Manhattan Club, Sweeny and Connolly were often seen at Harry Hill's.

Harry Hill's, a concert saloon on Houston Street, was a sprawling, two-story building, which admitted women free, but to keep out the riffraff, gentlemen were charged twenty cents admission. It had a national reputation for its women, dancing, hard liquor, and exhibition prize fights. One of New York's gaudiest "hells" was run by a God-fearing man who went to church and prayer meetings regularly, was a generous benefactor to charity, and fancied himself a poet. Harry Hill did a roaring business with the exception of one night every week when knowledgeable customers purposely went elsewhere. On this evening, Harry abruptly stopped the serving of drinks, stepped onto his stage, and delivered a long recital of his own poems. A sample of his work was inscribed on a sign over the front door lighted by a huge red and blue lantern:

> Punches and juleps, cobblers and smashes
> To make the tongue waggle with wit's merry flashes.[25]

Harry tried, not always successfully, to run a place that would not become completely unhinged by midnight. On the walls were written the strict rules of the house: "No loud talking; no profanity; no obscene or indecent expressions will be allowed; no man can sit and allow a woman to stand." Hefty enough to be his own bouncer, "he keeps the roughs and bullies in order," wrote a writer of the day, "he keeps jealous women from tearing out each other's eyes . . . he can be seen in all parts of the hall, shouting out, 'Order! Order! Less noise there! Attention! Girls, be quiet!' "[26]

What troubled one contemporary about Harry Hill's was not so much city officials consorting with known criminals, but women standing at the bar smoking cigars and drinking their whisky "straight," at ten cents a glass, and even worse, drinking absinthe. "Consequently," he said, "a woman with temperance proclivities would not be very acceptable."[27] Moreover, since during the past few years absinthe had become a favorite with the ladies, it "is a dangerous poison even for men, how much more harmful must the effects of it be on the more tender organism of females!"[28]

The slums served the rulers of Tammany well. From Tweed's Town were recruited the storm troopers of the Ring, the strong-arm toughs who were vital to the Ring at election time as bruisers and "repeaters." They were a lusty group of men (and women), some of whom have become a part of New York folklore. Unlike later counterparts, they had no Stephen Crane, O. Henry, nor Damon Runyon to immortalize them. Some acted individually, or led gangs of repeaters. There was William Varley, alias Reddy the Blacksmith, pickpocket, thief, murderer—"a villain of the deepest dye."[29] (He killed Wild Jimmy Hagerty in Patsy Egan's saloon when Hagerty had the bad judgment to try and make him stand on his head.) Reddy's excursion into crime was a family enterprise. His sister was a notorious shoplifter, confidence woman, fence, and a madam in a house on James Street. Powerful in the Fourth and the Seventh wards as leader of the William Varley Association, Reddy and his gang proved to be of immense help to the Tweed Ring in the elections of 1868, 1870, and 1871.

Also indispensable was Captain Isaiah Rynders, an ex-Mississippi River gambler, who led the infamous Empire Club at 25 Park Row. From the 1830's on, Rynders and his Empire Club proved particularly irritating to reform meetings: they broke up meetings of Whigs, of William Lloyd Garrison, and of assorted anti-Tammany-ites. With the help of Dirty Face Jack, Country McCleester, and Edward Z.C. Judson (who wrote Western dime novels under the name of Ned Buntline), he achieved immense power as the commander of the Five Points gangsters. So influential was he that a street was named after him (later renamed Center Street) and, despite his criminal connections, he became a United States Marshall.[30]

There was Bully Morrison, a vicious, usually drunken, red-whiskered thug, and a tough wiry hoodlum known as Pegleg Gordon, the "Terror of Battle Row," who unscrewed his wooden leg and swung. And there were the gangs of the slums, like the Gophers, Dead Rabbits, Gorillas, the East Side Dramatic and Pleasure Club, and the Limburger Roarers, who were adept in violence at the polls or among themselves.

Among the ladies, Gallus Mag, Sadie the Goat, Hell-Cat

Maggie, Battle Annie Welsh, and Euchre Kate Burns, whom a newspaper called the "champion heavyweight female brick hurler" of Hell's Kitchen, were all specialists in election day mayhem. Gallus Mag, who supported her skirt with suspenders, was a mean six-foot female who, armed with a pistol and a club, was employed as a bouncer at a dive called the Hole-in-the-Wall. Sadie the Goat, a prostitute and all around rough-and-tumble-fighter, ran with the Charlton Street Gang, a group of river pirates. She won her nickname by the way she would lower her head and butt like a goat in a fight. When aroused Hell-Cat Maggie looked like an enraged tiger. Her teeth were filed to points and over her fingers she wore sharp brass spikes. Even the bravest of men lost their poise when she charged screaming into a polling place. (In a celebrated fight, she bit off the ear of Sadie the Goat.) The huge and violent Battle Annie, "the sweetheart of Hell's Kitchen," was a terrifying bully. She commanded a gang of ferocious Amazons called the Battle Row Ladies Social and Athletic Club.[31]

The citizen in Tweed's Town most important to the Ring was not, however, the violent political mercenary; he was quieter, more troubled, more confused, and there were infinitely more of him. He was the newcomer, the immigrant, who particularly from the 1840's on swarmed into the town, into the rotting tenements, into the congestion, filth, and disease of the lower wards. The "uprooted," as Oscar Handlin calls them, faced a sustained crisis of movement, beginning with the severing of old familiar ties and a dreary ocean voyage; then, in a new unfamiliar world, they faced the crisis of adjustment, the difficulty of making new ties with a new people who often regarded them with distrust and contempt. That the Tweed Ring and Tammany Hall could help them, at least partially, to establish roots meant that the immigrant became the most important bulwark to the power of the Tweed Ring and the Democratic party.

> I s'pose you've noticed how that Pat
> Rhymes, beautiful, with Democrat.[32]

5

THE NEWCOMER

I was born in Mullion in the County Cork
Thirty-five hundred miles from gay New York
Me father never gave a good Goddamn
Because he was a real old Irishman.

Irish drinking song. Anon.

THE NINETEENTH-CENTURY IMMIGRANT was the disinherited of a new frontier. For thousands of them the frontier was not the wild, untamed wilderness and the hostile Indian. Their frontier was the city, where the dangers of the forest were substituted by exploitation by political machines. They faced the contempt of oldtimers —the rooted, established "native" American—and were forced to endure all the painful unexpected adjustments to American urban life. For some the new frontier meant a rebirth, a rich existence filled with opportunities unequaled in the Old World; for others it meant an existence of frustration and poverty, where the promise of American life ironically seemed closed to them. The growth of modern urban political machines, whether under the Tweed Ring or later machines in New York, was in large part determined by the adjustment of the immigrant to the city.

It was by no means a coincidence that a change in the character and pace of immigration in the 1840's eventually made its impact upon New York politics. Before this time, the English, Germans, and French, those who made up the great folk migrations of the eighteenth century, were the principal nationalities who migrated to the United States. Shopkeepers, professional men, farmers, and craftsmen, they were equipped by skill and capital to adjust to the New World and exploit its opportunities, either by moving on to the West or by easing their way into the middle-class life of the city.[1]

By the middle of the 1840's, this pattern changed drastically. Political upheavals and the great potato famines of 1846-48, which struck both Ireland and Germany, created for thousands a desperate need to flee to the New World. To use Oscar Handlin's words, "these people had no choice of destination. They were almost unique in the history of immigration in their intense desire to flee to America."[2] As opposed to the immigrants before the 1840's, they lacked skill and capital which made it extremely difficult for them to move beyond the city; indeed, the greater number had to remain in New York.[3] Consequently, immigrant population increased rapidly. The population of New York City increased from over 300,000 in 1840 to 942,292 in 1870. By that year, when the Tweed Ring was at the height of its power, there were more than 400,000 immigrants in New York, most of them Irish or German.[4]

The bulk of the immigrants found themselves painfully ill-equipped to survive in the new urban world. Landless peasants, rooted in a profoundly static rural environment, they found the skilled, specialized middle-class occupations closed to them. For most, only the more menial, dirty, poorly paying jobs were available. The women went into domestic service, and some—to prostitution. The men worked on the docks, swept the streets, or hired out as laborers in the building trades.[5] For the politically inclined, especially the Irish, the saloon, the police force, and the fire companies served them.

The newcomer found that he had escaped the poverty of the farm to find the poverty of the city. His home was that well-known New York eyesore, the tenement. His existence was barely marginal. His daily life was a constant harassment of a lack of water, sewage, ventilation, sanitation—and respect. Filth, disease, periodic unemployment, family disorganization, and despair, erupted into what particularly worried the native middle classes—disorder and crime. A large number of Irishmen were involved in the bloody draft riots of 1863. Of the 49,423 prisoners in city prisons for one year before January 1870, some 32,225 were of foreign birth, and of these 21,887 were Irish.[6] All this convinced many native-born Americans that the Irishman was indeed a particularly dangerous fellow. Yet Ireland itself was a notably law-abiding country having a lower crime rate than either England or Scotland.[7]

Buffeted by the distrust of the native and the challenge of the city, the immigrant joined his own kind in order to grapple with the pressures and anxieties of his life. By settling in ethnic clusters the immigrants gave the city on the East and West Sides the appearance of a collection of little "Europes." But this kind of solidarity by no means suggested that the immigrants had shut themselves off from American life. As one historian has noted with excellent insight, the immigrants "reflected widespread acceptance of the common middle-class ideals dominant in the society about them. Even the mass of former peasants, who could not in their own lives apply the American axioms of thrift, hard work, advancement, and progress, recognized that these were the keys to respect and status in the United States." [8]

Tammany Hall, with motives more expedient than altruistic, seeing the immigrants confronted with and often confounded by the hard problems of the city, came to their aid. While reformers preached about civic responsibility, efficiency in government, and particularly lower taxes, Tammany exchanged cheer, charity, and jobs for votes. The Tweed Ring learned the art of being ethnic brokers. When the steamers came in, Democrats flocked to Castle Gardens to offer the immigrant a bowl of soup, guide him to a cheap boarding house, and often find him a job. Tammany and its many affiliated ward clubs provided good fellowship, which usually revolved around the bar, where the newcomer could find a sympathetic ear for his resentments. Here, too, Tammany could strengthen group-consciousness by appealing to the immigrants' national pride. For example, on December 29, 1870, at a Democratic General Committee meeting, Grand Sachem Tweed presiding, Richard O'Gorman, who was not only an eloquent Irishman but also Corporation Counsel for the City of New York, offered these resolutions.

> The Democratic Party never fails to sympathize with all men who devote themselves to the cause of their country's independence, and
>
> Whereas, Certain Irishmen who have suffered painful imprisonment in various British prisons and were punished for their opposition to British dominion in Ireland, have been recently released and are expected soon to arrive in the City of New York; therefore;
>
> Resolved, That the General Committee of the Tammany Society, pledged as it is to the cause of freedom all over the world, tender to the Irish patriots a cordial welcome.[9]

The Boss himself began the celebration by giving $1000.

The generosity of the beneficent Tweed, however, should not belie the fact that Tammany ruthlessly exploited the immigrant. The fundamental interests of Tammany were not those of the immigrant but the cold, calculated pursuance of the narrow self-interests of Tammany Hall. If this coincided with the interests of the immigrants, all well and good; if not, the immigrant was either ignored or shunted aside. More often than not, the two interests did not coincide. Conservative Tammany Hall never undertook a sustained attack on the critical ills affecting the newcomer—poverty, housing, education, etc. Charity and patronage were doled out in bits and pieces for the purpose of strengthening the political position of the Tweed Ring's Tammany organization. Nor did the immigrant fare much better in other cities under different regimes, such as the venal Republican machine in Philadelphia.

To satisfy their need for companionship and organization, the immigrants formed mutual-aid societies, churches, newspapers, theaters, militia, and fire companies, many of which could provide strong political support. Politics offered one of the very few escapes from Wooster or Water streets, and Tammany enrolled the Irish and the Germans into the district organizations, rewarding zeal with a committee post and a public office. In the 1850's Fernando Wood made New York's "finest" into an institution to win immigrant favor and dispense patronage. On March 24, 1855, the German newspaper *Staats-Zeitung* published data which, while not altogether accurate, reflected the dispersal of immigrants on the police force.

Ward	*United States*	*Ireland*	*Germany*	*Elsewhere*
First	19	37	5	2
Second	28	18		1
Third	45	3		3
Fourth	18	32	3	3
Fifth	44	11	1	1
Sixth	21	32	1	4
Seventh	39	20	1	4
Eighth	41	7	4	2
Ninth	49	2	2	1
Tenth	37	2	2	4
Eleventh	40	7	3	
Twelfth	20	12	1	1
Thirteenth	35	10	3	2
Fourteenth	19	30	3	2
Fifteenth	40	1		
Sixteenth	30	14		2
Seventeenth	33	11	5	4
Eighteenth	36	10	1	3
Nineteenth	29	12		2
Twentieth	29	14	11	3
Twenty-first	42	7		1
Twenty-second	25	13	3	3

The Tweed Ring shrewdly went much beyond Wood and opened up an unusually large number of public offices to the Germans and the Irish. Indeed the Ring used the immigrant to help create the first modern city machine in New York and to streamline Tammany Hall. Never before had the Democratic party so effectively gained the support of the newcomer. The Tweed Ring provided an unprecedented number of jobs for immigrants. This is not to say, as it has been argued, that the Tweed days mark the coming of the immigrant, especially the Irish, into his own, politically.[10] True, the Irish were infiltrating almost every branch of government; true, the old Anglo-Saxon ruling class was leaving politics for industry and finance, and more and more Irish filled their places. But if the ethnic character of political leadership is any criterion, two Ringmen, Tweed and Hall, were of Scottish and English origin respectively, and the first Irish Catholic city boss did not emerge until John Kelly, after the Ring's fall. The Tweed era, therefore, marks a transitional stage which would culminate in Irish domination of Tammany Hall and New York City politics.

The *New York Times* published a list on September 17, 1869, which was not altogether accurate, but was precise enough to illustrate how the Ring gave the immigrant through patronage a role in city government.

Office	*No. of Germans*	*No. of Irish*
Mayor's office	2	11
Aldermen	2	34
Assistant Aldermen	1	37
Comptroller	2	126
Street Department		87
Law Department		8
Croton Aqueduct		76
Supervisors	2	14
Education	2	42
County Clerk	15	10
Surrogate	4	9

Office	*No. of Germans*	*No. of Irish*
Sheriff	1	23
Tax Commissioner	2	26
Coroner	1	3
District Attorney		19
Supreme Court	1	57
Superior Court	2	40
Common Pleas		26
Marine Court	4	18
Sessions	1	44
Police Courts	4	34
Superintendent of Buildings		31
Special Sessions Court		5
Commissioner of Juries		5
Assessments		6
Police captains		32
Almshouse		48
City Prison		20
Penitentiary		18
District prisons		10
Poor Department		18
Workhouse		12
Randall's Island		23
Lunatic Asylum		42

The *Times* admitted that the accuracy of the table was tainted somewhat by including "Americans" under the number of Irish; but the native-born, it hastened to add, did not constitute more than one-third of the list.

If these figures suggest the overwhelming preference for the Irish, the legitimate *voting* strength was not as much as popular myth has it. The 1870 census listed the State of New York's population as 4,382,759; 12 per cent of whom, or 528,806, were of Irish birth; 981,587 were males eligible to vote. In the total voting population of the State, the Irish immigrant accounted for 11.3

per cent, but in New York City they represented 21.3 per cent, or approximately 40,200 voters.[11] The *illegitimate* voting strength of the Irish was something else. The great virtue of the Irish vote was the discipline and cohesiveness of its rank and file. Complained an anti-immigrant rhymster about the Tweed Ring and the immigrant:

> Ever and aye as they come
> Thousand on thousand, more and more
> In crowds that are never clean or thin,
> The grand magnorums rake them in.
> Their hearts they twist, and their ears they fill,
> And their bellies, too; and to work their will
> They teach them lies of every hue
> Concerning the king. Oh, king, 'tis true!
> They bring them so to the polls; and then,
> For every vote of the loyal men,
> The grand magnorum slips in ten.
> The votes of the men beyond the seas
> Are many; but, not content with these
> Our gifts as voters they override....
> And the thing is a thing, oh king, that sours
> On us all, to find that the city powers,
> By the aid of the men from beyond the seas,
> Are from us reft by such deeds as these.[12]

The immigrant could be mustered readily into the ranks of the democracy not only because of the excellence of Tammany's recruiting methods, but also because of the temptation of public office the Ring dangled in front of him. It was a fine irony, and perhaps a fitting one, that the reformers themselves in many ways had as much to do with driving the newcomers into the outstretched hands of Tammany as did Tweed himself.

Before, during, and, indeed, after the Tweed era, there was a large migration into New York of upstate small-towners, and agrarians, New Englanders raised on high-toned moral imperatives. They brought with them the orderly, methodical, conscientious,

Cartoon by Thomas Nast illustrating the anti-Catholic reaction to Tweed's public school policy; courtesy of the New-York Historical Society, New York City

cold, and exacting Protestant ethic, which could rise to the heights of the evangelical when seemingly endangered. And danger there was, personified by the city, which represented a new way of life contrasting violently to the peace of the farm and the quiet of the village common. The immigrant, who seemed to bring with him from Europe all that was old and sour and evil, thus seemed to threaten the city, a way of life, and Republicanism itself. For many Protestant New Yorkers the suspicions aroused by the nativists in the 'fifties and the horrors of the draft riots of 1863 were greatly heightened by their awareness of the unholy alliance of the Tweed Ring and its minions, Catholic Irish and beer-drinking Germans. The old ideological contest between the Old and the New World seemed resumed; the battlefield was New York City.

The Yankee notion of political action—and many Yankees composed the ranks of reformers in New York—assumed that democracy worked only by widespread participation and eager civic interest. Politics was the duty, the business, the responsibility of all men; it was the Protestant ethic preached and practiced. The public good must be put before personal welfare. Politics must reflect correct business habits: efficiency and low costs; above all, the politician must be a moral man. To the reformer, as E. L. Godkin said, Tweed's Town seemed "as much a *terra incognita* as Montenegro or Albania. There could hardly be a more striking revelation of the sources of Tweed's power than is to be found in the gulf which still separates American families from their Irish servants." [13]

The reformer's fear, confusion, and distaste centered on the immigrant. "These newcomers," said one high-minded reformer, "were ignorant, clannish, and easily controlled. Their moral sense had been blunted by ages of degradation. . . ." [14] Protestant Yankee reformers saw them as ignorant foreigners; their case was hopeless. Printed matter could not reach them. "What honest men print they cannot read, what honest men say they will not hear." [15] They were untrained in the duties of citizenship. They were "entirely" unacquainted with republican government, and "utterly" unfamiliar with American political ideas.[16] The *New York Times,* spokesman for middle-class reform, found the immigrant the lowest and most ignorant class of the whole community, especially the Irish, who "always" ranged themselves on the side of reaction and absolutism, and whose "unquiet character" was made more obnoxious by whisky, religious fanaticism, and barroom politics. The Irishman never looked more the grotesque caricature of the ordinary human being than when he was "rigged out" in a long black coat and a new "silk hat," for a silly St. Patrick's Day parade. What to do about it? The *Times* suggested rescue by way of "industry and virtue," the public school system and Cooper's Institute, libraries, migration to the West, "where health and plenty greet the laboring swain," and more attention and control by the Department of Public Charities and Correction, "without involving any special drain upon the resources of the government." [17]

Not all reformers were intensely anti-immigrant. One, overpowered by a sense of guilt, said: "The poor immigrants coming to our shores found rich legacies—the privileges which our fathers had fought for but we neglected through money making and or indifference—like taxation, election of representatives, voice in expenditures of money, the ballot—these great privileges are cast into the streets as trash, like the broken toys of a spoiled child. . . . And we charge *them* with the crime of theft. We, who tossed these privileges away!" [18] And the *Nation* ruefully pointed out:

> It ought to be said for the Irish that two of the most respected judges, Daly and Brady, are Irishmen; the two noted judicial rascals are Americans; and the chief scoundrels of the City Hall are drawn almost equally from the Irish and Americans. The clearest brains of the Ring are Irish, but most of the money seems to go to the Americans, who, by the bye, are far more luxurious dogs than the Irish.[19]

But these examples were more the exception than the rule. Most reformers were anti-immigrant and anti-Catholic, and only succeeded in herding the immigrant closer to Tammany. One doesn't woo a girl by telling her how ugly she is.

The immigrant needed time to shed his European heritage. Coming from a peasant environment, often ruled by an autocracy, he was bewildered and alienated by the Yankee-Protestant notion of politics. He could be led by the Tweed Ring and later city bosses because in the past he had been led by one "boss" or another—the landowner, royalty, the aristocracy. Politics to him meant not some misty goal of high-sounding principles, but something that would specifically advance his welfare. An anti-immigrant spokesman would say, "The immigrant lacks the faculty of abstraction. He thinks not of the welfare of the community but only of himself." As Oscar Handlin points out, "it never occurred to this critic that precious little thought was given by others to the welfare of the newcomers."[20] Used to the paternalism of the Old World, he sought improvement through personal contacts and personal loyalties, something the Tweed Ring understood and exploited. The reformer simply could not break the communication barrier. When an "honest" man came among the citizens of the lower wards, speaking of temperance, Sabbatarianism, civic responsibility, the evils of patronage, the necessity of justice, and the logic of economy, the immigrant's reaction was one of suspicion and fear. The cry for efficiency and the end of patronage might mean the end of his job. Economy might scotch the building of a new school for his child. To him civic responsibility was an understanding of his plight, justice was a playground for the children, or something to eat when times were bad. With a certain qualification, not abstractions but basic needs were the critical issues of politics.

The qualification was that Tammany was not altogether above using abstractions. It is well known that Tammany used the devices of food, a job, and coal to win immigrant support. But it has not always been realized that Tammany used an abstraction, an idea that persuasively caught the minds and imaginations of newcomers—the abstraction of patriotism. It was heady stuff for the new immigrants after the 1840's because of their urgent compulsion to be a part of America, on one hand, and because of the constant ridicule and contempt of nativists on the other, who held that the immigrant was a threat to American ideals. Patriotism became a means for the newcomer to prove himself worthy, and Tammany Hall was the Pied Piper leading him on. The famed exponent of practical politics, George Washington Plunkitt, explained patriotism and politics in his own inimitable way:

> Tammany's the most patriotic organization on earth, not withstandin' the fact that the civil service law is sappin' the foundations of patriotism all over the country. Nobody pays any attention to the Fourth of July any longer except Tammany and the small boy. When the Fourth comes, the reformers, with Revolutionary names parted in the middle, run off to Newport or the Adirondacks . . . How different it is with Tammany! The very constitution of the Tammany Society requires that we must assemble at the wigwam on the Fourth, regardless of the weather, and listen to the readin' of the Declaration of Independence and patriotic speeches.
>
> You ought to attend one of these meetin's. They're a liberal education in patriotism. The great hall upstairs is filled with five thousand people, suffocatin' from heat and smoke. Every man Jack of these five thousand knows that down in the basement there's a hundred cases of champagne and two hundred kegs of beer ready to flow when the signal is given. Yet that crowd stick to their seats without turnin' a hair . . . for four solid hours . . . sittin' in the hottest place on earth . . . with parched lips and gnawin' stomachs, and known' all the time that the delights of the oasis in the desert were only two flights downstairs! Ah, that is the highest kind of patriotism. . . .
>
> And then see how they applaud and yell when patriotic things are said! As soon as the man on the platform starts off with "when, in the course of human events," word goes around that it's the Declaration of Independence, and a mighty roar goes up. . . . Tammany don't only show its patriotism at Fourth-of-July celebrations. It's always on deck when the country needs its services. . . .
>
> Now, a word about Tammany's love for the American flag.

> Did you ever see a Tammany Hall decorated for a celebration? It's just a mass of flags. They even take down the window shades and put flags in place of them. There's flags everywhere except on the floors. We don't care for expense where the American flag is concerned, especially after we have won an election.[21]

It would be easy to dismiss Plunkitt as being superficial, funny, and cynical. It might also be a mistake to do so. For all the exaggerations, no matter how much Tammany's motives for patriotism may be questioned, the super-patriotic appeal was an effective force in cementing the newcomer to the leadership of New York's Democratic party. The Tweed Ring controlled an organization that had from the very beginning posed as a patriotic society. To be sure it was an organization concerned not with the larger issues of national policy, but committed totally to advancing its own self-interest in the City and State of New York. But on national holidays or on days commemorating some heroic American achievement, Tammany reacted with the highest degree of patriotic fervor and purple prose. One has only to pour through the mountains of documents in the Kilroe Tammaniana Collection in the Columbia University Library that record the Tammany patriotic celebrations.

Tammany's nationalism was not a unique departure from practical politics, but rather a marrying of patriotism and politics to achieve local, practical ends. In effect, Tammany assumed the role of spokesman for American ideals. For the immigrant especially, it posed as the machinery behind the Americanization process. The Tweed Ring accepted and accelerated this tradition. It made Tammany the guardian of the ideals of American life so urgently sought by the newcomer. It combined the old traditions of Tammany—patriotism and anti-aristocratic appeals—with the ideals of the day: equal rights, free opportunity, free public schools, religious freedom—to be achieved, of course, only by following the guiding hand of St. Tammany. It exploited the immigrants' frustrations and despair and created, as it were, a politics of resentment. Enemies of Tammany and reformers in general were identified as the opponents of true patriotism and American ideals, and the source of all the immigrants' woes. All this plus free lager, free cigars on election day, free coal in the winter, a bail bond when in trouble, a kind word at a wake, and a job, proved irresistible to the immigrant and the native poor alike.

These appeals to patriotism were artfully combined with unflinching attention to the grass-roots of immigrant life. This approach represented a kind of revolution in New York politics. Prior to the reign of Fernando Wood, political factions were controlled by men belonging to the upper or middle class, who tended to see politics as a duty, not a profession. From the days of Tweed's Forty Thieves through the Civil War, a change was gradually occurring beneath the surface of political life. The old ruling groups, even the august Albany Regency, were being slowly displaced by a group not new, but different in numbers and the ranks from which it came—the professional politicians. As New York itself grew, politics became more centralized, more disciplined, more professionalized. It became more of a business, and despite the schemes of the Tweed Ring, not always a dirty business. It involved also the everyday routine of building an organization and a following, the often dreary, exhausting leg work of politics, which did not appeal to the "respectabilities." As the old ruling class abdicated from practical politics, visiting the lower wards only to deliver lofty moral manifestoes, the professionals moved in. Professionalization meant new opportunities for ex-firemen like Tweed or a poor boy like Sweeny, who would have found it difficult to compete with the gentry in former days. Importantly, it meant that the native-born Tweeds and Sweenys, the fagged-out symbols of respectability like Hall, the lawyers, doctors, merchant princes, shopkeepers, scions of old families—the old ruling groups—had to begin to move over and make a place for a new group, the Connollys—the Irish immigrant.

Tweed, Sweeny, and Connolly understood this. They studied the immigrants' ways, attended their weddings and funerals, participated in their club life, became specialists in personal relations and personal loyalties. Politics was a business, not business—

efficiency which often expressed itself in an inhuman regard for the individual—but the business of getting votes. Tweed understood this when in the winter of 1870 he gave $50,000 to the Seventh Ward to buy food and coal, something the reformers never understood. Nor would they understand how professional politicians made politics a thing of good fellowship—indeed fun—like an exciting torchlight parade for Tweed, Mike Norton treating 1500 supporters to a clambake, Slippery Dick Connolly's annual ward club ball. And certainly the do-gooders would find only contempt for this Irish drinking song:

A short time ago a gentleman named Darrity
Was elected to the Senate by a very large majority
He was so elated that he went to Dennis Cassity
Who owns a saloon of a very large capacity
He said to Dennis, "Just send out to a brewer
And get a hundred kegs of beer and give it to the poor
Then send out to a butcher shop and get a hundred tons of meat
And then ask the boys and girls to come and have a bite to eat
Send out invitations in a hundred different languages
And tell 'em to come and have a glass of beer and sandwiches." [22]

Thus the immigrants, undergoing a painful adjustment to American life, frustrated by the terrible realities of the city, alienated from the reformers, transferred their Old World loyalties to the professional politicians, who, while exploiting them, at least understood them. In the heavily-immigrant Seventh Ward the loyalty remained to the very end. In November of 1871, when the Tweed Ring was rapidly falling apart and the Boss was indicted a month earlier for fraud, when it was evident that the city had been looted, the Seventh Ward re-elected William Marcy Tweed to the State Senate. The reformers found it incomprehensible and paid the price for ignoring the newcomer. But the immigrants of Tweed's ward remembered the food, the jobs, the money offered in hard times, the compassionate interests in their problems. It was to the Boss that they gave the "last hurrah."

6

CITY GOVERNMENT

> With few exceptions, the city governments of the United States are the worst in Christendom—the most expensive, the most inefficient and the most corrupt.
>
> Andrew D. White

THE TWEED RING found in municipal government a machinery admirably suited to its purposes. The government of the City of New York, a thing of shreds and patches, offered a standing invitation to plunder. A man attempting to describe it paused after several thousand words to say that he had undertaken to write a discourse on the government of New York but was actually writing a discourse on stealing.[1] Another writer, dismayed by its complexity and inefficiency, chose a complex but nonetheless efficient metaphor to sum up what had happened to municipal government in New York by the time the Tweed Ring came to power.

> . . . the municipal structure has come to resemble one of those dwellings, begun in the olden time, built by piecemeal, at odd times, and patched and added to by fresh generations,—starting with some gabled cottage in the centre, with a Gothic addition in one direction, an attempt at a classic portico in another, a group of stables and styles here, a suite of new parlors there, while meantime some strong-handed neighboring baron has seized and held more than one choice apartment within the curtilage—till withal the whole collection has grown into a labyrinth so devious, that those who have lived their lives around it scarcely know how to find their way in or out of it.[2]

One group who could find its way in and out of this "labyrinth so devious" was the Tweed Ring, who made city government its own private bailiwick. The Ring exploited it not only to conceal graft but also to build the muscles and sinews of its political machine. No real understanding of the Tweed Ring, therefore, is possible without some understanding of the nature of city government under the Ring and the historical evolution that made it the way it was.

The Tweed Ring inherited a municipal structure, a legacy which went back more than two hundred years, beginning with the Dutch, who themselves for a brief time were confronted with a Tweed-type, seventeenth-century rogue named Willem Kieft, "a fountain of woe and trouble, a receptacle of wrath and a public plunderer," said a troubled cleric.[3] From the beginning, New York's political development was bedeviled by two woes: lack of experience in self-government and outside control. The British established two broad political divisions, the counties and the towns, but the two cities of Albany and New York were considered separate, distinct political entities.[4] Where the towns were able to enjoy the town meeting, that great institution for self-government and popular sovereignty, New York was not. Whether under Dutch, English, or American rule, she was controlled by an aristocratic elite to well within the nineteenth century. Despite her tremendous potential as the political, economic, and social center of the state, she had no training in governing her own affairs. Through the years, this authority rested upon the regulation and whims prescribed in either Holland, England, or at the Capitol in Albany. Thus from the seventeenth to the nineteenth century, the science of government did not keep pace with New York's expansion as a great commercial city.[5]

With the Dongan charter of 1686, the English created the basic pattern of city government. The city was divided into six wards. Citizens were allowed a marginal voice in government by being allowed to elect an Alderman and one Assistant Alderman for each ward.[6] But the major offices were controlled by the Governor and his council, composed of affluent gentlemen, since they could appoint the Mayor, Recorder, Clerk, and Sheriff.

As one of the most conservative states during and after the Revolution, aristocratic rule predominated until 1822, when democratic tendencies began to appear. The people were now permitted to elect the Common Council, Sheriff, and Clerk, but it was not until 1834 that the Mayor became popularly elected. The major democratic breakthrough did not come until the charter of 1847, which reflected the liberal State Constitution of 1846. Belatedly, the charter was an experiment in local self-government, modeled on the township and school district systems. It gave elective powers to the people for most of the important offices in the city.[7]

In the post-Civil War period, when the Tweed Ring entered politics, one thing was clear: democracy and self-rule did not produce better administration. City government became a curious variety of contradictory and temporary expedients, having no common principle. It was actually a crazy-quilt of petty sovereignties, each independent of the other, and all spending money without any accountability to anyone.[8] To make matters worse, the Mayor had little responsibility—he could not appoint or remove the heads of nine executive departments. The departments themselves were in administrative shambles, having powers that were either undefined, doubtful, or conflicting. Their executives, being independent of the Mayor's control and arrogant and jealous of their own power, built private empires. While the diffusion of mayoralty powers gave Fernando Wood a smoke screen behind which he would operate his corruption, the fact that he could never unite and control his executive departments was one reason he never achieved the power of a Tweed.

By 1857 when Tweed began playing a significant role in New York politics as a Supervisor, another change took place. Reaction against the corruptions of the Forty Thieves and Fernando Wood had set in and was encouraged by the Republicans, who hoped to enhance their position in the city. The result was a radically new city charter. It was a fateful decision, full of irony. The charter of

1857, designed as a reform measure, "reformed" city government by creating more administrative chaos, thereby setting the scene for boss rule. It gave the Tweed gang a Cause—home rule, dear to the hearts of New Yorkers. It was so skillfully exploited by the Ring that it led to a new charter in 1870, which consolidated the power of the Tweed Ring and raised it to the zenith of its power. Down to 1857, municipal authorities had some say in laws affecting city government, but with the new charter all power to change this government rested with the State legislature. James Bryce saw the charter of 1857 as a watershed in New York history. "Since this date," he wrote in the *American Commonwealth*, "the largest city . . . of the American continent has lain at the mercy of the State legislature; and the legislature has not scrupled to remodel and disarrange the government institutions of the city. Its charter has been subjected to a continual 'tinkering' that has made the law uncertain, and a comprehension of its administration extremely difficult."[9]

The growth of boss rule was further enhanced when the lines of authority and responsibility in city government were complicated and confused. A series of departments were created, partly with city and partly with state business, which were for all practical purposes independent and not accountable either to the Mayor or to the Aldermen. Heads of the Almshouse department, Board of Education, and the Croton Aqueduct Board, the Comptroller, and the Corporation Counsel, were elected directly by the voters, chosen and controlled, however, by party caucus. When the Tweed Ring came to power, it wasted little time in capturing the party caucus that made these nominations.

The most important alteration made by the charter of 1857 resulted from a move by the Republicans, led by Thurlow Weed, to change certain local offices into State offices, to be filled through appointment by the Governor. Ostensibly this was a reform, a proper check and balance against corruption in the city. Actually it was the attempt of the Republicans, who had swept the State in the recent election, to obtain a share of power and patronage which they needed badly in a city usually dominated by Democrats. Thus State boards or commission government arrived in New York. A Metropolitan police force, fire and health commissions, and a State board for the administration of Central Park were created. By 1867, Boards of Charities and Corrections, Education, Emigration and Quarantine, Taxes, and Assessors were added.[10]

There were well-established precedents for commission government. New York State in 1792, 1810, and 1816-17 had commissioners appointed to begin connecting the Great Lakes and Hudson River systems. All of this was lost sight of in the hue and cry that followed the 1857 charter. City Democrats, fearful that their power and patronage were in danger, argued vehemently that the city was now deprived of any home rule, and that interference from an unsympathetic, tyrannical Albany would be the rule of the day. Protest was translated into violence. The attempt to enforce the bill that created a Police Commission was resisted to the point of riot and bloodshed. For a while New York was treated to the spectacle of two police forces, which was just as if they had none at all, as the new Metropolitan police and the old Municipal police rioted and bashed each other's heads on the very steps of City Hall. When a ballot was taken from the old Municipal force to seek their opinion of the new police law, it was not altogether astonishing to find that out of 1100 policemen, 800 were Democrats who wanted the status quo; the 300 who wanted a change were Republicans.[11] The matter was finally decided in favor of the new police law by the highest court in the state.

The commission system worked in England, but it was not very successful in New York. It not only deprived the city of some measure of self-government but compounded a mistake long enduring in the state: there was no one uniform system for municipalities, for the legislature passed special laws regulating the frame of government in each of its cities. It gave the Democrats in general and the Tweed Ring in particular the emotionally charged issue of home rule. At the same time, the Ring increased its lobbying efforts at Albany and attempted to bribe the Republican commissioners in the city. The justification of "nonpartisan" given to the commissioners merely affirmed the old adage that you can't take politics out of politics. Politics became more foul; more Republicans became "Tammany Republicans"; and Tweed was given a chance in 1870 to present a new charter, not so much to decide home rule, as Carl Becker once said about the American Revolution, as to decide who shall rule at home.

This, then, was the general character of government that fell by 1866 into the hands of the Tweed Ring. New York had simply outgrown its government. In the years of expansion before and after the Civil War, the city was growing without plan or direction, bursting its old boundaries. There was an urgent demand for new streets, new buildings, better transportation, better welfare services. Reflecting a theme in other great American cities of the nineteenth century, there was an intimate connection between rapid growth and the emergence of powerful city machines. City improvements demanded an increased labor force, thereby offering greater opportunities for patronage. The political machine could build a following by controlling jobs and offering work to its followers in construction or on the city streets or city parks. Rapid urbanization brought crushing social problems beyond the scope of existing city agencies, allowing the political machine to operate as a kind of welfare organization, providing not only employment, but handouts in money and food to the needy, in exchange for a vote. Expansion provided increasing opportunities for graft involving contracts for new buildings or various city improvements, franchises for horsecar lines and ferry companies. Moreover, expansion helped create the perfect covering for a city machine: the rubble of an archaic, inefficient city government, where authority and responsibility were divided and confused. In effect, a wide gap opened between the city's ever-expanding economic organizations and its lagging, obsolete agencies of government. The man who could step into this breach and act as middleman between the economic and political institutions could have the title of City Boss. When the Tweed Ring did step into this breach, it inherited a system of government that would serve it well and cost New Yorkers dear.

It was a government lopsided and filled with loopholes in responsibility. Two differently constituted Boards of Councilmen had been established in succession. The affairs of the city were dominated by a rurally oriented State legislature, and the city was forced to turn lobbyist to protect itself. Power sputtered down irregularly from Albany and state boards, and spread unevenly from Mayor to city legislative officers. The city was hopelessly entangled in overlapping jurisdictions of authority concentrated in the Common Council, where Supervisors and Aldermen literally constituted a double government. Each had its own large battery of officials with high salaries, one government for the county, the other for the city. These governments were divided into sixteen departments. In five of them were as many as eighteen bureaus, staffed by a head with a fancy salary and an army of clerks. As a fitting touch to governmental chaos, all the departments were independent and not responsible to any central authority; and, to add chaos to confusion, independence was granted to the commissioners who owed their allegiance not to New York City but to Albany. No wonder James Bryce said, "The phenomena of municipal democracy in the United States are the most remarkable and least laudable which the modern world has witnessed; and they present some evils which no political philosopher, however unfriendly to popular government, appears to have foreseen, evils which have scarcely showed themselves in the cities of Europe, and unlike those which were thought characteristic of the rule of the masses in ancient times."[12]

If there was one branch of city government that best illustrated Bryces' dour interpretation it was the Aldermen or Common Council, or the "Board of Common Scoundrels." The Aldermen had varied greatly in number and function since the Dongan charter of the seventeenth century. In 1866 its two branches, the Board of Councilmen (or Assistant Aldermen) and Board of Aldermen, were executive as well as legislative bodies. Its two chambers were modeled after the Federal example, one to represent the majority and numbers, the other the minority and property. Its functions, as the Union League put it, were "official nominations, accumulations, and division of the spoils of office." [13] Aldermen did not have an exciting job; it was often routine, more often dull. The history of the Board was not a spectacular one, but it did have its special moments. In 1831 the Aldermen gave a charter to the Harlem Railroad Company for the "perpetual and exclusive use" of Fourth Avenue, and critics of the grant charged corruption. In 1842 a street cleaning contract was let for a period of years at $64,000 a year, although responsible contractors said the job could be done for $25,000 a year. Throughout its history, there were charges that appointments to the Board were sold. In 1861 P. T. Barnum, showman extraordinary, bribed the Aldermen to allow him to supply salt water from the bay to the Museum where he was exhibiting his marvelous whales. And then there were the Forty Thieves. But aside from these incidents business continued as usual: presentation of petitions, motions and resolutions, communications and reports from departments, unfinished business, and special orders of the day. When the Tweed Ring seized power, however, the dreary business of aldermanic duties was given a little zest.

The Ring controlled the Aldermen in much the same fashion as it did the Board of Supervisors. It didn't seek to win over the entire Board, but just the necessary few which by block vote could pass an extortive "cinch" bill or a lucrative franchise. The Ring was aided by two trends which had begun before it took power: the increase of professionalization in urban politics and the decrease of middle- and upper-class men in city government.

As politics became more of a business, politicians found more "business" opportunities in the Aldermen. Nor was the business always graft. They became more concerned in building political power in their own ward, as they used their position to grind out legislation favorable to their own followers. Their view of city affairs narrowed to the simple proposition that what was good for their ward was good for the city. If they had to give a little to gain a little, this easy compromise was useful to the leaders of Tammany Hall. Moreover, as politics became more centralized, many of the Aldermen owed both their nomination and election to the Ring. And political debts had to be honored.

This development, in turn, revealed a change in the kind of men who became Aldermen. Chancellor Kent wrote in 1835 that "the office of Assistant Alderman would be pleasant and desirable to persons of leisure, of intelligence, and of disinterested zeal for the wise and just regulation of the public concerns of the day." [14] The Alderman of the post-Civil War days was a considerably different creature from Kent's man of leisure. There was the story told during the Tweed days that "a certain wag" hired a newsboy to run into the aldermanic chambers shouting, "Mister, your liquor store is on fire!" All the Aldermen, it was said, leaped to their feet and rushed for the door "in undignified disorder and panic." [15]

Much of this was reflected in an article that James Parton, the so-called father of American biography, wrote during the early days of the Tweed Ring. By no means objective or impartial, the article registered the gentry's disgust as men of humble origins moved into power. But it did reveal to some extent the legislative process and techniques of the Aldermen as they practiced their politics. Parton decided that it was not enough to know the general history and nature of city government, not enough just to be indignant about the course of municipal government. It was necessary to go down to City Hall itself and observe a day in the life of a city legislator.

His first impression was of the City Hall. Passing by open doors, he was struck by the profusion of idle men, cigars, and smoke. There were few buildings in the world, he said, wherein the consumption of tobacco goes on more vigorously than the City Hall of New York. Even clerks were smoking cigars "of a flavor beyond that which the pursuit of literature allows."

Thinking his time would best be spent visiting the lower branch of the Aldermen, the Board of Councilmen or Assistant Aldermen, he went to the second floor, passing more idle men smoking cigars, and entered the Councilmen's Chamber. It was a large room, furnished with "preposterous magnificence," thick carpets, curtains "heavy with expense" but not "regardless of expense." The chamber was arranged on the plan of the Representatives' chamber in Washington. The President sat aloft; below him were four clerks; the members, thirteen Republicans and twelve Democrats, sat in two semicircles in chairs of expensive mahogany; the desks were of "solid elegance." To remind the members, "who all have gold watches," of the time, there was a great clock framed in gilt and carving. Portraits of Fillmore, Clay, and Hamilton Fish "disfigure" the walls, and George Washington looked "coldly" and apparently with disapproval down on the scene. "*He* never had such furniture either at Mount Vernon or at Philadelphia, nor did he ever have such at Independence Hall." On the ceiling was a gaudy fresco of an eagle spreading its wings. And to the side was a door leading to the Councilmen's private room, where there was a wardrobe for each member's belongings. "These wardrobes are very properly provided with lock and key."

Because the Board met only twice a week, with the average session lasting just an hour, Parton was somewhat astonished at the army employed to assist the Councilmen in their duties. There was a chief clerk, a deputy clerk, a first assistant clerk, a second assistant clerk, a general clerk, an "engrossing" clerk, all earning from $1200 to $3000 a year, plus other assorted bureaucratic folk like doorkeepers, messengers, and assistant messengers. To the salaries of these helpers were added several thousand more dollars for "extra services"; six or seven thousand more dollars to reporters of seventeen newspapers "for not reporting their proceedings," at $200 each. Even then, Parton suspected, the clerks were paid for not doing their work, for in June 1866 the Mayor complained that bills which came to him for approval were "so badly written that he could scarcely read them," and warned that if penmanship did not improve he would turn his attention to other things.

Looking over the Councilmen, Parton did notice some honest

men. There was Christopher Pullman, who led a minority of six; William B. White, manager of a printing office; Stephen Roberts, a "sturdy smithy," and Morris A. Tyng, unique for also being an honest lawyer. The majority of the Board, however, in experience and ability were equal "to the management of an oyster-stand in a market." The crowd of spectators outside the railing was no better. It looked like a rogues' gallery come to life, he said. Greetings and friendly chit-chat were passed between the members and the audience, and, once, a Councilman tossed a chunk of tobacco to a spectator, "who caught it with pleasing dexterity."

The session started. In "reckless haste" a member proposed that certain lots be provided with curbstones; another, that a free drinking fountain be built; another, that a street be paved with Belgian pavement. "The resolutions were adopted, usually, without a word of explanation, and at a speed that must be seen to be appreciated."

A member proposed to lease a building for a city court at $2000 a year for ten years. Christopher Pullman arose and carefully pointed out (1) the rents were already too high; (2) the lease was too long; and (3) he had seen the building and could prove that even $1200 for that rather shabby structure was exorbitant. He was immediately challenged by a man with a bull neck and "ungrammatical habits." Before Pullman could gasp air for rebuttal, a half dozen voices shouted, "Question! Question!" The question was immediately raised and a "perfect war of noes" voted Mr. Pullman down. In another "chorus of *ayes*" the motion was carried. ("In all such affairs, the visitor notices a kind of ungovernable propensity to vote for spending money. . . .")

Parton noticed how the device of the "previous question" was artfully used. One member introduced a resolution to annul an old paving contract and authorize a new one at higher rates. Anticipating graft, "honest" Stephen Roberts rose to his feet holding a bulky document containing the signatures of property owners who complained against any increase of rates. He stood waiting, eyeing the chairman, ready to present the remonstrance as soon as the clerk finished reading the resolution. "Fancy the impetuous

Roberts with the document held aloft, the yards of signatures streaming down to his feet and flowing far under his desk, awaiting the time when it would be in order for him to cry out, 'Mr. President.'" The member who introduced the resolution, however, was the one who caught the impartial chairman's eye and he moved the previous question. And that was that. In vain Mr. Roberts "fluttered and rattled his streaming ribbon of blotted paper."

A three-fourths vote was required to grant money—that is, eighteen members. If the Ring-controlled members could not muster the necessary strength, the tactic of "reconsideration" was relied on. If, for example, the Ring wished to pass an important money bill, but it was voted down, the member who introduced it made a motion for a reconsideration, which meant the bill was not dead but could be voted upon again at another time. A reconsideration required only a majority vote, which the Ring could usually raise. Usually, however, parliamentarian finesse was not necessary. Corruption was simpler and more direct—the Ring bought the required Republican votes.

Thus James Parton witnessed the carrying of a number of extraordinary measures that day. A resolution directed the Street Commissioner to make a contract with the lowest bidder for lighting the whole island with gas for twenty years, the price fixed at the moment when gas and labor were twice their usual price. A young Councilman returned to his ward a hero by having the Board pay $900 to a drunken hackney driver who had driven his coach and two horses off a dock into the river. Particularly annoying was a resolution to appoint a messenger to the City Librarian, "who had perhaps less to do than any man in New York. . . ." The resolution failed the day Parton was there, but later he had to report that "perseverance meets its reward. We hear that this messenger is now smoking in the City Hall at a salary of fifteen hundred dollars."

After the provocative session with the Assistant Alderman, Parton felt he could hardly endure a round with the Aldermen. But curiosity triumphed over disgust. In the room where the Aldermen met, he noticed that instead of pictures there were busts on each side of the President's chair, one of John Jay, one of John Marshall. Parton found the same wild profusion of clerks, engrossers, readers, messengers, and assistant messengers. Except that the Aldermen were a little older and better dressed than the Councilmen, he could find no other difference between the two. Whatever dubious scheme was hurried through one body was rushed through the other. "Sometimes the Councilmen point the game, and the Aldermen bring it down; and sometimes it is the Aldermen that start up the covey, and the Councilmen that fire." [16] Parton would have agreed with the jingle, many years later, commemorating the final end of the Board of Aldermen.

Farewell the Board of Aldermen
Whose word no one relied on
Who seldom did an honest thing
And never did a wise one.[17]

But James Parton himself had a parting shot. After a day with the Board of Councilmen, a day of acute exasperation, he said of the assistant city fathers, "There will be moments when a person of vivacious turn of mind will feel an almost irresistible impulse to throw something at the head of those insolent young barkeepers. . . ." [18]

PART TWO

BUILDING THE ORGANIZATION

7

THE TIGER

Tammany, Tammany,
Swamp 'em swamp 'em, get the "wumpum," Tammany . . . .
Tammany, Tammany, your policemen can't be beat.
They can sleep on any street . . . .
When Reformers think it's time to show activity,
They blame everything that's bad on poor old Tammany . . . .
They say when a bad man dies he goes to Tammany Hall . . . .
On the level you're a devil, Tammany.

From the song "Tammany, A Pale-Face Pow-Wow"
by Vincent Bryan and Gustave Edwards

ONCE UPON A TIME, a long, long time before De Soto or La Salle, a great Indian chief lived in the land west of the Allegheny Mountains. He was a famous hunter, warrior, and statesman. He was called by his tribe the "savior of his country" because he defeated the Evil Spirit in a series of great battles. When the Evil Spirit caused sickness and drought by making the plants spew poison in the air, the Indian chief set fire to all the prairies in the land, burning the plants and even singeing the Evil One himself. Very angry, the Evil Spirit sent an army of rattlesnakes against the Indian chief, who laughed and killed them by dancing on their heads. Very, very angry, the Evil Spirit sent out a host of mammoths. But the chief dug deep pits and put sharp spears inside and salt licks just behind. The mammoths fell into the pits trying to get to the salt licks. They were all killed. Now the Evil Spirit was so angry that the skies turned black, and thunderbolts shook the land, and it rained and it rained. And while it rained, the Evil Spirit built a dam across a lake near Detroit, and the dam and the rain caused all the Great Lakes to flood and to threaten the chief and his tribe with drowning. But the chief fought back. He scooped out a ditch, which is now the channel of the Ohio River. The rain ended and the lakes gradually subsided, but the rapids of Detroit and Niagara Falls still remain as monuments to this great Indian Chief, whose name was Tammany.[1]

So went the legends of Tammany. Two weeks after the inauguration of George Washington, an organization was permanently established in New York City which, borrowing the name of the fabled warrior, called itself the Tammany Society or Columbian Order. In later years it seemed to many that this political tribe of warriors had at last ended the heroic struggle with the Evil Spirit, had, in fact, admitted it as a member in good standing. "Tammany Hall," said the crusading cleric, C. H. Parkhurst, "is a form under which the Devil disguises himself." [2] Be that as it may, the organization became one of the most durable institutions in the history of New York City, "at once a study and a wonder" in American political life. Thus George Washington Plunkitt could say: "I've seen more than one hundred 'Democracies' rise and fall in New York City in the last quarter of a century. At least a half dozen new so-called Democratic organizations are formed every year. All of them go in to down Tammany and take its place, but they seldom last more than a year or two, while Tammany's life is like the ever-lastin' rocks, the eternal hills, and the blockades on the 'L' road—it goes on forever." [3]

The origins for the New York Tammany Society go back to before the American Revolution. On the first of May, Middle Atlantic Societies held a festival called "Saint Tammany Day." This custom originated with the Schuylkill Fishing Company, a social club organized in Philadelphia in 1732, which adopted Tammany (or Tamenend) as the club's patron.[4] The custom spread, and other clubs sprang up and adopted the same name. By May 1,

1772, the first permanent society was established in Philadelphia under the name of "The Sons of King Tammany." As opposition to the British intensified, Tammany societies multiplied and assumed a prominent part in revolutionary sentiment. During the Revolution "Saint Tammany"—he had now been popularly canonized—was regarded not only as the patron saint of the Continental army, but was popularized further as the hero in John Leacock's poem, "The First of May, a New Song, in Praise of St. Tammany, the American Saint." Leacock used the title "Saint" as a device not only to establish an Indian, a truly 100-per-cent American, as a genuine, home-grown American guardian, but also to ridicule such Tory societies as St. George's, St. Andrew's, and St. David's. Thus the first stanza:

> Of St. George, or St. Bute, let the poet Laureat sing,
> Of Paroah [*sic*] or Pluto of old,
> While he rhymes forth praise, in false, flattering lays
> I'll sing of St. Tamm'ny the bold, my brave boys.[5]

And more than a hundred years later, foreign saints were still getting the worst of it:

> Let Erin praise St. Patrick,
> Who forced the snakes to flee
> Let Scotland praise St. Andrew,
> And France her St. Denis;
> These saints had some good features,
> But these we won't discuss,
> For, blessings on St. Tammany,
> He's saint enough for us.[6]

By the end of the Revolution the societies, whose patriotic objectives had been achieved, passed from view. With the change of national government from Philadelphia to New York, the movement, however, was rejuvenated under the leadership of the Tammany Society of New York. A society had existed in New York as early as 1787, but under the leadership of William Mooney and John Pintard the society in New York was permanently established. Its members were sworn to uphold the Constitution and to preserve the liberties of the land. At that time it was more of a social than a political club. While its members were of different political persuasions, all shared the goal of protecting the United States against the ideals and institutions of a monarchy. The "best" people were attracted to its ranks and the society assumed a prominent position in the social life of the city; its festivals were events of considerable pageantry, attracting large audiences. If the society had been left in the hands of Mooney, it would have continued as a kind of eighteenth-century Rotary Club, with an elaborate and somewhat preposterous mimicry of Indian customs and rituals, and as a source of patriotic prose on July 4.

As the classic struggle between Jefferson and Hamilton unfolded, the society took on an increasing political complexion. The majority of the members, imbued with an anti-aristocratic tradition which suggested that centralization was a species of monarchy, supported Jefferson. Enthusiasm for the French Revolution provided more ideological fuel for the society as did its role as counterweight to the aristocratic Society of the Cincinnati. As the political tendencies of the society became more pronounced and its partisan character accentuated, its branches spread north to Rhode Island and Massachusetts, south to Virginia, and west to Kentucky and Ohio. Under the impetus of the patronage of Jefferson, its chain of branches foreshadowed the establishment of national political parties.

In New York, it was the keen political sense of Aaron Burr which first recognized the potentials of Tammany Hall. Although Burr never joined the Hall, the braves did support him vigorously in the election of 1800, when he won both the city and the state against Hamilton and Jay.[7] From this time on Tammany became more enmeshed in city politics, although the sachems continued the charitable activities of the organization. At the time, however, this did not mean that Tammany combined charity and politics to organize the poor in order to win public office.

With the disruption of party lines following the fall of the Federalist party, the struggle that had stimulated the growth and power of the movement abated; the branch societies found little inspiration in politics, and many societies withered away. Only the society in New York remained secure. It was sustained not only by local politics but also by patriotic and philanthropic ideals. It contributed to public celebrations, city affairs, and national holidays and became more powerful in city politics. Known for a while as "Bucktails," Tammany found De Witt Clinton disguised as the Evil Spirit, and for years Clintonites and Tammanyites fought for control of New York. Clinton, an early student of the art of patronage, was able to hold his own with some success. Tammany resisted his policy of internal improvements until it recognized its overshadowing popularity; then, typically Tammany, it changed policies in mid-stream and appeared as a better friend of state canals than Clinton himself.

The 1840's mark a turning point in the history of the Hall. By this time the Hall was distinctively known as "the champion of the poor." Right up to the present day the myth has persisted, encouraged by Tammany itself, that Tammany Hall has *always* been the champion of the poor in terms of organizing them for political action. This is not true. From the very beginning until 1837, the Hall was dominated by upper- and middle-class merchants and bankers, who were fiercely proud of their roster of distinguished gentry, like Cadwallader Colden, Davis L. Matthew, John Adams Dix, Edward Livingston, Morgan Lewis, Peter R. Leonard Gansevoort, and others.[8] Tammany had attracted some of the working class, mainly the skilled artisans, for until the 1820's even the workingman had to be somewhat affluent in order to vote, since he had to possess a certain amount of property.

Nor was Tammany always the champion of the immigrant. In the first decades of the nineteenth century, Tammany was a non-Catholic, non-foreign organization. "Not only did the extreme prejudice against holding of office by Catholics and foreigners cause it to nominate exclusively Protestants and natives for office, but a foreigner was not even allowed to hold any important post in the organization."[9] It was only when immigration increased and immigrants became more important politically that the Hall took an interest in them.

After the 1820's, as the base of suffrage was constantly being broadened, Tammany was reluctant to champion further extensions. It only did so when the popular demand for it became so strong that it was politically expedient to become more democratic.[10] Between 1824 and the Tweed era there was a major change in the appeal it made for support. In the former year, St. Tammany was still the enemy of monarchy and Old World aristocracy. In 1868, the rhetoric of the Hall was more demagogic. Tweed directed the general committee to advocate the election of John T. Hoffman as Governor in these terms:

> He is the friend of the poor, the sympathizer with the naturalized citizen, and the foe to all municipal oppression in the form of all odious and other excise requisitional laws. . . . Is not the pending contest preeminently one of capital against labor, of money against popular rights, and of political power against the struggling interests of the masses?[11]

The social, ethnic change from a party of Protestant conservatives to a party championing the poor and the immigrant began in the 1820's and culminated in the lusty years of Jacksonian Democracy.

The strength of the lower classes was considerably strengthened beginning in the 1820's as their ranks were bolstered by an increasing swell of immigration and their power enhanced by an extension and liberalization of the suffrage. With the coming of Jackson they were in a position to square off and challenge the conservative merchant-banker control of Tammany Hall. Excited by the Jacksonian appeals for the ending of special privilege, especially corporation privileges, mainly in banking, the lower-class and lower-middle-class rebels tried and failed to reform Tammany from within. Disenchanted, they deserted the party and joined first the Workingmen's party, and by 1834 the formidable Equal Rights party, both of which were under the leadership of middle-class intellectuals. It was a trying period for the braves, who had to face splinter parties, the Whigs, reformers like William Leggett, and the Locofocos. Through the struggle the society wore two faces. On one hand it issued a host of proclamations against the monied aristocracy; on the other hand, most of its chiefs were members of that aristocracy. "Nearly every one of the thirty-six members of the general committee was a president or a director of some corporation enjoying great legal powers; and nearly every prominent Tammany man had voted or lobbied for measures creating banks or other corporations, measures often evoking great popular criticism and discontent." [12] It was not until the Equal Rights party demonstrated its ability to defeat Tammany in a three-cornered contest in 1837, with much furor and a riot or two, that the radicals seized power in Tammany and allied themselves with Martin Van Buren, whose methods and point of view were largely similar. As a result many State-bank owners withdrew from the Hall.

By the 1840's the Hall had established another characteristic to be passed on for greater fulfillment by the Tweed Ring. It acquired the reputation for having a stupendous appetite for graft. But even here myth distorts the case. For years Tammany opponents with an anti-immigrant and upper-class bias, and Tammany men themselves, who were denied patronage or admittance to leadership, have argued that only when the immigrant and the lower classes joined the Hall in increasing numbers, beginning in the 1840's, was Tammany besmirched with foul deeds. Before that were the good old days of integrity, honor, honesty, and the respectability of conservative, upper-class rule.

The fact is the old leadership had as much hunger for graft as the "new" ruling elite, except it lacked the strength and the political, social, and economic evolutions in New York that made graft more possible and more extensive. For example, in 1809, the "respectable" Benjamin Romain, many times Grand Sachem of Tammany Hall, was indicted for fraud while serving as Comptroller. Even William Mooney himself was caught with his fingers

The Tammany Tiger Loose; one of Thomas Nast's most famous cartoons; courtesy of the New-York Historical Society, New York City

in the till. As Superintendent of the Almshouse, he dipped into the funds reserved for the poor. Samuel Swartwout, an eminent Tammany chieftain, gave the language a new verb to describe corruption. As Collector of the Port of New York, he "collected" $1,250,000 and fled the country in 1838.[13] Impressed, New Yorkers coined the verb "to swartwout" to describe a Tammany brave in action. If Tammany had its embarrassing moments, it could also demonstrate that its moral aspiration was not lacking. In 1817 it went on record against the "foreign" game of billiards, because it might undermine the morals of the young.

With all these changes and supposed changes, one thing remained consistent in the Hall's history: the importance of the Tammany building itself, as a meeting place, as a headquarters, as a symbol of unity and awesome power.

In 1928 an old, ugly brick building in the worst black-walnut period style, on Fourteenth Street east of Irving Place, was being torn down. A familiar landmark in the city, it was the headquarters of Tammany Hall, now being moved to a new site. The old building was in a dreary setting, with the Central Family Hotel next door, and the "Surprise Shooting Gallery" opposite. Years back the neighborhood had been lively. Tony Pastor once had a theater next door; close by was the famous saloon "Sharkey's Place," and not many steps away another landmark, the Rialto Theatre. Around the corner on Irving Place was a little Spanish hotel where O. Henry heard his stories about Central American conspirators.

For the most part, the inside of the Tammany building was drab. Upstairs was "the most dismally hideous ballroom in New York, but also the most historic."[14] Downstairs there was a large room, decorated with a multitude of flags, and off to one side, a fine paneled safe with Indians painted on it. Here and there were spittoons, some with bunches of blue grapes painted on. On the wall were the portraits of former mighties of the Hall: Murphy, Croker, and Kelly—William Tweed's picture had long since been removed. When the building was destroyed, the cornerstone was discovered. Alongside was a heavy lead box which held, among other things, a copy of the ode delivered by De Witt Van Buren when the cornerstone was laid, a three-dollar gold piece, an autographed photo of Boss Tweed, and two ten-cent "shinplasters." [15]

July 4, 1867, when the cornerstone was laid, had been a splendid day for the wigwam. The Grand Marshal of Tammany Hall, Andrew Garvey (later indicted for overplastering the new County Courthouse), led the band and the parade to the new site. Windows and roofs of the surrounding buildings were crowded with spectators. Grand Sachem John T. Hoffman, Mayor of the City of New York (who owed his election to Boss Tweed), dug a hole with a trowel made of polished silver with a handle of pure ivory. Somewhere in the midst of a ponderous dedication, he said that the new building "will, for the next half century at least, be the headquarters of the Democracy of New York, wherein the great principles of Civil and Religious Liberty, Constitutional Law, and National Unity, which form the great corner-stone of the Republic, will always be advocated and maintained." [16] Nearby fluttered a banner with the words, "Civil Liberty, the Glory of Man."

Laying of the cornerstone not only symbolized the establishment of the Tweed Ring as the first dynasty in Tammany Hall, but also it pointed up the importance of the building itself in the rise of Tammany in New York politics. The building itself was the symbol of party regularity: the standing claim that Tammany was *the* Democratic party in the city. When dissident groups split from the parent organization, mainly because their appetite for patronage had not been satisfied, and set up headquarters in an Irving or Apollo Hall, they were dwarfed by the Fourteenth Street monstrosity. The possession of such a building proved a great advantage in perfecting the organization. There was a place and room for strategy.

Infinitely more important was what went on inside, the character of the organization itself. Here was the heartbeat and the pulse of Democratic power in the city. Here was a superb organization, moving year after year and day after day with a unity, consistency, tenacity, and effectiveness unknown before in city politics.

The executives of the Tammany organization were thirteen sachems who constituted the Grand Council of Sachems, who in turn elected a presiding officer called the Grand Sachem. Real power, *the* power of the Hall, was contained in the General Committee. The constitution of the organization was of a peculiar dual character. The Society was a distinct and separate body from the General Committee. The Society owned the building, which from 1817 had been known as Tammany Hall, and leased it to the General Committee. Since the latter met at the Hall, it was known as the "regular" organization.

The General Committee, established in 1803, was composed of three elected members from each of the ten wards in the city. Up to 1822, there was some democracy in the Hall when the General Committee worked closely with all members at a general meeting, submitting its decisions and recommendations for their approval. This was changed in 1822, when the general meeting was replaced by a representative general committee whose members were selected in primary elections. The result was that the General Committee became more and more independent of the rank-and-file in the Hall. As the General Committee assumed the business of nomination, platforms, and other important matters, it evolved into a well-organized hierarchy of politicians.

While Tammany tried to beguile the public into thinking that Tammany was a dual society, fraternal and political, in practice it was not. The public knew that Tammany and the Democratic party in New York City were closely stitched together. Those who rose in Democratic politics joined the Society, and the ruling elite of the Society usually controlled the committees in the political organization, meshing the two, for all practical purposes, into one political and social organization.[17] Until the coming of the Tweed Ring, authority in the General Committee was divided among continually shifting cliques engaged in constant battles with each other, profoundly frustrating strong leaders like Fernando Wood who tried to centralize power in themselves. One reason the Tweed Ring founded the first real dynasty in New York City was that Boss Tweed adroitly managed to centralize power in Tammany by dominating the General Committee, other critical committees, and the Tammany Society itself.

Indeed, it was under the Tweed Ring that the classic Tammany structure emerged, not under Tweed's successor, "Honest" John Kelly, as it has sometimes been argued, although Kelly did improve on his inheritance. One of the major devices the Tweed Ring employed to fashion the first modern city machine was its streamlining of the internal structure of Tammany, the ward committees, the position of the ward leaders, and the election machinery.

Domination of Tammany Hall began by capturing and consolidating the Hall's committee system. Control of the General Committee, the Committee on Elections, the Committee on Finance, were avenues to formidable power. But the Ring further centralized its influence by controlling the Committee on Organization, sometimes called the Executive Committee. It was an elite committee because it was composed of all the city's twenty-two ward leaders (equivalent to district leaders). As one writer described it:

> This body was the absolute slave of the Boss-in-chief. Every member of it either held office, elective or appointive, at the Boss's hands, or else was a favored contractor of public works, or was in some other position of political advantage. The Boss not only held every one of them responsible for his own vote and conduct, but for the vote and conduct of the members of his Ward Committee, and further, for the vote and conduct of every member of the Election District Committee of his Ward. When I say conduct, of course you understand that I mean political conduct. So you see, the Boss-in-chief held the whip-hand over every member of the General Committee as well as of the Ward and Election District Committees.[18]

If the General and Executive Committees were the brains of the Hall, the wards were its arms, legs, and muscles. Wards had always been a vital foundation in Tammany for it was here that the Hall marshaled its rank-and-file support. Under the Tweed Ring the wards were modernized into a highly organized network for grass-roots political action. No other political enterprise could match it. Rival Democratic groups might oppose it in a moment of pique, reformers might loudly complain, but all sooner or later proved ephemeral. They came and went while Tammany, stubborn and persistent, stayed on, working toward the day that gave reason for its existence—election day.

In 1868, when the Tweed Ring was consolidating its power, there were twenty-two wards and a total of twenty-one Assembly districts. Each ward was divided into election districts. The General Committee determined the number of delegates each ward would have on the General Committee. The Republican party followed the same procedure. Representation was based upon the number of Democratic or Republican votes cast in each ward at the last gubernatorial election.

The efficiency that the Ring brought to ward organization can be seen in Peter Sweeny's Twentieth Ward. As ward leader, Sweeny chaired four of the most important committees, the most powerful being the Ward Committee which represented the ward's election districts. There was a recruiting agency within the ward, a sort of "get-them-while-they're-young" agency, called the Young Men's General Committee. There was a maze of committees prepared to select delegates to School, Constable, Councilman, Alderman, and Judiciary conventions; plus county, congressional, and assembly committees.[19] One device that was particularly effective in tying the wards closer to Tammany Hall was the Election District Committee, which furnished voters for the primary elections. In the event of an intraparty dispute, it could also supply "shouters" at nominating conventions.

Political life in the ward revolved around the political club, an old institution in New York which spawned such pre-Civil War clubs as the Huge Paws, the Indomitables, the Ring Tail Roarers, and the Empire Club. In the past, however, the saloon tended to be *the* grass-roots center of political activity. During the Tweed Ring's era, the ward political club was replacing the saloon as this grass-roots center. A historian of New York club life, in fact, declared that in no time in the history of the metropolis had there been such an expansion of club life.[20] For good reason; practically every ward leader organized his own ward club, like the Young Men's Democratic William M. Tweed Club, Slippery Dick Connolly's St. Patrick Mutual Alliance, the Jefferson Club, the Unique Club, the Michael Norton Association. The club was the bastion of a ward leader's power, his headquarters, his second home. From here he built his power as ward leader in the first place, from here he built a following to stay politically alive, and from here he could advance (especially with a strong showing on election day) to sweeter political plums. William Marcy Tweed, for example, never could have reached the summit of New York politics without the backing of his Seventh Ward and the club that made it so potent.

The ward captain was to Tammany what the sergeant was to the army—the backbone of the organization. He was responsible, and held to strict account, for the vote of his election district. If the Democratic vote fell off without reasonable explanation, or through his own lack of skill, he was removed with dispatch. All the ward captain needed for success, said the *New York Times*, was a certain bonhomie with men, generosity, audacity, skill in his job, and "an entire forgetfulness that there is such a thing as honor and conscience."[21] He had to know his neighborhood thoroughly. He had to have a keen perception of human nature. He was often a Councilman, Alderman, contractor, or saloon-keeper, who ran his club like a petty baron, or if he was particularly powerful, as a duke of the realm. He cultivated a following by dispensing favors, by catering to local interests and problems. He found jobs for needy families, or loaned them money, honored them with his presence at weddings and wakes. For businessmen and saloon-keepers, he granted relief from some law or city ordinance; for gamblers, prostitutes, and gangsters in trouble, he found bail, or if the person was particularly favored by the Tweed Ring, he could arrange for the "right" lawyer and the "right" judge, who would arrange for the "right" sentence; for the particularly loyal, obedient, and dedicated followers, he buttressed his own power by advancing them as precinct captains or high officers in the ward club. If he could "swing" the faithful in the beneficent direction of Tammany Hall on election day, he was rewarded with patronage for himself and, if powerful enough, for some of his followers, such as a place in the street-cleaning department or a minor clerkship. If continually successful, he could convert his club into a powerful instrument for control of nominations to local offices. It was a simple political formula: the more neighborhood statesmen that advanced to office, the more powerful the club and the ward leader became.

If the ward leader was shrewd, he made his ward clubhouse into a pleasant place where a tired Manure Inspector or an Assistant Health Warden could find relaxation at the billiard table or at the bar where he could chew over the latest political gossip. If he was particularly canny, he would create a neighborhood *esprit de corps*, which paid off in political dividends, by having his club sponsor clambakes, picnics, summer outings, and at least two "balls" a year, one between New Year's Day and the beginning of Lent, and one between election day and Christmas. If he had any political sense at all, he used the club to celebrate his and Tammany's good name in torchlight parades and rallies just before election day. And on election day itself, he converted the club into a kind of battlefield headquarters, turning out the neighborhood vote, dispatching "repeaters" to selected voting booths, marshaling all his skill to destroy in his ward the Republican party, rival Democratic groups, or any reformers courageous or foolish enough to contest his power.

Deeply political as it was, the ward club did not rank finally and ultimately just as a political phenomenon. It served as a social institution as well. The clubhouse, like the saloon, was a haven for recreation and good fellowship, and a refuge from wives. And the club itself provided a means by which the native poor, or an immigrant Irishman or German, could advance to some social standing and status.

A good example of a successful ward club was the Young Men's Democratic William M. Tweed Club, of the Seventh Ward. Started initially on a $10,000 loan by the Boss, it moved into new headquarters at 105 East Broadway just before the fall 1871 election. Tweed spent $20,000 to have it repainted, wallpapered, and furnished. On the first floor was a handsome parlor, with rosewood furniture covered with scarlet velvet, a grand piano, "magnificent" mirrors, and "handsome" chandeliers of bronze and gold. The light-tinted carpet was "sumptuous." In back of the parlor stood a bar and billiard room. A stairway covered with a fine velvet carpet led one to the club meeting room upstairs, where, on the same floor, there was a bath and "retiring rooms." The floor above had two card rooms and the office for the club secretary.[22]

Aside from the grand balls and picnics that Tweed sponsored, each club held its own rallies. Michael Norton, the mighty lord of the Eighth Ward, could even outdo the Boss on such rallies. On April 21, 1871, the Michael Norton Association thought it appropriate to welcome State Senator Norton home after he finished another tiring but dedicated stint in the State legislature. The club rented two barges and the steamboat *Sleepy Hollow* to meet the Senator at Yonkers and escort him home. Enticed by the prospect of a free ride, free drinks, and free food, nearly 7000 people appeared. In triumph the good Senator was escorted to headquarters in Hudson Street, where amid a fireworks display his admirers consumed such items as 100 kegs of beer, 50 cases of champagne, 200 gallons of chowder, 50 gallons of turtle soup, 36 hams, 4000 pounds of corned beef, 20 gallons of brandy, 10 gallons of gin, and a barrel of whiskey, and smoked 5000 cigars.[23]

Ward clubs like the Michael Norton Association, while officially not a part of Tammany Hall, were nevertheless critically important in sustaining its power. But the club could also shatter the unity of Tammany. Ward leaders were often prima donnas, their puffed egos sensitive to real or fancied criticism and their appetite for patronage not easily satisfied. The history of the Hall is packed with episodes in which ruffled ward leaders sheered off from the Hall, founded their own organization (usually giving it some melodious name), and went on to wage war with Tammany. But the Tweed Ring was able for most of its reign to work with the ward leaders, binding them to the goals of the Ring and Tammany. As the Ring centralized power within the Hall, it centralized the power of the ward leaders and their clubs. It was not easy to do. It required delicate tact, persuasion, generous gifts of patronage, and, if need be, iron discipline. When the time did come for several of the more powerful ward leaders to revolt, the Ring was ready and able to quell the insurrection and, importantly, make the kind of peace that left the ward leaders reasonably satisfied, but put them back in their place, subordinated by the Tweed dynasty.

The Ring had other ways of harnessing potentially rebellious spirits. It dominated two other clubs, the so-called Stable Gang and the Americus Club, which brought the "executive" leadership of the Tammany domain together in good fellowship, where ward leaders, city officials, businessmen, police officers, municipal and state judges, and gang leaders of the underworld, could get to know each other better, work in closer harmony, and share a collective *esprit de corps,* the antidote to the independent, querulous spirit of rebellion.

The Stable Gang (William Tweed, founder) was not strictly a club, having no formal organization; it was, to use Francis Gerry Fairfield's phrase, "a sort of nursery of clubs," bringing together certain key leaders of Democratic ward clubs with leaders of the Democratic "social" clubs, such as the Oriental, Blossom, and City Clubs. Aside from strategy, the chief function of the group seemed to be to keep important people happy. It was a kind of mutual-congratulatory society, where through the ritual of celebrating the birthdays of its members, all were infused with harmony and warm affection.

The Americus Club (William Tweed, president) was the pinnacle of Tammany club life. The sumptuous clubhouse, located in lovely Indian Harbor, Connecticut, offered a cool refuge from New York's summer heat. Its membership was limited to one hundred of the most important of the Tweed Ring organization, from ward leaders, officers in state and city government, to judges, businessmen, and even "Tammany" Republicans. Behind the pomp and frolic of the Americus Club lay essentially the same strategy that underscored the meaning of the Stable Gang, only on a higher level.

Other clubs, not exclusively political, also helped the Ring enhance its position and streamline Tammany. Ring members sought out the target companies, with their parades, picnics, contests, and the honor that went with becoming a crack shot. Ingeniously, the Tweed Ring, using the machinery of Tammany, took an inordinate interest in making their life even gayer and more colorful. In the past, ward leaders usually sponsored the clubs, digging into their own pockets to finance the fun, knowing the members would repay their generosity by waving a banner with the right name on it on parade days, and voting the right ticket on election day. With the coming of the Tweed Ring, Tammany Hall replaced the individual ward politician as the great benefactor by digging, as it were, into the pockets of the taxpayers. To recruit and maintain the target companies, members of target companies now got ten cents a week, $6.50 per parade, a uniform furnished by Tammany, and on "muster day" rations of whisky, food, and cigars. The Tweed Ring's target was election day.

Tweed, Sweeny, Connolly, and especially Oakey Hall, also infiltrated the rarefied atmosphere of some of New York's largest plush "social" clubs, among whose members were prominent figures in politics, law, business, and arts and letters. The Ring was able to make important contacts here, outside the political world. Men of affairs, sitting in overstuffed chairs or leaning on a mahogany bar, chatted with civil servants about their problems, and problems had a way of instantly dissolving when the city government performed a special favor. The Ring enjoyed doing favors—for a profit, a market tip, or a donation to the campaign fund.

The Manhattan Club, founded in 1865 as the Democrats' answer to the Republicans' Union Club, was a favorite social center, where Tammany chiefs rubbed elbows with railroad kings like Vanderbilt and Drew, and Wall Street plungers like Fisk and Gould. Or in its restaurant, one of the finest in the city—epicures, it was said, preferred it even to Delmonico's—one might see Samuel Barlow, one of the owners of the *New York World*, or General George McClellan. "For the rest, political celebrities, by the dozen or hundred, look down from the walls on the weaving of political webs by their successors in business; and, on any evening of the week, one may here meet any number of famous political spiders."[24] The Manhattan Club never attained the elegance of its Republican counterpart, as is suggested by certain strict rules: no liquor was to be served in the reception room; all damages to crockery or upholstery had to be settled before leaving; and no members were allowed to sleep on lounges or sofas—except on the third floor.

The Blossom Club (William M. Tweed, vice president) had one of the best wine cellars in the city and the most profitable bar, "the Winter Paradise of the 'soakers,'" as the *Times* called it. As Francis Gerry Fairfield, the chronicler of social custom in that day, described it: one entered into an elegant reception hall where on the right "a Titanic portrait of Mr. Tweed stares you in the face, and with the imperturbable good humor of the Napoleon of Democratic politics, appears to be saying, 'You're welcome, my dear fellow; pray help yourself to a look at the club-house.'"[25] The *New York Sun* tried to describe its luxury by saying that if you struck a sledge hammer on the floor, it would not be heard a yard off because of the thickness of the Turkish carpets.[26] At the City Club, a very fashionable and stylish organization, one would frequently find the millionaire Tweed Ring contractor James H. Ingersoll, "once a leading society man . . . ere his fate overtook him"; while at the Lotos Club (Abraham Oakey Hall, president) one would find the membership restricted to men of arts and letters. At the suggestion of President Hall, Saturday evening of each week was set apart for a general reunion of members, and the "Lotos Saturday Nights" became famous.[27]

All these steps toward consolidating power would have gone for naught if the Tweed Ring could not capture and turn to its own use the central factor in Tammany's existence, the election machinery. When election time approached, the Tammany machine started to move, shifting its gears, meshing its parts; sometimes it purred; sometimes it sputtered. The objective of the campaign was first to control the nominating convention and the primary elections, since winning in the primaries was often tantamount to election.

The Tweed Ring worked over the election machinery like skilled engineers, oiling and greasing its parts. To make it run with more efficiency and less rattle, the Ring tried to impress upon the entire Tammany organization the necessity of sending reliable men as delegates. It was accomplished by an order, by persuasion, or by promise of patronage. It was very important to control the nomination of the temporary chairman who would organize the convention. As the fictitious Boss Blossom Brick put it, "The temporary chairman is the Convention. He's an 8 to 7 man all the time." [28] If a revolt appeared, the chairman, who appointed the doorman of the convention, made sure he selected a man who would not admit a contesting faction. If a reformer group, for example, complained that many of its delegates were left off the official roll (the roll made by a secretary appointed by the chairman), the chairman could rule that such a complaint was out of order, and that he (the chairman) certainly did not make the rules.

For the primary elections, the Ring had remarkable powers of anticipation. The procedure to select delegates to Assembly District conventions who, in turn, would elect delegates to the Democratic State convention was started by order of the State Central Committee in a primary convention. Each ward leader through his Ward Committee named three inspectors to preside over the primary in his ward. On the eve of the election that decided who would be the delegates to the primary convention, the ward leader simply seected the "winners" in advance. They were carefully chosen for their loyalty and reliability. His lieutenants, the inspectors of the primary, signed a document stating that these delegates had been "duly elected" to the Assembly District Convention. The contest was over before it began. The "election" was held, the inspectors "counted" the votes and announced the previously selected delegates. Any question of election fraud was referred to the Committee on Credentials, a futile gesture, because by this time the Ring not only controlled this committee but the convention as well. The same procedure for State primaries was used for local primaries which nominated the mayor, judges, and various city officers like the Aldermen. By controlling the ward leaders the Ring controlled the naming of the delegates and hence the convention itself.

Witnessing Tammany at work at election time, even the *New York Times* was forced to admit that here was "a wonderfully and admirably-constructed and conducted machine . . . the wheels work smoothly, the pulleys run without a jar, the cogs slip into one another perfectly, while everything is kept well oiled and greased from the public funds of our wealthy citizens." [29] To keep the political wheels, pulleys, and cogs in running order required discipline. The bane of Tammany Hall was not so much the reformer, but the ambitions of its leaders, who could throw the machinery out of gear. "The Ring and the Boss," said one perceptive writer of the period, "command an army composed of elements as dangerous as those which make up the crew of a pirate ship. The instant the slightest sign of weakness is shown, each man aspires to be commander, and is willing to sink the ship and all on board rather than to forego his own ambitious schemes." [30]

Party regularity became Tammany's byword, its first commandment, its discipline, particularly under the Tweed Ring. "Tammany men," said a historian of the Hall, "never forgave the crime of individuality in defense of sentiment or ideals." [31] When its regularity was questioned, when its position as *the* Democratic party of New York was challenged, it could expose the heretics with such manifestoes as this:

WE ARE AGAIN THREATENED WITH
A FACTIOUS OPPOSITION.

Those misguided members of our Order who have been mainly instrumental in creating and upholding the *BOGUS* Democratic Organizations now existing—those malcontents whose exertions have been continually arrayed against our country and our party—will endeavor to subvert your interests and secure the control of our patriotic and venerable Order. *YOUR VOTE AND INFLUENCE* will materially aid in defeating the malevolence and ingratitude of our enemies.[32]

Throughout its reign, Tweed's Tammany was challenged by Democratic splinter groups. There were all kinds of Democrats, said Joseph H. Choate, "hailing from all sorts of halls, generally with harmonious and musical names, but not very harmonious spirits." There were Apollo Hall Democrats, Irving Hall Democrats, Mozart Hall Democrats, Reform Democrats, German Democrats, Independent and Union Democrats, "lukewarm Democrats and Democrats fiery hot, but none . . . professedly cold-water Democrats." [33] The Tweed Ring, more emphatically and effectively than any of its predecessors, used Richelieu's maxim to handle factions. First, do everything to conciliate; if that fails, do everything to crush. The motto: United we stand; rule or ruin.

What, then, was Tammany; and what was the basis of its success? Mark Twain held one view, common to many. Tammany had

> but one principle, one policy, one moving spring of action—avarice, money-lust. So that it got money it cared not a rap about the means and methods. It was always ready to lie, forge, betray, steal, swindle, cheat, rob; and no promise, no engagement, no contract, no treaty made by its Boss was worth the paper it was written on or the polluted breath that uttered it.[34]

This was not altogether fair to Tammany, for the Hall did not have a monopoly on venal techniques and fraudulent practices; its rivals often acted the same way. The Whigs and the Know-Nothings vied with Tammany in election frauds and raids on the city treasury. The Republican party might hold its nose and point with horror at the New York City Democrats, while at the same time, the Republicans who controlled the State legislature performed intricate and blatant corruptions in Albany. Tammany did not have any peculiar flair for graft, but it did have more ingenuity and better management than its rivals. This common view holding Tammany as a mere "plunderbund" distorted and obscured other characteristics, as Gustavus Myers pointed out.

> One class of the voters may be mercenary and actuated by the lowest and most selfish interest. But it would be an unwarranted assumption to stigmatize as such the entire voting element supporting Tammany. Beneath all that organization's known record of continued corruption and pretense, there must be intrinsically strong qualities and popular currents to have guaranteed it its virile existence.[35]

Edward Cary, another student of the Hall, said that while the chief motive power of the machine was self-interest,

> by this is not meant the greed of money alone. It includes ambition of a not discreditable sort, vanity, social aspirations no less real and effectual because incomprehensible to those who think that they constitute the only "society," and the love of distinction . . . [a Tammany leader] may be selfish. He may be crafty, deceitful, unscrupulous, greedy, a swindler, a thief, a perjurer: but service he must render, at all times, in a thousand ways, to as many men as may be; and it must be a substantial service which they recognize and are willing to repay.[36]

Tammany, then, was an organization engaged in politics as a business. It resembled a great feudal system with a complete hierarchy running from Boss to sub-bosses, committee men, ward captains, precinct captains, and workers. It was autocratic and demanded the most unequivocal servility. While often engaged in plunder, it still was held together by the powerful bonds of ambition, loyalty, tradition, and the great game of politics. It was the product of the political, social, and economic conditions of the City and State of New York. Its success, under the Tweed Ring, was fostered by the chaos created through the overlapping and competing demands of state, city, and county governments. This success was reinforced by its organization and discipline, which, said Peter Sweeny with pride and some exaggeration, was second only to the Roman army under Caesar. The organization sustained its power at election time with gangs of repeaters, thugs, corrupt election officials, who were protected by the courts, and winked at by the police, 80 per cent of whom in the days of the Tweed Ring were Democrats.

Fundamentally, however, its success rested on the common people. Tammany's sympathy and understanding for them were mixed with ruthless self-interest, but Tammany's concern for the common man, compromised as it was, meant something infinitely more to those in Tweed's Town than lofty manifestoes issued by reform groups who preached ideals but seldom practiced practical politics. But the common man could also be the Achilles' heel of Tammany Hall. Once disenchantment shattered apathy and party partisanship, even Tammany Hall—for all its power and techniques—could not withstand the verdict at the polls.

8

THE SHINY HAT BRIGADE

Letter of recommendation for a political appointment:

Dear Tit:

The bearer understands addition, division and silence.

Appoint him!

Your friend,
Bill

Rufus E. Shapley, *Solid for Mulhooly*

UPON READING Voltaire's history of the reign of Louis XIV, a student of mid-nineteenth-century American politics concluded that many Americans would have smiled at the ridiculous catalogue of offices in bureaucracy. In Paris, in the year 1710, counselors of the king had such posts as hog-inspectors, inspectors of calves, wigs, and slaughter-houses, inventory-drawers, measurers of firewood, deputy measurers of firewood, pilers of firewood, unloaders of firewood, comptrollers of timber, charcoal-measurers, grain-sifters, comptrollers of poultry, barrel-gaugers, butter-testers, beer-testers, brandy-testers, linen-measurers, unloaders of hay, and removers of boarding. "But how mild and trivial was their abuse of kingly power," he said, "compared with the hordes of superfluous officers that swarm in the public buildings of the city of New York!" [1] In the office of the City Comptroller there were 131 clerks, many holding ingenious titles. The Street Commissioner alone employed 60 clerks. The Corporation Manual listed a host of puzzling positions: twelve "manure-inspectors," twenty-two "health wardens," seven "assistant health wardens," twenty-two "street inspectors," seven "assistant inspectors of meat," seven "inspectors of encumbrances," twenty-two "distributors of corporation ordinances," and that was only the beginning of the catalogue. "Who has ever seen any of these wardens and inspectors?" [2] The Citizens' Association tried, but found, much to their disgust, that these offices were filled for the most part by saloon-keepers, immigrants, "low ward politicians," gamblers, pugilists, and assorted hangers-on. The analogy to Louis XIV was apt. Under King Tweed and his counselors, practically every office and department in the city was invaded by an army of political mercenaries with ragged reputations. These officeholders constituted the Tweed Ring's spoils system. And because of their preference for tall sleek hats, they were called the Shiny Hat Brigade.

It was not necessary to go to the Old World for a proper comparison for the spoils system in New York under the Tweed Ring. Spoils and patronage attended the birth of the Republic. Jefferson and Jackson made appointments for party reasons. By 1828 every state throughout the North and West had established a spoils system.[3] But it was most firmly entrenched from the Civil War to roughly 1885.

The Tweed Ring, as political architect, did not create its own materials. For example, by capturing Tammany Hall it had at its disposal a ready-made political machine. It was in the enlargement and redesigning of that machine, as well as in extending its power beyond Tammany, that the Ring's talent lay. Its members demonstrated a keen appreciation of political architecture by astute applications of the spoils system. Through patronage, a system of punishment and reward, they built a vast network of followers which enveloped the public administration. Control of the inner springs of city government, and of Tammany, and their own official positions, gave them the power to dispose of a multitude of city jobs. But whom to reward, whom to trust, whom to punish, these were the delicate decisions. In building their organization, the Tweed Ring played a dynamic game of power politics on a municipal level, which required the same kind of judgment, subtlety, and finesse used in power politics on a state and even the national level.

Control of patronage enabled Tweed to become New York's first absolute boss. Before his appearance, a clique of leaders divided the emoluments of public office, but with complete control in the hands of the Ring, the powerful Tammany chiefs, the ward leaders and their following were made dependent on the good will of the Ring. From the ward leader down to the precinct captain, power depended on the ability to supply patronage to the faithful. No jobs, no power—and a new leader would take their place. Unfortunately, there was never enough patronage to go around, and the kingdom of St. Tammany, a kind of feudal system, was always vulnerable to a powerful baron who might organize a Runnymede. Tweed, therefore, was less the absolute autocrat than the prime minister, bringing his court together by using patronage as a gentle or a harsh persuader, as a gift, as a promise, as a threat. That the Tweed Ring built a successful empire is attested by the fact that through patronage alone it employed at least 12,000 people; that 33 per cent of the money supplied to the city departments was stolen, in the sense that it went to men listed on the payrolls who did no work, or to payroll names which were fictitious. The *Nation* noted "that the number of votes the Ring controlled or influenced by various instruments at its command—offices, sinecures, contracts, public works, untried indictments, suspended sentences, penalties, licenses, ordinances, and so on—was not less than 60,000."[4] It was enough of an empire to inspire Charles Graham Halpine, a Tammany man never invited to join the charmed inner circle, to pass as poetry these patches of doggerel, entitled "St. Tammany and the Nabobs."

> These nabobs have shirt-fronts with diamonds a-gleam,
> And their Verzenay bubbles, an amber-hued stream;
> Grand junction, commercial politicians they are,
> And in "selling for cash" each shines like a star,
> Singing tooral, tooral, tooral.

They sit in gay rooms under glass chandeliers,
And each bulbous-nosed squatter at Tammany sneers;
Oh, they look with big eyes on political jobs,
And then rattle the tin in their corpulent fobs,
  Singing tooral, etc.

Big chunks of a golden humanity these,
Fat ingots with heads swelled as big as a cheese;
They twiddle their thumbs as they dream of their checks
And 'tis they hold the people ker-chuck by the necks,
  Singing tooral, etc.

Greedy handlers of bullion, bold signers of bills,
Immense in the matter of cleaning out tills;
The masses are asses—so Nature ordains,
For we all know that cash is the measure of brains,
  Singing tooral, etc.[5]

The first principle guiding the Ring's patronage system was to reward the important men in the organization: the Congressmen, State legislators, important ward leaders, friends in the Republican party, co-operative contractors, the General Committee of Tammany Hall, and department heads. For example, Mike Norton ("the far-famed thunderbolt of the Eighth Ward") was Corporation Livery Stable Keeper, Baggage Agent at Castle Garden, Commissioner of the new Court House and of Jefferson Market Court House (but represented here by a dummy), contractor for the sprinkling of Harlem Lane ("for which he gets $30,000 a year and it costs about $5,000 to do the job"), furnisher of hacks and carriages to the Common Council at funerals and official junkets. He also held several sinecure clerkships in the name of his livery stable bookkeeper. The *New York Times* estimated that his city jobs yielded him some $50,000 a year.[6]

There were plums for those who represented New York and the Ring in Albany. Dennis Burns, for example, was both an Assemblyman and docket clerk in the County Clerk's office. "What the duties of a 'docket clerk' are nobody can tell," said the *Times*.[7] The honorable Timothy Campbell, a member of the Assembly, "who became noted . . . for appearing on the floor with a fast female," sponsored a bill in the Assembly creating the position of Mechanic's Lien Clerk in the County Clerk's office, paying $5000 a year. "Astonishingly," Campbell himself got the job. It was rumored that the only duty he performed was to draw his pay, his face never having been seen inside the County Clerk's office.[8]

Richard O'Gorman, an important man as Corporation Counsel, received $1791 to maintain his office and staff, and a monthly allowance of $1000 for the puzzling reason, "in lieu of clerk hire." He was suspected of pocketing most of this, hiring a horde of clerks who came from wards of political friends, and then officially listing their wages under the head of "Contingent Expenses—Law Department."[9]

The Mayor's office offered a harvest of patronage. Of the twenty persons in this office, there were six marshals, a record clerk, copying clerk, sergeant-at-arms, interpreter, two messengers, a private secretary, five clerks with varying titles, and one Timothy Golden, the Mayor's man Friday, a kind of court jester. But it was the Permit Bureau of New York City, under the direct control of Mayor Hall, that was a classic example of patronage in action. It was estimated that under any honest management the amount paid for permits could not be less than $100,000 a year. Yet in 1866, the return was $23,077.72; in 1870, $13,749.95; and in 1871, only $11,924.92. No amounts were rendered by the Mayor or his bureau showing the itemized receipts. No deposits were made in the city treasury until the end of the year. Where had the money gone? The Union League found, to their astonishment and indignation, it went for the most part to pay the salaries of twenty-two political appointees when six men could have done the job. It was estimated that in February 1871 the expense of receiving $194 was $2,840.66. In March, the Tammany appointees were more energetic. The expenses of receiving $145 were only $2,843.70. In April, however, a record was made. It cost $2,842.64 to receive just six dollars! "Truly," said the Union League, "it is a very expensive business." [10]

The second principle of patronage was to reward business friends. For instance, Charles E. Wilbour, president of the Manufacturing Stationers' Company, of which Tweed was part owner; editor of the *Transcript*, of which Tweed was part owner; president of the New York Printing Company, which Tweed owned, also held three positions on the public payroll: stenographer in the Bureau of Elections ($3000), stenographer in the Superior Court ($2500), and Examiner of Accounts in the Bureau of Accounts in the Tax Commissioner's office ($3500).[11]

Andrew Garvey, Grand Marshal of Tammany Hall, gave another side to the workings of patronage during the investigation of Tweed in 1877.

> Q. Besides those dividends or commissions, or whatever you call them, what you paid to members of the Ring and others, did you make any presents to officials or others, to control patronage during those years?
>
> A. I subscribed for presents to various officials, but it was voluntary. We had the patronage already; but it was the fashion to make presents at that time, so I did so with the others.
>
> Q. To control patronage?
>
> A. No, it was the fashion to do so. Everybody was doing it. So I made presents with the others. . . .
>
> Q. To whom were they given?
>
> A. There were subscriptions got up for silver sets to various persons; besides which, we had to pay into the fund to be used at Albany to influence legislation. Ingersoll subscribed $50,000; Keyser and Miller $25,000 each, and, as Mr. Tweed says, everybody that did business down there had to subscribe, and they got it back in the same way that I got mine back.[12]

The king of the sinecure holders was Cornelius Corson—significantly, a boyhood friend of William Marcy Tweed. He began as bartender for a saloon on the High Bridge Road; advanced to foreman on the *Evening Express*. His political ambitions began when he was a messenger for the Common Council. He married "a most estimable lady," the sister of Superintendent of Police Kelso. During the Civil War, Corson was profitably engaged as a recruiter for bounty-jumpers. During the high days of the Tweed Ring he served as clerk to the Commissioners of the Ninth District Court House ($10,000); Chief of the Bureau of Elections ($5000); clerk to the Board of County Canvassers ($2500); as a clerk for the Board of Supervisors he received $2500; as official reporter to the Board of Aldermen he received $2500; as stenographer to the courts, $2500; and to boot he was a school trustee, Tweed's secretary, a lobbyist at Albany, figurehead owner of the New York Printing Company, and a shareholder in the *Transcript*.[13]

The third principle underlying Ring patronage was that charity began at home. Nepotism was as much a feature in the Ring organization as in a seventeenth-century English court or the palace of a Turkish potentate. William M. Tweed, Jr., was an Assistant District Attorney, a Commissioner of Street Openings, a receiver in the Pacific Railroad. As a general in the State Militia, appointed to the Governor's staff, he delighted in wearing the uniform, whether the occasion called for it or not. Richard Tweed, the Boss's brother, was a Tax Assessor and his son a first assistant clerk in the Department of Public Education. Alfred Tweed, another son of the Boss, was a clerk in the district court, and William H. King, Jr., a nephew of Tweed, Deputy Commissioner of Public Works.

Henry Starkweather was appointed to the lush post of Collector of Assessments. He received as fees 2.5 per cent of all the monies he collected, and 2 per cent on the monies he did not collect. It was estimated that one who held this job for four years would receive $544,237 in fees for simply sitting in an office and seeing to it that certain notices were sent out and monies paid in by property owners assessed for local improvements.[14] "Who is Henry Starkweather? Who ever heard of him?" asked the *Times*. He was the father-in-law of John Hoffman, the Governor.

For all his faults, Peter Barr Sweeny loved his family. Four of his relatives employed in city government were paid in just one year a total of $164,112.[15] Nepotism continued on down to the "mute inglorious Tweeds," the judges and ward leaders. This is not to mention all the relatives of Ring members who were made referees and receivers by the Ring judges.

"When Rome had left far behind her traditions of republican freedom," said the *New York Times*, "she became cursed with a precious set of rascals, known . . . as the Praetorian Guards. These men were the true originals of the modern 'loafer,' the difference being the Praetorians could fight bravely."[16] The *Times* was angry with New York City politics, and usually when in this state of mind, it sought the proper analogy with either classical times or oriental despotism. In this instance, the newspaper was referring to the horde of Tammany supporters, the small-fry politicians of the Shiny Hat Brigade who, thanks to Tammany's patronage, were swarming into the offices of city government.

These were the rank and file of the Tweed Ring's army, the political sharpshooters, guerrillas, bushwhackers, and light cavalry. These flamboyant statesmen were on "call" throughout the city, their job was "maintaining order—or disorder—thereat as the occasion required; be delegates to local conventions; keep track of the voters; see that they would vote 'right;' . . . threaten and intimidate the recalcitrant; praise . . . and sing paeans of adulation and triumph to the Boss-in-chief, William M. Tweed."[17] For these valuable services they were rewarded with positions in the city government.

When a sergeant in the shiny hat brigade dressed up, he might wear, said a contemporary, plaid breeches and a plaid cutaway coat, a red silk cravat, tall black hat, yellow kid gloves, and a fancy cane. He walked with a swagger, black hat jauntily cocked, puffed on black cigars, and could be seen drinking in the saloons or lounging on street corners. Once a boss from another city looked on a Tammany supporter and gave the group another name. "Pah!" he said. "Paint eaters!" The name stuck and became a kind of political slang for those political small-fry who, as the Boss said, would eat the paint off a house if he did not hold them in check.[18]

One member of the shiny hat brigade was Tim Donovan, a saloon-keeper in the Nineteenth Ward, once a well-known prize-fighter. During the time of Fernando Wood he achieved notoriety through biting off one of the ears of the Honorable Thomas Connor.[19] In the summer of 1870, the police at Saratoga made a "terrible" mistake by thinking he was a three-card monte sharper. For $1000 a year he was Deputy Clerk of Fulton Market. "He is never seen at work."[20] "Oofty Gooft" Phillips, a comedian by trade, had larger talents: he was a clerk to the Water Register and in the winter months a correspondent in Albany, where he wrote complimentary articles on Democratic rule in New York.[21]

The city employed as public officials a number of men with interesting backgrounds: George Hill, a gambler known better as "Cooley Keys"; Maurice Daly, a professional billiard player; and Jim "Maneater" Cusick, a frequent inmate of Sing Sing, aptly appointed as clerk to a city court and, to boot, holding a position in the Sheriff's office.[22] For removing garbage from the Fulton Market, Thomas Canary was paid $1250. "How faithfully he does his work the entire community will attest."[23] George H. E. Lynch held sinecures amounting to $14,000 minus eight cents, an amount that fascinated members of the Jackson Club, a reform group. They formed a special committee, a subscription was taken up, and the committee called at the offices of the *Times* to leave eight cents for Lynch to pick up.[24]

Political machines of the present day still follow the ancient practice of patronage, but they tend to appoint trained men capable of doing the job. In the days of the Tweed Ring, however, the procedure was not so sophisticated. In these days before civil service, every job was a political plum. A man was appointed on the basis of who he knew, not what he knew about the job. In his *Autobiography*, Andrew D. White illustrates a classic example of this brought out in an investigation of a "Health Inspector" appointed by the Tweed Ring. He was questioned about a case of smallpox in his district.

> "Did you visit this sick person?"
> "No, sir."
> "For what reason?"
> "I didn't want to catch the disease myself."
> "Did the family have any sort of medical aid?"
> "Yes."
> "From whom did they have?"
> "From themselves; they was 'highjinnicks.'" [hygienics]
> "What do you mean by 'highjinnicks'?"
> "I mean persons who doctor themselves."

Intrigued, the judge asked other health inspectors if they had had any experience with "highjinnicks." According to Andrew White, "some answered that they had them somewhat; some thought that they had them 'pretty bad,' others thought that there was 'not much of it,' others claimed that they were 'quite serious'"; and finally, in the examination of a certain health officer who was very anxious to show he had done his best, there occurred the following dialogue which brought down the house:

> "'Mr. Health Officer, have you had any "highjinnicks" in your district?'
> "'Yes, sir.'
> "'Much?'
> "'Yes, sir, quite a good deal.'
> "'Have you done anything in regard to them?'
> "'Yes, sir; I have done all that I could.'
> "'Witness, now, on your oath, do you know what the word "highjinnicks" means?'
> "'Yes, sir.'
> "'What does it mean?'
> "'It means the bad smells that arise from standing water.'"[25]

While the reformers held mass meetings, and identified their organizations as being endorsed by wealthy, prominent, and respectable citizens, the Ring leaders met with the ward leaders, the ward leaders met with the precinct captains, and the precinct captains bought drinks for and votes from the rank and file. When a reform group, such as the powerful Citizens' Association, became unpleasantly vociferous about city government, Tweed went to some of the important members of the reform organization and exchanged patronage for less talk.

> "Were you able to convince them, after a time, of your way of thinking?" he was asked during an investigation.
>
> "Yes, sir."
>
> "By what means did you effect that change of sentiment?"
>
> "I think we took care of most of them." [26]

There were three payrolls for the County Bureau: the regular roll, and two "temporary rolls, half the names on which were fictitious. Many of the clerks who were legitimately employed had not learned how to read or write. Money for the last two payrolls was not taken out of any appropriation, but was part of a fund raised on the sale of Riot Damages Indemnity Bonds." [27]

The Tweed Ring survived through patronage. To keep the organization happy and working smoothly, it had to satisfy the almost insatiable appetite for patronage of its underlings. If the jobs ran out, the Ring invented new ones. Thus there were only three water pumps below Fourteenth Street, yet twenty men were employed at $1000 as "pump inspectors." Nor were the ladies slighted. Many Tammany men were good family men, as a favorite toast, "To Our Squaws and Papooses," attests. "May our chief pleasure be in providing them with fur, with venison and with wampum—we know theirs is to please and make us happy." [28] And the squaws went forth and earned their wampum chiefly as cleaning women, and in some offices it seemed there were as many cleaning ladies as public employees. It required twelve women to clean the rooms in which the Supreme Court held sessions, and five to clean those of Common Pleas and the Superior Court. "It will be seen that if the Court-house is not one of the cleanest places in the world, it is not because money enough is not spent upon it," said an unhappy newspaper.[29]

In 1857 work was begun on Central Park, the pride of New York, an attempt to capture and preserve the Arcadian loveliness of rural America amid the confines of her greatest city. Here with its brooks and its trees, its quiet paths, and its sense of freedom that Nature suggested was the symbol of an older, vanishing America, the simplicity, honesty, and integrity of Jefferson's yeoman farmer. Here was the antidote to the crushing, ugly, cruel, and impersonal forces of urbanization. To preserve God's handiwork, however, a price common to both rural and urban America had to be paid, the price of patronage. It was something the Superintendent of the Park, Frederick Law Olmsted, one of the greatest landscape artists in the United States, never understood.

Confessedly "a wholly unpractical man," Olmsted was astonished to find, especially with the coming of the Tweed Ring, that the park was becoming less an oasis of Arcadian virtue and more a refuge of hungry job-seekers and unprincipled politicians. He once received in just six days more than 7000 letters, mostly from politicians, requesting jobs for their followers. When he was not compliant, a candidate for a magisterial office gave a speech to a horde of unemployed laborers from Olmsted's own doorsteps, telling them that the Superintendent was obliged to give them jobs, and if he were slow about it, a rope around his neck might make him reconsider. One Sunday morning, a dozen men forced their way into his house begging for work. When Peter Sweeny became president of the Department of Public Parks, the situation—at least to Olmsted—became intolerable.

Up to 1870, Central Park had been under the control of a commission appointed by the governor. With the new city charter of 1870, pushed through the State legislature by the Tweed Ring, the functions of this board were transferred to the Department of Public Parks, which was administered by one outstanding public servant, Andrew H. Green, and three Tammany chieftains, Peter Sweeny, Henry Hilton, a former judge, and the powerful ward leader, Thomas C. "Torpedo" Fields. Green was allowed to serve only to give the board some respectability, but any power he might have exercised for good deeds was completely nullified when the other commissioners constituted themselves as an executive committee and thereby captured the administration of the public parks system. Sweeny was made president and he directed the board with an understanding of his job not unlike that of the Health Inspector's understanding of "highjinnicks," as the distinguished naturalist, Waterhouse Hawkins, discovered much to his grief.

Before the Sweeny administration, the Park Commission had asked Professor Hawkins to prepare a special exhibition for Central Park. He was to create out of plaster large skeleton models of some extinct animals which had once existed in America. The dedicated professor worked for almost two years and at the cost of some $12,000 completed the skeletons of two huge vertebrates. When the new commission came into being, Commissioner Henry Hilton demanded that Hawkins stop his work; and then with the blessings of Sweeny, Hilton ordered that his vertebrates and his molds be totally destroyed by sledge-hammers and buried. As Hilton explained it to the astonished naturalist, "he should not bother himself about 'dead animals,' when there were so many living ones to care for." [30] To add insult to injury, Sweeny and Hilton ordered that a bronze statue and a skeleton of a whale donated by Peter Cooper be painted with a glaring coat of white paint.

Sweeny and his commissioners were not interested in skeletons, they were interested in patronage. Under the Sweeny regime it was reported by the *New York Times*, with perhaps some exaggeration, that 4000 laborers were employed in Central Park.[31] Along with patronage came plunder. In the four years prior to the coming of Sweeny, the average annual cost for maintaining Central Park was just $250,000. From April 20, 1870, to November 1, 1871, however, Sweeny and Company in executive sessions spent $6,000,000. They left behind them liabilities amounting to over

$1,500,000, contracts amounting to another $500,000—a total expenditure of $8,000,000 of the public's money.[32] This was more money than had been spent in the preceding thirteen years for the whole cost of creating as well as maintaining Central Park. What particularly rendered Olmsted and others speechless was the fact that Sweeny could veto the building of a much-needed Paleontological Museum, at the estimated cost of $300,000, because it was too expensive!

After 1870, the machinery of patronage was further centralized and geared to an operation never before experienced in New York. Thanks to the Tweed charter of 1870, the former center of patronage was merged with the old Croton Board and other "rarebits" to become the Department of Public Works, William M. Tweed, president. The department controlled more patronage than any other office in the city. With hundreds on the payroll it cost up to $1,200,000 a year to maintain. As president of the Department of Public Works, Tweed received a salary of $10,000, with an almost unlimited amount for "contingencies." Actually the position was supposed to be worth $100,000 a year to the man who ran it. It was the most popular department in the city, and every day men came to seek jobs. As a newspaper described it, "the stairs and corridors were thronged with diamonds, shiny hats, dirty hands, and dyed moustaches, and a cloud of cigar smoke hung like a protecting curtain over the political element that pushed and crowded in the hallways." [33] As Boss Blossom Brick said, "If you want office, young man, kneel to the Boss first, then to the Leaders, then to the people, and afterwards to the Lord, if you have any spare time left!" [34]

Years later Tweed was asked about his activities in the Department of Public Works.

Q. "During the existence of the Ring, were there not quite a number of persons upon the pay-rolls, who were regularly paid as if they were doing service to the city in one capacity or another, who actually didn't do any service at all?"

A. "Or very little."

Q. "Was it understood that they shouldn't do any service at all?"
A. "Yes, sir."
Q. "Now, at this time, can you recollect any such persons?"
A. "In my time, I also had a private pay-roll of my own—some forty or fifty, or sixty thousand dollars paid out of my own pocket, but letting them think that they were paid by the city. Disbecker, who used to be Police Commissioner, I paid forty or fifty dollars a month, out of my own pocket, for a year or two. He thought it came from the department."
Q. "What was he supposed to do?"
A. "He was appointed Inspector of something or other, he thought—something that didn't exist at all. All the work he did was to get his pay every month.... I had E. K. Apgar I think, the Assistant Secretary of State...."
Q. "What was he on the roll for?"
A. "To draw his money...."
Q. "Well, what was he doing?"
A. "Spouting—talking—making speeches." [35]

The lack of organization, independence, and working habits of those who labored in the Boss's vineyard—the streets and city parks—suggested that Tweed was carrying out Artemus Ward's happy idea to save jealousies by making his regiment all Colonels. A newspaper, curious about the state of civic improvements, sent a reporter to investigate. Washington Square was a labyrinth of winding paths, heaps of dirt and rubbish, where two to three hundred men stood with spades and pickaxes, "striking picturesque attitudes." The scene remained delightfully pastoral and primitive because there was no lively stir among the laborers. In another public park the amount of energy expended by eight men in retarding each other's efforts to fill a car "will dawn upon the reflective lounger... like a new revelation in natural philosophy." Gingerly handling pickaxes, men tapped the ground gently "as if it were hallowed, and... gazed long and earnestly at the impression they made as if they expected to find among the dust some of the Bowery pennies." [36]

On pay day, the strength of the Tweed Ring's army made itself painfully evident. A reporter visiting the City Chamberlain's office found an awesome line, stretching from the cashier's desk down and around the staircase into a basement crowded with laborers. He interviewed an Irishman who worked on the city streets.

> "I suppose there are a great many who get paid for working on the pipes and boulevards who never go to work at all?" the reporter asked.
>
> "They are obliged to answer roll call and show themselves sometimes, but then they can loaf if they have a mind to."
>
> "I suppose these foremen want a man to work all the time?"
>
> "Yes," said the laborer, "I got sacked once by a foreman because I had some words with him. I laid down my spade and went to lay off, and he told me to go to work. I told him I wouldn't work for any foreman, and I was sacked. He came down into our Ward afterward, and we laid for him, and he got punched in the head. I've been sacked often, but can get work whenever I want it."
>
> "How often do they call the roll?"
>
> "Twice a day. I go up there in the morning and answer roll call, and then I take a pick, spade or wheelbarrow, work a little while, and then I go and take a sleep somewheres, and sometimes I answer roll call and sometimes I don't; if I don't the foreman answers for me. . . ."

Curious about how he could be re-employed after being fired several times, the reporter asked him how he did it. The laborer replied that he did it by presenting letters to the foreman.

> "Who do you get them from?"
>
> "Oh, from the politician chaps in the Ward, Aldermen and other fellows."
>
> "The foremen of the gangs always take you back when you show them the letters?"
>
> "Yes; if the first letter don't bring it, the next one will and three he can't get over. It shows too much weight." [37]

Thus the Tweed Ring helped to establish the pattern of patronage in New York that lasted well into the twentieth century. Reformers found the machine evil, Republicans cried shame, and uninvited Democrats called it un-American, but all would turn its gears and move its wheels when it came their turn (if only momentarily) to use it. Patronage was part of politics in a democracy; it was necessary for party leadership and discipline. But the venality of the Tweed Ring made it also into an instrument for massive corruption; indeed, a vicious kind of corruption because it confounded even further some of the city's critical problems, such as health, sanitation, and law enforcement, by placing incompetent political hacks into those public offices requiring expertness, integrity, and responsibility. The spoils system in New York was unique only in its vastness; Philadelphia had its Gas Ring; St. Louis, its Whisky Ring; Chicago, Long John Wentworth; and even in Brooklyn, New York's illegitimate child, the victors gathered in the spoils. If the practice brought a touch of evil and shame to New York, it accomplished one thing at least; it gave a hungry Irishman, a German with a big family, a migrant New Englander, a native but unfortunate New Yorker, a job.

9

CRIME AND PUNISHMENT

The kind of justice is queer and low,
And comes, like the temple building, slow;
And ever there lingers a dismal stench
Of fraud and guile around every bench.

C. Robbins, *The Royal Decrees of Scanderoon*

Responsible men in New York City felt that the Tweed Ring would bring about the collapse of republican institutions and civil liberties in the city and state of New York. The Ring had captured not only City Hall and Tammany Hall but also that seemingly impregnable fortress, the Hall of Justice.

Oldtimers recalled the traditions of the bench and bar: the majesty of justice, the love of right because it was right, the protection of property, the outspoken denunciation of corruption. Their memory was warmed with nostalgia for the good old days—Kent, Josiah Ogden Hoffman, Oakley, Jones and Duer, stalwarts of the New York bench, impeccable, impartial, and invulnerable, of course, to political influence. Those were days when justices knew the law, were appointed for good behavior, and, again, were completely free of the political arena. But now all that was a thing of the past, or so it was thought. It had changed with too much democracy, when judicial offices became elective. And here the nostalgic oldtimers remembered Tocqueville on this subject, and perhaps for a moment forgot he was an aristocrat: "These innovations will sooner or later be attended with fatal consequences; and that it will be found out at some future period that by thus lessening the independence of the judiciary they have attacked not only the judicial power, but the democratic republic itself."[1]

The infusions of democracy that affected the New York judiciary from 1846 on, when many judicial offices were made elective, did not immediately make real Tocqueville's gloomy prediction. The judges that were first elected to the Supreme Court of New York were men of unusual ability and integrity. After 1846, the Superior Court actually achieved a better reputation than it had when judges were not elected by the people. Nor did more democracy cause "fatal consequences" for the Court of Common Pleas, which showed no signs of decay after 1846. As for the Surrogate Court, it went on to gain a national reputation for excellence. The only exceptions were the police and justices courts, which continued to be a legal disgrace. They were as bad under the new system as they were under the old.[2]

Thus the year 1846 did not represent a sudden turning point from good to evil. New York had had unprincipled men on the bench before the judiciary was democratized. Moreover, judicial corruption had been a problem in times and countries never troubled about the implications of suffrage and elective legal offices. It was a long old story. Democratization of the New York judiciary, for better and for worse, did bring important changes, but these reflected similar changes occurring in other phases of public life. Like city government, the judiciary reacted to economic growth and the increasing flow of immigration. Its organization became bloated, jurisdictions overlapped, responsibility became divided; its offices, like civil offices, became more and more the domain of professional politicians. Too much democracy was not the exclusive bane of the judiciary as it appeared under Ring rule, but it did allow legal machinery to fall more and more into the hands of those who controlled political nominations. This was particularly true for control of the civil and police justices, elected from small districts, comprising two to four wards. These justices could often control the destiny of a petty criminal, the fortunes of the local boss's supporters, the overzealous partisan who had voted too early and too often.

The Ring captured the judiciary as it had captured city government. Just as the chief design for New York's first modern city machine was centralization of the vital sources of political power, so indeed was the judiciary modernized and streamlined. Where before, a local ward chief might control his own police justice, the Ring sought to centralize such power by managing all judicial nominations, or at least enough to give it the controlling interest. This first step was achieved with the control of Tammany. The second step was to place the faithful in positions from the lowest to the very highest in the legal system. A bill was passed to create additional clerkships for practically the entire judicial system. Individual courts increased their payrolls. In the Trial Term, Part III, of the Supreme Court, for example, there was a complete set of officers, including clerks and stenographers, which seemed a burden on the taxpayers, since in 1868 it had met for only one session and was never deemed important enough to be given a regular meeting room. In 1871 the civil and police courts provided eighteen additional sinecure positions worth $3000 each, even though it was apparent their departments were already overstaffed.[3] There was no central, co-ordinating department to supervise court payrolls, thus allowing several legal departments, particularly the District Attorney's office, the Superior Court, and the courts of General and Special Sessions, to operate as separate, individual dynasties. Payrolls therefore became swollen with names both influential and fictitious. James Sweeny, as a result, acquired the powerful post of Clerk of the Superior Court; Nathaniel Jarvis, Jr., became Clerk of the Court of Common Pleas; and William M. Tweed, Jr., was appointed Special Clerk in the District Attorney's office. It was estimated that almost half the names on court payrolls came from the rich imagination of the Tweed Ring.[4]

The *New York Times*, attempting to estimate the depth of the Tweed Ring's invasion and the generosity of their patronage, said that twenty officers were sufficient for each court, yet the Superior

Court had forty-three, the Supreme Court fifty-two, the Court of Common Pleas thirty-six, the General Sessions thirty-seven, and the Marine Court thirty, making a total of nearly 200 sinecures in official positions alone, and not including the appointments to minor posts.[5] A superabundance of sinecures could prove embarrassing. On one occasion, in a district civil court, a case required the immediate services of a stenographer. Not one could be found, although the court listed eight on the payroll.[6]

Nor did expanded payrolls necessarily reflect a population growth which would require a larger legal staff. Before the Tweed Ring, the Superior Court, for example, had a calendar of around 5000 cases; it convened at 10 A.M. and closed at 4 P.M. With the advent of the Ring, its calendar shrank to 2500; it convened at 11 A.M. and closed at 3 P.M.; but its expenses increased $26,400.[7]

The appointment of the "right" men to key posts was the third step in making the law as much a matter of politics as of justice. In this instance the Ring depended upon the old Tammany gambit of appointing respectable men to enhance the public's sense of complacency and divert attention from appointments less respectable. John O'Gorman, a henchman of Tweed, once gave much publicity to the "respectabilities" adorning the bench. How, he said, could it be said that the judiciary was corrupt when these men of great legal experience and proper breeding were on the bench: John R. Brady, "a man whom every member of the Bar delights to honor"; Judge Van Brunt, "who even now is beginning to make his mark upon the Bench"; and Hamilton W. Robinson, "a lawyer of ripe experience"? Every good appointment, however, was balanced by placing on the bench a man faithful to the goals of the Ring. The men who best represent the state of the judiciary under the Tweed Ring were two judges of the Supreme Court, George Barnard and Albert Cardozo, and John H. McCunn of the Superior Court, City Recorder Hackett, and the Corporation Counsel, John O'Gorman.

A dictionary defines "venal" as "that can readily be bribed or corrupted; mercenary: as, a *venal* judge." Of all the venal judges who in the long history of New York have disgraced its bench,

George Barnard ranks as one of the most notorious, and possibly the most colorful. He made a striking appearance. He was a handsome man with the tall, erect figure of a soldier; a sallow complexion highlighted black eyes and black moustache; a fine head was covered with wavy, jet-black hair. He preferred black suits, expensive frilled shirts, and tall white hats, cocked over an eye. Arrogant, obscene, witty, he looked like a gambler, fancied himself an aristocrat, and had a passion for low women, late hours, and hard liquor. Tweed found him useful, but exasperating: "You had to waste much time with him—be around with him a good deal, coax him, and make him believe he was a great man—pat him on his back." [8] Of his legal abilities, his own brother was supposed to have said, "George knows about as much law as a yellow dog." [9] As for his gamy reputation, at the trial following his impeachment, his attorney William H. Beach made this defense, which deserves a special place in the literature of the law.

> I am frank to say I do not approve all the acts of this respondent. I think, sir, bad mannered as I am, I might be able to improve him in dignity of demeanor and suavity of address. He has been educated, as have been many of our sons, in a rude school. He is a man of action, bold in his convictions, fearless in their expression. He is not the kind of metal of which tools and instruments are made. He might become a daring leader of bold adventurers, were he not well grounded upon principle. But never, sir, could he be made the petty and insignificant puppet of meaner men. If he descends to crime, it will be with a bravery which sometimes adds dignity to its commission.[10]

Barnard's early education was hardly in a rude school. Born in 1829 of good family in New York, he was graduated from Yale and went to California. There he was an unsuccessful prospector, a "shill" in a gambling house, a member of a Negro minstrel troupe. He drifted back to New York and the ruder elements of politics. In 1858 he was elected Recorder and, taking a cue from his predecessor Recorder Riker, he made a reputation for judicial capacity by imposing severe sentences on criminals. By 1860 he had caught the eye of Tweed, who successfully backed him for the State Supreme Court, which was made somewhat easy since Tweed was the presiding officer at the nominating convention. Tweed himself described how he managed it.

> So I took the chair, and wasn't very comfortable in it, either. A man from California, by the name of Doyle, was running against Barnard. . . . I saw, as the roll call proceeded, that Doyle had the majority of delegates. Said I to a secretary, "Have a motion made to dispense with calling the roll!" It was done. "All in favor of Mr. Barnard as the nominee of this body say aye. Carried! The meeting is adjourned!" Well, there was a riot and I was driven into one corner; Isaiah Rynders [who backed Doyle] had a pistol as long as my arm drawn and cocked. Said he, "I'll pay you for this!" I was scared, but I didn't say so. "I'm not afraid of a whole ward of you fighting villains," said I, and we all got out.[11]

It was in court that Barnard acquired part of his reputation. A reformer said with some understatement that his habits on the bench were all his own. He usually entered the courtroom wearing a huge white hat, which more often than not, remained at a rakish tilt throughout the session. He would sit down, prop his feet (one of which had the aristocratic gout) on the desk and motion to a clerk to bring him some pine sticks. Throughout the session he would whittle, make bawdy jests, and take large, conspicuous gulps from his brandy bottle.[12]

Matthew Breen claimed seeing Barnard in action in the court of the General Term of the Supreme Court. He was giving oral examinations to attorneys seeking admission to the bar.

> "Senator," said Barnard, addressing the trembling candidate, "do you know there is such a thing as the State Constitution?"
>
> "Yes, sir."
>
> "If a proposed bill came up for consideration, which you knew was in violation of the Constitution, what would you do?"

Without hesitation: "I would move to suspend the Constitution; same as we sometimes suspend the Rules of the Senate to pass a bill."

"Stand aside," said the Judge with a snicker, "you will make a profound lawyer."

Next candidate.

"Now, sir," said the Judge, "if you had a claim for a client of $50,000 against the City, what would be the first step you would take to recover it?"

Without hesitation: "I would go and see Bill Tweed."

"You will make your mark as a Corporation lawyer," said Barnard, amid much laughter.[13]

But Barnard's reputation was not built on such details. Boss Tweed introduced him to James Fisk, and Barnard became a leading actor in the famous Fisk-Gould-Drew battle over the Erie Railroad.[14] As a Supreme Court Justice he was invaluable to the Ring in seeing that the right men were appointed to street commissionships, receiverships, and as legal referees. If any Ring supporter was arrested and tried before Barnard, "Tweed's intercession was equivalent to a dismissal of the case." [15] George Barnard was amply rewarded for services rendered. When he died, a total of more than one million dollars in bonds and cash was found among his effects.

Albert Cardozo was a striking contrast to Barnard in everything but a capacity for corruption. Where Barnard was large, boisterous, hard-drinking, and conspicuous for his lack of legal knowledge, Cardozo was slight, quiet, hard-working—a gentleman and a scholar. Indeed, he was thought to have one of the best legal minds of his day. This courteous, beardless man, with thick curly hair, would hardly be noticed in a crowd, said one opponent, but one with a sense for evil would notice one distinguishing feature. "He had the eyes of a serpent, looking from the face of a corpse." [16]

Cardozo was born in 1830 in New York of a Portuguese-Jewish family. After being graduated from Columbia College with high honors, he entered law practice. Fernando Wood saw him as a useful tool and nominated him as Judge of the Court of Common Pleas. Tweed also recognized his usefulness and elevated him to the State Supreme Court after the Civil War. Cardozo made the transition from Wood to Tweed deftly. His intense ambition steered him to Tweed, who seemed to be the one man who could make possible Cardozo's dream of securing a seat on the bench of the Supreme Court of the United States. But Cardozo never forgot Wood. When Wood, no longer a power in New York, brought suit against the City, Cardozo, who presided over the case, awarded him a judgment of $180,000 for the rent of buildings not worth over $35,000.[17]

Cardozo's office, Room 13 during Ring rule, was called the "Star Chamber" by reformers erudite enough to suggest a comparison to an old English court of the same name, known for its violations of justice. Like Barnard, Cardozo was extremely useful in appointing the proper Commissioners, Receivers, and Referees. Moreover, since Governor Hoffman appointed both to the General Term of the Supreme Court, which reviewed decisions of that court, and where in many cases no further appeal was allowed by law, they made a formidable partnership in obstructing or guiding the law as the Ring saw fit. While Cardozo never shared in the Erie Railroad harvest, he did develop a specialty of his own. He became a kind of escape hatch for criminals; through his good offices he pardoned or dismissed several hundred known criminals who were or might be useful to the Ring.

Barnard and Cardozo constituted a strong bench for any political machine; backed up by Judge John McCunn it took on even more awesome proportions. John McCunn, a poor Irish immigrant, clawed his way from the tough world of the city docks to city politics and a law degree, and by 1863 he had made his way to the Superior Court. Outwardly good-natured and even jovial, he "could talk so smoothly and act the whole-souled Irishman so well, that he deceived respectable men into thinking him honest and desirous of improving himself." [18] Behind this wholesome exterior was a seedy morality. As a lawyer, McCunn often sold his clients' secrets to the opposing counsels. And once, as Judge, he persuaded a close relative to transfer property to him, and then asserted his title to it, even dispossessing his compliant kinsman. His personal appearance was peculiar. A story was told of an eminent foreigner who, at a public gathering, expressed the greatest curiosity to know something of "that remarkable-looking man with the head like St. Just." When he was told that he was looking at a colleague of William Tweed and friends, "the tourist's faith in craniology is supposed not to have survived the shock."[19]

McCunn's knowledge of law was even less than that of Barnard. It was said he employed eleven lawyers to write his opinions for him.[20] As a Superior Court Judge, he was particularly useful in his supervisory capacities. In one instance, which the *New York Times* called the "Singular Proceedings of a Democratic Judge," on election day in 1869, at Jefferson Market Police Court, Justice Dodge was presiding over a busy court. During the first part of the day, repeater after repeater appeared before him, and there were alarming symptoms that he intended to do all in his power to enforce the law and punish offenders, as he held all offenders for $500 bail. Perhaps because of these inconveniences, Judge John McCunn appeared and with "vigor" and "such energy" succeeded in getting the repeaters out of jail on various pretexts.

Recorder John Hackett, a man of easy conscience, was another key gear in the Ring's legal machinery. He was known as the "poor man's judge," because the majority of his cases were either the poor or the criminal. He was thus in a position to render favors to those ward chiefs whose followers found themselves in trouble. His record for dismissals was unsurpassed. "Recorder Hackett," said one indignant investigator, "without the slightest legal authority, has in a large number of cases, after the accused had been regularly convicted of serious offences, assumed to suspend sentence *and has discharged them from custody without the slightest punishment.*"[21] For example, within a year and ten months Hackett dismissed 170 cases. Twenty-eight of this number had been found guilty of grand larceny, fifteen of burglary, and others were adjudged guilty of forgery, assault with intent to kill, keeping disorderly houses, and the like. On one day alone, three burglars, one forger, and four criminals were let loose after conviction.[22] A newspaper was thinking of him when it said that three things never failed to influence a city judge—political pressure, a woman's tears, and the cup of friendship.

Hackett also distinguished himself in other respects. Of forty-nine appeals taken from his decisions, no less than twenty-two reversals occurred, whereas decisions of his colleagues, Judges Bedford and Sutherland, had been reversed but eight times. Other aspects of Hackett's legal ability left something to be desired. He once sentenced one Charles H. Madden to twenty years' imprisonment for entering his mother's room and taking eight dollars. Another man was given life imprisonment for setting fire to his store.

Hackett, who had held other judicial positions before becoming City Recorder, entered that office in March 1866 through the insistence of A. Oakey Hall, at that time District Attorney. One of his first acts as Recorder was to claim and receive $1166 for salary from January to March 1866, a period in which neither he nor anyone else was Recorder![23] On July 31, 1866, he was appointed to a commission entrusted to lay out a public place known as "The Circle," at the intersection of Eighth Avenue and Fifty-ninth Street. The Commissioners were delegated to estimate the value of the private property taken and to assess the cost upon the property benefited, a simple task, since the amount of condemned private property was very small; in fact, it was less than two acres. Such a challenge, however, apparently required expert opinion, and hence Hackett and his two fellow Commissioners gathered a staff of one surveyor, one clerk, one assistant clerk (James M. Sweeny), and nine appraisers. At the end of fifteen months a ponderous report was submitted. The cost of maintaining the Commissioners and their staff to estimate and take over two acres of property was $26,331.91. The Citizens' Association gagged, but Judge George Barnard allowed the sum.

For his service as Commissioner, Hackett received $3000. Asked how he could claim such a sum in view of the law restricting the fees to 30 cents per lineal foot, he replied, "We measured a spiral line commencing at the center and screwing its way out." This impressed one writer to say that it "would certainly seem to be a 'ring' and not merely a circle proceeding."[24] In addition, Hackett held down several other well-paying city jobs, and still found time to maintain a lucrative law practice.

Another prominent Ring judge was a huge, hairy, eloquent Irishman named Richard O'Gorman, a master of political blarney. A former prominent Fenian leader in Ireland, O'Gorman came to New York and made a reputation for himself as a crusader against corruption. The high-minded Citizens' Association along with other anti-Tammany organizations backed him successfully for Corporation Counsel. On November 6, 1865, he wrote the Citizens' Association, acknowledging his gratitude. "I would be as earnest as yourselves to its [the office of Corporation Counsel] rights, assert its honor and protect its finances from adverse influences, from whatever quarter, or in whatever shape they may assail it."[25] A year and ten months later, a disillusioned Citizens' Association circulated a pamphlet appropriately entitled "How the Money Goes," giving a detailed account on how both the taxpayers' money and O'Gorman's promises went.

O'Gorman was adept at making friends and influencing people. One of the more sophisticated techniques of graft exercised by the Tweed Ring was to allow warm friends to file fraudulent claims against the City, pay them off, and collect a commission. O'Gorman, as Corporation Counsel, had a pivotal role in these schemes. The Citizens' Association pointed out that judgments obtained against the City during O'Gorman's reign reached an all-time high of $474,589.78. Of this amount, $200,000 in judgments was obtained in defiance of the law, and should have been reversed on appeal, but O'Gorman himself, the legal officer of the City, advised that they be paid in full. In one instance, O'Gorman retained a law firm to defend the City; this firm, in other cases, was engaged in recovering heavy judgments against the City. The Association also referred to the unusual procedure of O'Gorman's certifying a bill in his own favor for $10,000 for extra services rendered by himself in arguing the case of the Taxation of Bank Stockholders, at Washington, in addition to paying from the city treasury $20,000 for two lawyers to assist him.[26]

What was particularly galling was that, while the City lost over $400,000 in judgments, expenses to maintain O'Gorman's office also reached an all-time high of $152,974.32. Although O'Gorman was seemingly employed full time, he spent from his office fund $86,611.50 for professional advice and clerk hire. As previously mentioned, Hackett received $21,727.50 of this, or about two-thirds as much as O'Gorman earned and four to five times as much as the City deemed adequate compensation for his duties as Recorder. It seemed strange that O'Gorman, a reform candidate, who drew more than a hundred dollars a day for attending to the lawsuits of the City, should need professional aid to the sum of two hundred dollars a day, and clerk hire to the value of about seventy-five dollars more a day. "Cannot the city," said the *New York Herald* "get beaten in its lawsuits at a cheaper rate than five hundred dollars a day?" [27] It was estimated that O'Gorman, who once said, "I pledge . . . if elected to this office, to devote all the strength and energies I possess, and to use all the powers the office may afford . . ." pocketed at least $33,833.32.[28] Richard O'Gorman was to prove invaluable later during the investigations of the Tweed Ring, when he persistently piled a multitude of legal roadblocks in the path of justice.

The few historians and political scientists who have paid any attention to the Tweed Ring have been dazzled by its plundering of the city treasury. Moreover, students of the relations between crime and politics in New York have centered their attention for the most part on the late nineteenth and twentieth centuries, with the Lexow, Fassett, Massett, and Seabury investigations, and with such criminals as the Eastmans, Lepkes, and Lucianos. Little attention has been given to the fact that petty and important criminals, involved in vice, gambling, confidence games, and the like, were tributaries of the Ring. Indeed, one of the first large-scale investigations of crime in New York came in 1875, as an aftermath of the Tweed Ring exposures.[29] To be sure, crime was not so highly organized nor so intimate with politics in the Tweed Ring era as it was from the 1890's on; nevertheless, the basic pattern existed. The criminal depended upon political protection for his crimes. The control and protection of crime was, in fact, one of the Ring's sources of power, not only as a means of building and modernizing the machine, but also as a source for exacting tribute. On election day gangsters repaid the Ring for services rendered. For example, men like Reddy the Blacksmith, who cut his political teeth upon breaking up abolition meetings before the Civil War, beat up anti-Tammany voters for the Tweed Ring after the war. Some authorities, in fact, date the emergence of the modern criminal gangs back to the early repeater gangs.

Boss Tweed's New York was as wicked as the New York of the 1890's during the Reverend Charles R. Parkhurst's crusade or that of the early 1930's that Seabury exposed. In 1872, William Evarts estimated that more crime occurred in New York, with a population just over a million, than in London, with a population of three million. During the Tweed era "covert crime," practiced by confidence men, pickpockets, burglars, and sneak thieves, increased enormously, while crimes of violence did not, largely because, said one contemporary, "the thugs of the city found employment in politics equally congenial and more remunerative."[30] At that time there were about 30,000 professional thieves and 2000 gambling dens.[31] In 1868 a total of 78,451 crimes were reported. During 1870, in the vicinity of Water Street and the waterfront alone, 17,000 sailors were robbed. "It was a fairly average year for this sport."[32] Thieves, prostitutes, medical quacks, and abortionists like the notorious Madame Restell openly advertised in the newspapers, and particularly in the *New York Herald*. "Wanted immediately," one advertisement said, "twenty-five or thirty young and stylish girls to go South; one good piano-player and singer."[33]

Prostitution was a rich source of revenue to the Ring. As one reformer announced with some astonishment, "Startling as is the assertion, it is nevertheless true, that the traffic in female virtue is as much a regular business, systematically carried on for gain, in the city of New York, as is the trade in boots and shoes, dry goods and groceries." [34] Within three miles of City Hall were 400 brothels, housing 4000 "abandoned" females. In a rare investigation in 1873, the police department found on Wooster Street alone that there were nine brothels, two saloons, a meeting place for professional thieves, and a public school with an attendance of 1200 children. Behind the school were seven more brothels.[35] Brothels paid $600 a week to policemen for protection, who in turn split their fee with politicians, and the infrequent raids were more for blackmailing than for abolishing vice. Some houses of prostitution, it was claimed, had telegraphic communication with the police, who were summoned to help them in the event of a disturbance.[36] Many notorious madams, like Adelaide Beaumont, were forced not only to pay tribute to police and the District Attorney's office, but also extra fees to police justices to resume business as usual.[37]

Gambling, like the theater district, moved uptown. During the Civil War and for years afterward, the gambling center was in the lower part of town, on Ann, Barclay, and Chambers streets, Park Row, and Park Place. John Morrissey, a Tammany stalwart and Congressman, whom Tweed employed as a repeater before he became affluent as a leading gambler, ran a faro game with John Petire in Barclay Street, where guests of Astor House were accommodated. There were a few elegant establishments like Chamberlain's, with imported carpets, valuable paintings, rosewood furniture, and smartly dressed servants, which catered to the respectable element. By the time of the Tweed Ring, professional gamblers had gained a strong hold on the underworld, and a particularly strong hold on the courts. Several judges obtained office through the influence of these gamblers, "and their [the judges] indisposition to execute the law against their best friends is not a matter for surprise." [38]

As any modern expert on crime knows, machine rule in American municipalities has been made possible only through control of the police. From the days of Fernando Wood, down well into the twentieth century, it was exemplified by a long line of predatory police captains whose motto, "Hear, see and say nothin'. Eat, drink and pay nothin'," seemed to characterize New York's "finest" at their worst.

The Tweed Ring inherited a police force that already had a painful history of shake-ups and reorganizations. The first real beginnings of a modern police force occurred in 1826, in an effort to cope with a growing crime problem which was beyond the easy-going means of a force which was still eighteenth-century in character. But this was accomplished only after a long controversy over whether policemen should wear uniforms. It was finally compromised by their wearing leather badges on their hats; subsequently the officers were called "leatherheads," and a popular phrase of the time, "lazy as a leatherhead," tells us something about them. After a shake-up in 1843, George Washington Matsell organized the Detective Bureau and in 1844 formed the Municipal Police, the first organized police force in the United States. After another shake-up in 1845, the police emerged with a uniform and a label, "the finest." A massive reorganization occurred after the riot of 1857, when the force was taken out of the hands of municipal authorities and placed under the control of a state commission chosen by the Governor. The Metropolitan force survived until 1870, when the Tweed charter, by delivering the appointment of police commissioners into the Mayor's hands, returned control to the City. Whether under the authority of the State or the City, Wood or the Tweed Ring, the confounding problem persisted: the force could not stay free from political influence.

While the police achieved some measure of discipline and effectiveness under State authority, the appearance of the Tweed Ring and its capture of key administrative posts converted the force into a political football, and as a result it experienced gloomier days than it had even under Fernando Wood. Henry Smith, the

Republican and great friend of Boss Tweed, was made a Police Commissioner, as were Abraham Disbecker and G. W. Matsell, whose talents for police administration had been replaced by political ambition. John Kelso, a brother-in-law of Cornelius Corson, a close friend of Boss Tweed, was made Superintendent of Police, and it was common knowledge he regularly met Tweed in Room 112 of the Metropolitan Hotel.[39] The force became demoralized as promotions were made by political favor and not on merit. Carrying on the practice of Wood, but more extensively, the force opened its ranks to Tammany supporters and thieves. Gamblers and criminals were given freedom and immunity from arrest. It was not that every policeman was dishonest; it just seemed to New Yorkers that every time a policeman was seen, "he was browbeating a saloon-keeper for a free drink, extorting money from streetwalkers. . . . [or] running errands for politicians." [40]

Under the Tweed Ring, the police department became a patchwork of almost independent kingdoms, where the Captain was autocrat and ruled, it was said, by divine right. The Captain and his favorite subordinate often took exclusive control of cases, removing the task from the patrolmen; thus some cases would be dropped for political reasons. The honest policeman was relegated to the trivial cases, or as the *Times* put it, sent "to follow in the trail of a chemise, stolen from a clothes line." [41]

During the great investigation of 1875, one Captain testified that he "thought" there were gambling houses in his precinct, but he was not "sure of it." At any rate, he had the singular record of never having arrested a gambler. Another Captain allowed seven brothels to run in his district, and when a citizen called for an investigation, the police beat him up. During another investigation, Alexander "Clubber" Williams was asked why he did not close up the brothels. He gave a classic answer: "Because they were kind of fashionable at the time." [42] On many occasions, police magistrates, "in the bright heyday of suddenly-developed virtue," committed notorious thieves without bail, but the next day they were on the street again. In 1868 a total of 5423 cases of crime evaporated into nothingness between the police station and the courts.[43] Perhaps the best example of political interference with the law was the career of one Patrick Duffy, brother of a former Alderman, Peter Duffy.

In 1857, on a drunken spree down Broadway, Duffy without provocation shot and killed a Negro. Tammany friends intervened, he got bail, and the case never came into court. In 1859 after assaulting and nearly killing a captain of a Long Island Sound steamer, he was tried before City Judge Russel and fined exactly six cents. From 1867 to 1870 he killed a gas fitter in front of the Eighth Precinct Station House, a Negro barber, and a restaurant owner. The owner's wife, a witness, disappeared. After each act Duffy was arrested. He received bail, however, and was never brought into court. In 1870, now a member of the General Committee of Tammany Hall, the same Duffy pleaded guilty to stabbing and killing a police officer. He was sentenced to nine years and six months in Sing Sing. His friends again exerted their influence. Less than a year later, William Tweed persuaded Governor John Hoffman that Patrick Duffy deserved a pardon.[44]

The District Attorney's office was a refuge for many criminals. "Up to the point of obtaining the indictment," said a newspaper, "indeed nothing can exceed the ardor with which our indomitable legal functionaries push prosecutions," but once the criminal was arraigned, "a kind of languor steals over the proceedings; the case is never ready for trial, witnesses do not come forth, or disappear, and the culprit goes free." [45] One fork in the path was the District Attorney's office. In 1868 it was estimated that 10,000 indictments were quietly pigeonholed.[46] Hundred of indictments against lottery dealers, bawdy proprietors, and "other disorderly persons," were never tried.[47] The *Times* said:

> The District Attorney, however, hoping they will reform, refrains from bringing them, and waits year after year for the benign influences of our Christian civilization to soften their hearts. They naturally feel grateful for this forbearance, and depraved though they be, appreciating the purity of his motives, testify their gratitude by working for him at elections.[48]

The last vital link in the chain of politics, crime, and injustice, was the lawyer himself, or, as the ones who served the Ring and criminals were called, "Tombs Shysters," "Tombs Lawyers," "Tombs Harpies." Along with political influence and corrupt judges, it took a good lawyer to make sure the Ring's minions would be out of jail on election day to work for Tammany. No law firm ever gave more aid to the Tweed Ring and Tammany than the firm across the street from the Tombs, on the corner of Leonard and Center streets, where a huge sign announced the "Howe and Hummel Law Offices."

The firm of Howe and Hummel was so much a part of the New York scene, said Samuel Hopkins Adams, that the wag "invariably answered his drinking companion's 'Here's how' with 'Here's Hummel.' "[49] They were the most famous criminal lawyers not only of their day but possibly in the history of American criminal practice. Between 1869 and 1907, when District Attorney William Travers Jerome destroyed the firm, Howe and Hummel dominated criminal practice in New York, defending more than a thousand people indicted for murder or manslaughter.

They defended bankers, brokers, society women, and especially theatrical people, like Edwin Booth, Tony Pastor, John Drew, John Barrymore, and Lillie Langtry, as well as the famous of the underworld. Mother Mandelbaum, the leading "fence" of the age, paid the firm a retainer of $500 a year to defend her and her army of thieves. One of William Howe's greatest feats was to make a jury believe, as Richard Rovere put it, "that Ella Nelson's trigger finger had accidentally slipped not once but six times." For every big name there was a host of petty criminals of all kinds, including Reddy the Blacksmith, a capital Tammany repeater for the Tweed Ring, whom Howe and Hummel rescued.

William Howe began practice in New York in 1859 when criminal law was conspicuous for its lack of ethics. A mountain of a man, Howe's taste in clothes made him the Oakey Hall of the New York bar. A typical attire was multi-colored pantaloons, a brilliant purple vest, a billowing blue satin scarf, and diamonds—

diamonds on his fingers, watch chain, shirt studs, cuff buttons, and, in place of a tie, diamond clusters. He was, said one later writer, "something from the dreams of an English bookie," and his oratory was "as purple as anything from his wardrobe." [50]

If rhetoric or bribery did not win his case, Howe could always resort to tears. He was not only a magnificent shyster, he was also a magnificent ham. Samuel Hopkins Adams said that Howe was "the most accomplished weeper of his day. He could and would cry over any case, no matter how commonplace. His voice would quaver, his jowls would give, his great shoulders would shake, and presently authentic tears would well up in his bulbous eyes and dribble over. It was a sickening spectacle, but it often carried a jury to extraordinary conclusions." [51]

Where Howe was huge, loud, and gaudy, Hummel was small, cool, and tidy. Where Howe was ponderous and forceful, Hummel was quick and subtle. A little less than five feet tall, Hummel had a grotesque little body and often was taken for a hunchback. A black derby hat was perched on his bald head; instead of diamonds he wore a death's-head watch charm.

If Howe's specialty was the King's English, Hummel's was breach-of-promise blackmail. On the theory that last year's infatuations could be converted into next year's fur coats (to use Richard Rovere's phrase), he had "the girls rummaging around in their memories for old seductions the way antique dealers get home owners tearing up their attics in search of old glassware and ladderback chairs." [52]

The "magnificent shysters" were never directly related to the Ring in the sense of sharing the plunder from the city treasury, but with their quick ways and sharp practices, they were invaluable to the Tweed Ring. It was on election day that the lawyers were particularly valuable to the Ring. If a repeater got caught, the shysters were there to get him released—and back to work. Their "good" connections made them the vital liaison men between the Ring and the underworld. Their clients were often the means of maintaining corrupt politicians and judges in office, especially by strong-arm tactics at the polls. In return the Ring provided the necessary protection the criminal world needed to survive. That Howe and Hummel were the brokers in many of these transactions is testified by the fact that the Ring Judge Albert Cardozo alone was bribed on more than 200 occasions to release clients of Howe and Hummel.[53]

The Tweed Ring, then, in consolidating its power, seized the legal machinery of New York to make it the backbone of its organization. Without it other operations like election fraud were in danger of exposure and prosecution. Thus the Ring helped to establish one of the classic patterns of a corrupt political machine. Its alliance with venal judges, the underworld, the police, and shyster lawyers kept the machine moving, providing not only patronage, jobs, and graft, but also the means to protect and control organized crime. Fundamentally, however, it provided security and safety—the legal obstructions to obscure public plunder. If anything, it confirmed the old adage so vital to a political machine: "It is better to know the Judge than to know the law."

10

THE OPEN DOOR POLICY

Keep the people quiet and do a lot for the churches.
Political axiom, *New York Times*, Aug. 26, 1923.

There's always a certain number of suckers and a certain number of men lookin' for a chance to take them in, and the suckers are sure to be took one way or another. It's the everlastin' law of supply and demand.

George Washington Plunkitt,
Plunkitt of Tammany Hall

THE WINTER OF 1870 was bitterly cold. Sidewalks were covered with ice, and starving women and children were desperately seeking food and coal. And Boss Tweed came forth and donated $50,000 to buy groceries for the poor. In 1878, when the Boss died and the enormity of his plunder was known, many people said, "Well, if Tweed stole, he was at least good to the poor." [1] Forty-three years later, a newspaper remembered the great philanthopist as being as big in heart as he was in body. "Bill Tweed, to the world may have been a grafter, but to the poor people in the Bowery section ... he was the greatest and most generous man in the world." [2] And more recently John Pratt said, "While more prosperous citizens howled for economy, only the Tweed organization seemed to care for the needs of the underprivileged. It is a phase of the Tweed story that has never been revealed by the host of Tweed's critics." [3]

Regardless of Tweed's motives, John Pratt was right. Historians have neglected this side of the Tweed Ring. It created a public works program, an extralegal social security plan which was more extensive than anything else offered until the 1930's, when Tammany was forced to compete with the New Deal. Nothing seemed to escape the Boss's generosity—hospitals, orphanages, religious schools of various denominations, churches, cultural projects, soldiers' homes—all were grist for his charity mill. A clergyman aptly described it as "the open door policy in State Aid." [4]

Unlike some bosses of other cities, Tweed did not depend on just his own city organization for handouts to the poor. When he took his seat as State Senator in 1868, he secured a place on the important Charitable and Religious, Finance, Internal Affairs of Towns and Counties, and Municipal Affairs committees, and was in a position to place the considerable financial power of the state behind his public works program. On the Senate floor he announced, "I believe in supporting all deserving charities, without asking what denomination control [*sic*] them. . . . We, on this side, are in favor of aiding all the charities. So now, gentlemen on the other side, offer your amendments, inserting deserving charities, and we will accept them." [5]

Few politicians could resist such an offer. The extent to which the politicians jumped on the charity bandwagon can be seen from the fact that in the seventeen years between 1852 to 1869 the State appropriated a little over $2 million for private charities. However, in just three years, from 1869 to 1871, when the Tweed Ring reached its greatest power in the State legislature, the State spent $2,225,000.[6] The number of institutions receiving State aid was expanded. By 1871, orphanages and homes for the aged had increased from 68 to 106. A great amount of State aid went to religious institutions, especially the Catholic parochial schools, orphanages, and hospitals. This was good politics because a good deal of the Ring's support came from the poor Irish-Catholic. While non-Catholic institutions resented this generosity mightily, they were not forgotten, for Presbyterians, Baptists, Methodists, and Jews benefited as well.[7]

Catholics had long argued that their parochial schools should receive at least some part of the money allotted for public school education. For years they had been blocked by a Protestant-dominated State legislature and by religious and political groups who insisted that no State aid should be given to religious education. It was a familiar phase of a long struggle, with the Catholics arguing that, since they were taxed for schools, their parochial schools should receive some of the tax dollars.

Sensing a political opportunity to increase support from Catholic followers, from church officials down to the Catholic Irishman in the street, Tweed tried a tricky maneuver to give State aid to parochial schools. In May of 1869, Tweed's own Committee on Municipal Affairs prepared the tax-levy legislation. Cleverly hidden in this complicated budget statement was a proposal to make the City and County of New York assume portions of the yearly expenses of the city's parochial schools. Because of previous opposition to any State aid to Catholics, the legislation was skillfully worded to omit any specific mention of Catholic schools. Aid was to be given to schools that were not public or charity schools. Thus disguised it was passed. Since the funds would be administered by a Ring-controlled school official, the parochial schools would get their money.[8]

It was not long before it was discovered, however, and the Protestant community in city and state rose in righteous wrath. The ensuing public storm had the same thunderbolts seen in the anti-Catholic, nativist movement of the Know-Nothings in the previous decade. To the influential Methodist journal in the city it was not a Good Thing, but a Burning Issue—clearly "a Papal conspiracy."[9] The New York Council of Political Reform said, "Here, then, we are brought face to face with this night-mare of the world's peace—Church and State." The Catholic Church was being preferred by law, where other sects, namely Protestant, "are confessedly more American...."[10] The *New York Times* and *Albany Evening Journal* joined by the Republican-controlled Union League Club began a campaign for repeal.

The result of the uproar was inevitable. The legislature of 1870 was deluged with petitions against the law. Even Governor Hoffman, who usually sniffed and snuffed over problems like an elderly spaniel, thumped for the law's repeal with uncharacteristic vigor because he was fearful the law might affect his re-election in the fall. Tweed was forced to retreat, reluctantly but skillfully, avoiding condemnation from his Catholic constituents by putting all the blame on the Republicans. A repeal was presented in the form of an amendment, which prohibited any future grants to parochial schools. But the Tweed forces were not to be completely vanquished. The amendment was changed to permit schools already receiving aid for 1869-70 to get their subsidy for the coming year. Thus Tweed still managed to get funds for religious schools for at least two years. If this seems a paltry accomplishment, it was, nonetheless, "the only time in New York's history that Catholic parochial schools received regular public grants avowedly intended for general instructional purposes." [11]

Senator Tweed used methods other than direct contributions to help religious bodies. For example, he supported acts incorporating the Fulton Benevolent Association to incorporate the Ursuline Convent, to enable the trustees of the Mendon Central Congregational Society to sell their church property, plus three more bills allowing Protestant churches to sell their property, an act for the relief of St. Mary's Church, and the like.[12]

Religious institutions were not the only ones to benefit. Tweed sponsored an act allowing the Society for Relief of Poor Widows to acquire property, another to establish a home for indigent and disabled soldiers and sailors, another creating an orphan home, a bill establishing the Buffalo State Asylum for the insane, and others.[13]

Significantly, Tweed did not limit use of the State treasury to currying favor with the poor or with religious and charitable institutions alone. He also backed the pet charities and cultural programs of the gentry and threw a few sops to the business community. By so doing, he adroitly placed the respectable groups in a position where they were indebted to him and his friends. Thus on February 25, 1868, Bill No. 62, introduced by William Tweed, passed the Senate. It was a measure to establish the Presbyterian Hospital of New York, a project long sought by the better element of the city. Tweed made sure some of the most influential names of New York society were named as trustees—James Lenox, John Taylor Johnston, Robert L. Stuart, Morris K. Jessup, and Marshall S. Bidwell.[14] Tweed could also please the "respectabilities" and pose as a cultural benefactor of New York. Thus few people realize today that it was the Tweed Ring which introduced an act to incorporate the Metropolitan Museum of Art.[15] Tweed's benevolent hand seemed to spread its blessings everywhere. Mount Sinai Hospital, a favorite charity of the gentry, benefited through the Ring's charity, as did the Hudson River State Hospital.[16] Some business groups received a certain kind of "charity" through such bills as an act to incorporate the Guardian Savings Institution, an act to exempt certain property from taxation, and, to boot, legislation incorporating the Whitehall Savings Bank.[17] Nor was organized labor forgotten. The Tweed Ring made it possible for the Watch Case Makers' Benevolent and Protective Union and the Working Women's Protective Union to incorporate.[18]

If Tweed used his position in the State legislature to make charity a kind of political cement, he was equally active in the city, using "contributions" from Tammany and, indeed, money from his own pocket which had originally rested in the city treasury. On January 18, 1869, he gave a check for $10,000 to Isaac Bell, Commissioner of Public Charities and Correction, to spread good-will among the poor.[19] Some of the best proof of his largess was found by Mark Hirsch, biographer of William C. Whitney. Among Whitney's papers Hirsch found a tin box containing some Tweed papers. One envelope entitled "Charities, Donations, etc." contained eighty-seven canceled checks and one promissory note. These sums totaled $288,805 and were paid out during the years 1866 to 1873.[20]

There were other ways, aside from direct contributions, for the Tweed Ring to be the benefactor of the needy or worthy and win support or create complacency. For example, with his power in the Common Council, or Aldermen, Boss Tweed allowed the Sisters of Mercy and the Nursery and Child's Hospital to execute leases for a term of ninety-nine years for a generous rent of one dollar per year. Reformers complained to no avail that this was in direct violation of the city charter, which provided that the city should not lease its property for a term longer than ten years and that all leases of public property should be made at public auction.[21] Nor could the reformers do more than gasp when Tweed provided a lavish feast and an entertainment at his estate at Greenwich, Connecticut, for hundreds of orphans from Randall's Island nursery.

Confronted with the Ring's public welfare program in city and state, the reformers reacted in horror. To many of the middle and upper classes, in America during and after the Tweed era, reform was a matter of retrenchment and sharp economy. Many reformers considered poverty a just retribution for idleness and bad habits. Poverty was testimony to a profound lack of character. Self-help was the ideal of the day. These attitudes were highlighted in the winter of 1870, when Boss Tweed personally donated $50,000 to provide the poor with Christmas dinners. This event attracted both local and national attention. To the *New York Times*, the *Wilmington Daily Commonwealth*, the *Rochester Express*, and the *Cleveland Daily Leader*, it seemed that such outright charity would undermine what little moral stamina the poor had. When a man can plunder the public at the rate of $75,000 to $80,000 a day, said the *New York Times*, it doesn't cost much to give a few odd thousand dollars to the poor. "This is conscience money, if Tweed has a conscience."[22] We shall live to see, said the *Times*, Tweed give us Louis Blanc's national workshops; flour for the poor means a flood of corruption.[23]

Particularly appalling to economy-minded reformers was the presentation on Christmas night of a $16,000 diamond to the Boss as a reward for his generosity to the poor, which set an example some other politicians tried to follow. Not to be outdone by the Boss, Jimmy O'Brien, ward boss, ex-Sheriff, and the darling of many an Irishman, offered to distribute coal in one-ton quantities to needy families. But since those who needed coal the most did not have cellar room for an entire ton, O'Brien's bounty was not severely strained.[24] Charles Nordhoff, the eminent editor and newspaperman, reflected the views of many when he recalled with approval a statement of a city missionary, who said that charity "is almost always a curse; that to give money or the means of living to the poor has been, in the majority of cases known to him, to make them paupers, at least gravely to impair their efficiency; and that when he [the missionary] had once supplied a measure of coal, or any other indispensable means of life, he found, almost always, that he was called upon to repeat the gift year after year . . . how demoralizing must be the whole attitude of the rich towards the poor in a great city like New York, where Tweed was praised last winter, because he gave out of his ill-gotten millions a few thousands to those of his followers who chose to call themselves 'poor.'"[25] Memory of the welfare program died hard. Fearful of corruption, wedded to the politics of economy, the State legislature did not pass any charity measures for three years after the fall of the Tweed Ring. It was a bleak period for the hospitals, orphanages, aged, the benevolent religious organizations, and, above all, the poor. When this proved to be bad politics, charity appropriations were resumed, "but with great caution and never again with the complete abandon of the Tweed years."[26]

The Ring's welfare policy, despite its intense political aims, was a boon for the poor and infirm. It eased life for those who knew, to use Ruth Gordon's phrase, the dark-brown taste of being poor. New York was choked with peasant immigrants; rapid urban growth was placing impossible demands on private charitable institutions. The "good" government of the reformers was not a very human government. Arrogant, intoxicated by their own moral righteousness, steeped in extravagant puffery about the good old days, lacking both a sense of compromise and compassion, the reformers were outwitted and outmaneuvered by professional politicians.

But there is another side to the coin. Long before the rise of the Tweed Ring, Tammany Hall originally opposed such reforms for the lower classes as universal manhood suffrage, abolition of imprisonment for debt, and a mechanics' lien law, although later with hypocrisy it would claim credit for these reforms.[27] Tammany bent with reform only under pressure or when it could enhance its self-interest, such as by building parks, schools, and playgrounds. It was the same with the Tweed Ring and later city bosses.

It must be said for the reformers that they never lost a sense of reality, as have some sentimental apologists of the old-fashioned city boss. The reformers did recognize in the city boss's supposed altruism the inner core of cynicism. The Tweed Ring may have stolen from the rich and given to the poor, but it also stole from the poor. The conditions that contribute to poverty, the everyday plagues of living conditions, rents, disease, sanitation, were never the concern either of the Ring or of Tammany Hall. The privileges of the rich were protected. The Ring never contested exorbitant rents, the foul decay of tenement houses, or the excessive charges for coal and water. Criminals were allowed a field day in spreading vice and crime in the neighborhoods of the poor. There was no pretense of cleaning the streets of stench and garbage. Health inspectors, political hacks, rarely did their job. Moreover, workingmen, small shopkeepers, and pushcart operators constantly had to dig deep into their slender savings of hard-earned money to help pay for Tammany social events. If they dared oppose the Ring and Tammany, they were liable to persecution by police, city ordinances, or hired thugs. The impoverished might receive occasional food, jobs for those with the right connections, a steamer ride or a picnic from a ward boss—but it was usually just before election time. With some truth the *Times* compared the Ring to the barons of the medieval age, "who swept a man's land of his crops, and then gave him a crust of dry bread." Edward Cary, never a stern critic of

Tammany, sums it up and dispels some of the myth of Tammany's humanity toward the masses:

> The basis of the power of the Tammany organization is the hold it has on large numbers of the poorer classes. To these classes as a whole it is, nevertheless, always and entirely an evil. It robs and cheats them at every turn. It makes heavier the already sore burdens that they must bear. It increases the cost of the living which at best is so hard to get. It tends to make health more difficult and deaths more frequent. It levies toll on their contributions to the public treasury, and denies them their fair share of the public employment. In the enforcement of the laws in which they are most deeply interested justice, order, and decency have no place. In quarters where the poorer classes are compelled to dwell it pollutes, by the sale of license for the grossest immorality, the surroundings in which their children must be reared.[28]

Thus neither the cynical "open door" policy of the Ring, nor the callous "no door" policy of many of the reformers, answered the problems of the poor. The former was at least a masterful political technique, and as long as the Tweed Ring could deliver, the poor would sing its praises and vote for Tammany. Few agonized over the morality of the open door policy. For those who lived dingy lives in Tweed's Town, a vote for a handout seemed to be a fair swap.

PART THREE

ROGUES' HOLIDAY

11

"HONEST" GRAFT

> Grafting used to be open and above board,
> Like it should be if it's fairly honest.
>
> Dick Butler, *Dock Walloper*

Post-Civil-War New York has been described as being encircled by a host of political rings, rings within rings, each depending on the other. There was the Gravel Ring, the Detective Ring, the Supervisors' Ring, the Courthouse Ring, the Albany Ring, the Street Commissioners' Ring, the Manure Ring, the Market Ring, and, consolidating and hovering above all, the Tweed Ring. And what was a political ring? It was the source of "magic wisdom" that made Tammany Hall a political power, said a big chief of the Tammany braves. Samuel Tilden, who almost became President of the United States on the claim he had smashed a "ring," said:

> The very definition of a "Ring" is that it encircles enough influential men in the organization of each party to control the action of both party machines; men who in public push to extremes the abstract ideas of their respective parties, while they secretly join their hands in schemes for personal power and profit.[1]

Scholars and public alike have generally accepted Tilden's definition of the Tweed Ring. Why was it that later city bosses like Croker had a "machine," while Tweed had a "Ring"—a word, as it were, with a more ominous ring, a political synonym for conspiracy, venality, and corruption? If the Tweed Ring's skills at organization have never been rightfully emphasized, its achievements in corruption certainly have, although large-scale graft existed before the emergence of the Tweed Ring, and continued after its downfall.

We shall probably never know exactly how much the Ring stole. Calculations have run as high as $300 million, which was probably too high, even for the Tweed Ring. The *New York Evening Post* estimated it at $59 million; the *Times* thought it was more like $75 million to $80 million.[2] The Booth Committee, a group of citizens and Aldermen who investigated the Ring, reported that the city debt on January 1, 1869, was $36,293,929.59; by September 4, 1871, it had grown to an enormous $97,287,525.03.[3] The committee published a report which was by no means complete, but it did give some insight into the magnitude of the frauds.

	Cost	*Value*	*Deficit*
Courthouse	$13,416,932	$3,000,000	$10,416,932
Armory repairs	3,200,000	250,000	2,950,000
Unoccupied armory rents	190,000	——	190,000
Lumber account	460,000	48,000	412,000
Printing, stationery, advertising	7,168,212	1,300,000	5,868,212
Total	$24,911,644	$4,820,500	$20,091,144

Years after the fall of the Ring, Matthew J. O'Rourke, who had made a study of the Ring's plunders, estimated that if fraudulent bonds were included, the Ring probably stole about $200 million.[4] Henry J. Taintor made the closest study. For six years he had been employed by the City to determine the amount of the Ring's graft. It cost the City over $73,000 to maintain Taintor's investigation, and for a moment during the Tweed Ring investigation in 1877 there was the suspicion, later dispelled, that a dreadful irony had occurred: that Taintor, in investigating graft, had been tempted himself, and had padded his bills. At any rate, he testified his research showed that the Ring had stolen at least $60 million, but even this was not an accurate figure, he said, because he did not possess all the records.[5] Whatever the figure, in order to maintain a political machine as well as to increase their personal fortune, the Tweed Ring's operation was on a gigantic scale.

There were three primary sources of graft: the city, the state, and the business community. In the city, the Ring's control of the key legislative and financial agencies, from the Supervisors and Aldermen to the Comptroller and Mayor, gave it command of New York's financial machinery and bountiful opportunity for graft. Every warrant, then, charged against the city treasury passed the Ring's scrutiny and was subject to its manipulation. Every scheme for city improvements, be they new streets, new buildings, new city parks, had to be financed from the city treasury, controlled by the Ring. The results were often graft, reflected in excessive charges and needless waste. Every charter and franchise for new businesses had to meet the approval of the city legislature and the Mayor, and many companies, therefore, had to pay the tribute of the bribe to get them passed. All the city's financial affairs, such as bond issues, tax-collecting, rentals on city properties, were vulnerable as sources of graft. In effect, there was a direct relationship between power and graft. The Ring's political influence was so extensive that one roadblock to graft, the check and balance system—pitting the upper house of the City legislature against the lower house, and the Mayor as a check to the combined houses of the legislature—was simply nullified. When this happened, the city's financial operations became an open target.

This was largely true for the State legislature as well. Any check and balance between state and city, governor and legislature, was nullified. The Ring controlled the governor, John Hoffman; it controlled the powerful block of city Democrats in the State legislature. When he was elected State Senator in 1867 (and assumed office in 1868, when the Senate convened), Boss Tweed, as Chairman of the influential State Finance Committee, and as a member of the important Internal Affairs of Towns and Counties, Charitable and Religious, and Municipal Affairs committees, was in a commanding position to influence tax-levies, bond issues, and special projects for the city—all sources of graft. As the leader of the Black Horse Cavalry, a corrupt band of State legislators, he could control legislation leading to graft.

Not all the money came from the City and State treasury. The business community was an important source of profit, both as allies and victims. The Tweed Ring operated as lobby brokers for businessmen seeking to pass or kill legislation vital to their interests. Services rendered for the Erie Railroad, for example, brought in thousands of dollars. Businessmen provided large "kick-backs" in payment for receiving profitable contracts. The "cinch" bill, legislative extortion threatening business firms and individuals, was used extensively by the Ring through both the City and State legislatures.

Unlike the sly, sophisticated tactics of modern-day graft—the highly complicated dummy corporation, the undercover payoff via the "respectable" attorney—the Ring operated in a remarkably open and straightforward fashion. In effect, the shortest distance to the city treasury was a straight line. While the Ring used several methods for plunder, the largest share of the booty was gained by a method simple, direct, brazen, daring—and often sloppy. Every person who received a contract from the city, whether for supplies or for work on the city buildings and public works was instructed to alter his bills before submitting them for payment. At first the tribute was levied somewhat irregularly at 10 per cent, then it was raised to 55 per cent; in July 1869 it jumped to 60 per cent; and from November 1869 on, the tradesmen received 35 per cent and the Ring 65 per cent on all bills and warrants.[6] When bills from contractors and tradesmen did not come in fast enough, Tweed ordered vouchers to be made out to imaginary firms and individuals. On large contracts, Tweed acted directly and got immediately to the point. When he was told that electric fire alarms would cost the city $60,000, he asked the contractor, "If we get you a contract for $450,000 will you give us $225,000?" No time was wasted. The contractor answered with a simple yes and got the contract.[7] Nor did the Boss quibble over small sums. Once a merchant told Tweed that Comptroller Connolly had refused to pay his bill. Only by "kicking-back" 20 per cent of the bill, would the merchant ever get paid. Tweed wrote Connolly: "For God's sake pay ——'s bill. He tells me you people ask 20 per cent. The whole d——d thing isn't but $1100. If you don't pay it, I will. Thine."[8]

The division of the spoils varied: Tweed received from 10 to 25 per cent; Connolly from 10 to 20 per cent; Sweeny 10 per cent; Hall 5 to 10 per cent. There was a percentage for the "sinking fund," and James Watson and W. E. Woodward shared 5 per cent. These last two, clerks of the gang, did the paper work and forging. "You must do just as Jimmy tells you, and you will get your money," was a well-known saying among Tweed Ring contractors.[9]

James Watson, the Ring's bookkeeper, was City Auditor in Connolly's office. He first demonstrated his talents while a convict. In 1850 Watson was an agent for a prosperous firm which suddenly began to experience severe losses that Watson found inconvenient to explain. He fled to California. He was brought back to New York in irons and clapped in Ludlow Street jail. An active fellow with pleasant manners, he soon won the friendship of the warden. He took charge of the prison records and performed with such admirable efficiency, especially in calculations, that he was released, with the warden's help, and was appointed a collector in the Sheriff's office. He held that position under three Sheriffs. When the Tweed Ring was formed in 1866, he was made City Auditor, a position that paid a small salary. Four years later, he was worth anywhere from two to three million dollars. It was said that he was a simple man and lived in a curious state of "ostentatious modesty." He had only one luxury—fast trotting horses, a passion that later helped to ruin the Tweed Ring.

W. E. Woodward occupied a key post as clerk to the Supervisors; he helped to rig the percentages of the business that came through that office. At the time of the Aldermen's investigation of the Ring in 1877, the Aldermen were curious how a mere clerk could own a $150,000 home, the best home, in fact, in Norwalk, Connecticut. Asked how he could do this on a salary that never exceeded $5000, Woodward gave a straightforward answer. "I used to take all I could get, and the Board of Supervisors were very liberal to me." [10]

In the Comptroller's Office, Slippery Dick Connolly performed feats that justified his name, as his successor in 1871, the reformer, Andrew Green, confirmed when he found the treasury thoroughly sacked. As Comptroller, Connolly served the Ring three ways. He spent the money collected through the city's regular channels of revenue—taxes, rents from such city properties as markets, docks, armories, etc. While some of the money was spent legitimately, a good deal of it was either embezzled or found its way into fraudulent contracts, excessive rents, or padded payrolls, a percentage of which was "kicked-back" into the Ring's coffers. However, only about a third of the city's money came from taxes or rents; the rest came from securities. Thus when a tax-levy of some $30 or more million was spent, usually at a brisk pace, Connolly's next job was to realize $30 to $50 millions more by issuing stocks and bonds.[11]

Connolly performed this task like a financial conjuror. He created a litter of stocks and bonds raised for every conceivable project, ingenious in wording and intent. There were Accumulated Debt Bonds, Assessment Fund Bonds, Croton Aqueduct Bonds, Croton Reservoir Bonds, Central Park Improvement Fund Stocks, City Improvement Stocks, Street Improvement Bonds, Fire Department Stocks, Tax Relief Bonds, Bridge Revenue Bonds, New Court House Stock. Repairs to the County Offices and Building Stocks, Dock Bonds, and bonds for the Soldiers' Relief Fund.[12] The war chest to provide funds for padded payrolls, for example, was raised by the sale of appropriately named Riot Damages Indemnity Bonds. As a result of Connolly's various enterprises, the city groaned under a debt which increased by nearly $70 million from 1869 to 1871.

Finally, it was Connolly's responsibility to mask the Ring's fraudulent expenditures by slippery accounting techniques. In this, he was helped by the extensive power of the Ring which nullified an elaborate series of regulations established to prevent fraud. By state law, every warrant and claim drawn against the City must be itemized and accompanied by a signed affidavit certifying its authenticity. Before it could be cashed it must be thoroughly examined and signed by the Comptroller, City Auditor, the Board of Supervisors, and the Mayor. But since the Ring "owned" all these offices, it was relatively simple to rig a phony warrant and get the required signatures. Indeed, the Ring became so powerful that it owned its own bank, the Tenth National, to ensure the safe deposit of its booty. (Tweed, Connolly, Hall, James Ingersoll, and James Fisk, Jr., were the Tenth National's distinguished directors.)

Aside from his own ingenuity, Connolly was also helped by the city's complicated financial machinery, which was so complex as to baffle even the well-informed citizen and so decentralized as to allow room for deceptive maneuver. There were two financial bureaus, one for the city and one for the county, from which not only stocks and bonds were issued but claims were audited and paid as well. With the aid of the City Auditor, stocks and bonds issued from one bureau could be duplicated in the other, or fictitious accounts could be set up in both. It was no wonder that it took Taintor six years to make some sense of the Ring's financing, for Connolly created an accountant's nightmare by juggling and duplicating accounts. "Adjusted Claims" for one bureau, for example, became "County Liabilities" for the other. Slippery Dick, in fact, created a smoke screen for the Ring's schemes by manipulating money back and forth from "County Contingencies," "Contingencies in the Department of Finance," and "Contingencies in the Comptroller's Office," as if he were playing a kind of financial shell game.[13] "You must not attempt to raise the thimble and investigate the progress of the little game," said the *New York Times*.[14]

To complicate matters further, each bureau had two separate sets of books, one for warrants drawn on the appropriations account, the other for warrants drawn on the so-called Special Account, whose funds came not from any appropriation, but out of monies raised by the issue of stocks and bonds. The trick here was to spend money quickly and lavishly, exhausting the appropriations account, and then drawing further funds from the Special Account, a wondrous financial gimmick which yielded nearly three million dollars.[15] In his official report of 1870 (ten months late), Connolly, perhaps wearied of this frenzied finance, placed everything of a suspicious character in an account called "General Purposes," a heading that lacked his usual imagination.

Added to all this was another lush source for graft. Connolly and his lieutenant James Watson were in a position to audit and pay off fictitious claims against the city. With logic, the New York City Council of Political Reform said: "In a sound fiscal system one officer *adjusts* claims and another *pays* them. From the weakness of human nature it is not deemed wise or prudent for the government of any great city or county to allow the *same* officer to adjust a claim *who* is to *pay* it; lest he may be tempted by a share of the money to conspire with the claimant and allow an unjust claim. But in our city, in 1868 and 1870, a *single* officer, the Comptroller, *adjusted* and *paid*, by adding so much to the permanent debt, $12,500,000 of claims!"[16]

The Comptroller's office was also a point of frustration for those with legitimate claims against the city. They were kept waiting sometimes for years, before they could get their money. Subsequently, they often sold their claim to one of the Ring's agents for 50 or 60 cents on the dollar. Immediately after the transaction took place, the new owner was promptly paid. A clerk in Connolly's office, named Mike Moloney, was in charge of this branch of business.

> Moloney sits opposite the door by which his victims enter and watches for them with all the avidity that a spider might watch the approach of a fly. The moment an unlucky claimant makes his appearance Moloney jumps on his feet and steps forward to the counter to meet him. Bending forward he listens to the application of the victim, and then by a series of ominous shakes of his head, and "the oft-told tale" repeated in half-smothered

> whispers, he tries to convince the applicant that there is no prospect of him receiving his money for some time to come, and that, if he really needs it, he had better go over to City Hall and see Mr. Thomas Colligan. (The victim sees Mr. Colligan) . . . and comes out feeling much the same as if he had lost his pocketbook, while the genial Mr. Colligan pockets the "little difference," invites Moloney to dinner, and quietly divides the spoils while sipping Champagne or smoking a Havana.[17]

It is difficult to know where to begin in dealing with the many specific schemes of the Tweed Ring. Perhaps it is best to begin with what E. L. Godkin once called "one of those neat and profitable little curiosities of fraud which the memory holds after graver things are forgotten."[18]

In 1841, a man named Valentine, a clerk in the Common Council, persuaded the city to finance the publication of a city almanac which he would edit. Initially, it was a small volume of not quite 200 pages, which had a map of the city and a list of all persons associated with the government of New York City and their business and home addresses. Although the City Directory contained the same information, for some obscure reason the almanac seemed valuable. Down through the years, the almanac increased in bulkiness, and, more important, in cost to the taxpayers, until it became "a manual of folly, extravagance, and dishonesty."[19] By 1865, *Valentine's Manual*, as it was called, had become a 879-page monument of costliness and superficiality. Among 141 pictures was a large, folding four-page lithograph, illustrating—"O precious gift to posterity!"—a facsimile of each Alderman's autograph. Expensive lithographs covered a number of vital subjects: a fur store built in 1820; a house that Valentine had once lived in; a grocery and tea store of ancient vintage; Tammany Hall as it looked in 1830; a Fifth Avenue billiard saloon; and a host of "portraits of undistinguished persons." Well over 400 pages were cluttered with extracts from old government documents, newspapers, and "memories." The cost of printing was $57,172.30; the number of copies printed, 10,000. A few copies found their way

Cartoon by Thomas Nast; courtesy of the New-York Historical Society, New York City

into secondhand bookstores, which paid two dollars apiece for them, $3.36 less than a copy cost the city. An outraged public opinion forced Mayor Hoffman to veto the resolution authorizing a similar expenditure for 1866. He found that Appleton's or Harper's would have published the same number of copies for $30,000 instead of $53,672.[20] The Aldermen, however, overrode his veto.

When the Tweed Ring captured this lucrative enterprise, certain changes were made. In previous editions, a list of city offices and official salaries had been published. The Ring decided to omit this section. The avalanche of new offices it had created, and certain generous increases in salaries ("when and who increased salaries of Police and Civil Justices from $5000 to $10,000?" asked the *Times*) might be embarrassing. Instead, critically important historical reminiscences were printed, such as the various marriages in the family of Jacob Leisler—"antiquarian rubbish," said a newspaper.[21] There were other changes. Tweed's New York Printing Company was now authorized to print the *Manual;* subsequently it cost the city $90,000 to print it in 1869, and around $150,000 in 1870. Fifteen thousand copies were printed; the Comptroller and the Mayor alone received 5000 copies between them.[22] Local politicians apparently used their copies as gifts to friends and relatives. The *Times* reported that a gentleman who traveled extensively in the south of Ireland said about the only book he encountered in the cabins there was the *New York Corporation Manual.* The natives there called it the "Book of Kings"—meaning the "Irish kings of the New World."[23]

Another access to the city treasury, which allowed a privileged few to stuff their pockets, was the contracts for city printing. Tweed went on to explain how the fraud worked:

> For instance, any department in the city, say your department, required stationery; a requisition would be made. Some young man from your department would go over to them and deliver the requisition. Jones would say, "Well, this is a very nice requisition," and then he would try if possible to have a larger requisition made out; and whether or not, he would invite this

> young man to go in, and show him a lot of fancy goods and make him presents of them and enlarge the requisition that way, or else not furnish the full amounts of the requisition. . . . I may say that everybody who furnished requisitions to Jones and Company for stationery and supplies received such presents. Received furniture, bridles, saddles . . . Russian leather . . . robes for carriages, and sleighs and everything—fancy writing desks. . . . Yes sir, for I know persons, bringing requisitions, got what they desired in that line—books and everything. When I say books, I mean novels—libraries.[24]

The Tweed Ring created several companies which moved in to monopolize every phase of city printing as well as city advertising. One such firm was the New York Printing Company. Its expansion reflected all the gusto of American business enterprises. It began in a shabby little office on Centre Street, but almost at once business became so good that it absorbed three of the largest printing establishments in the city. The New York Printing Company was growing, said a newspaper, "but like other mushrooms it grows in the dark. It is spreading under the cover of night, and running its roots into the Treasury by deep underground passages." [25] On a capital stock of $10,000 it paid a dividend of $50,000 to $75,000 to each of its stockholders.[26] The city apparently liked its work, for during 1870-71 the firm obtained $260,283.81 of its business.[27] All these amounts incorporated a 25 per cent tribute to the Ring. The company became so versatile in printing all kinds of material that the city paid it another $300,000 for printing in book form the records of New York City from 1675 to 1776. Nor did the firm confine its customers to the City and County. Insurance companies and steamboat and ferry companies were extremely vulnerable to a legislative bill which, in the public interest, could hurt them by regulating their activities and profits. Hence, they all received a notice that the New York Printing Company would be happy to do their printing.[28]

The Tweed Ring composed the major stockholders of the Manufacturing Stationers' Company, which sold stationery supplies to city offices and schools. In 1870 the City and County paid it over $3 million.[29] Among its many bills, there was this interesting one: for six reams of note paper, two dozen penholders, four ink bottles, one dozen sponges, and three dozen boxes of rubber bands, the city paid $10,000.[30] James Parton singled out the Manufacturing Stationers' Company for its treachery.

> We have before us a successful bid for supplying the city offices with stationery, in which we find the bidder offering to supply "blue folio post" at one cent per ream; "magnum bonum pens," at one cent per gross; "lead pencils," at one cent per dozen; "English sealing-wax," at one cent per pound; and eighty-three other articles of stationery, at the uniform price of one cent for the usual parcel. This was the "lowest bid," and it was, of course, the one accepted. It appeared, however, when the bill was presented for payment, that the particular kind of paper styled "blue folio post" had never been called for, nor any considerable quantity of the other articles proposed to be supplied for one cent. No one, strange to say, had ever wanted "magnum bonum" pens at one cent a gross, but in all the offices the cry had been for "Perry's extra fine," at three dollars. Scarcely any one had used "envelopes letter-size" at one cent per hundred but there had been countless calls for "envelopes note-size" at one cent each. Between the paper called "blue folio post," at one cent per ream, and paper called "foolscap extra ruled," at *five dollars and a half*, the difference was too slight to be perceived; but every one had used the foolscap. Of what avail are contracts, when the officials who award them, and the other officials who pay the bill, are in league with the contractor to steal the public money?[31]

As the fictional Boss Blossom Brick said, "Official advertising is the Pain Killer of Politics."[32] During the Civil War three men started an insignificant newspaper titled *The Transcript*. They were George Stout, "a journalist unknown to fame," Charles E. Wilbour, a court stenographer and "literary man, somewhat less unknown," and Cornelius Corson, "an employee in the City Hall, and not devoid of influence in that quarter."[33] When Tweed,

Connolly, and Sweeny became their partners, business, but not circulation, picked up. The Common Council (the Aldermen and Assistant Aldermen) ordered that a full list of all persons liable to serve in the army, amounting to some 50,000 names, should be printed in the *Transcript*. Later, thirty-five copies of the list were published in book-form, "though the bill was rendered for a large edition." [34] From then on the *Transcript* enjoyed days of high prosperity. It published the major share of all "city advertising," which meant official records of the courts, and official statements and declarations, statistical reports, new ordinances, in effect, the facts and figures of city business. The rates were exorbitant enough to ensure a heady profit; for example, messages from the Mayor cost a dollar a line. A great deal of the advertisements came from Tweed's Department of Public Works, and from the Bureau of Assessments, where Richard Tweed was in control. Although the newspaper never sold more than a hundred copies, the city paid it $801,874 from 1869 to 1871 for publishing its official business and advertisements.[35] The December 3, 1870, issue, for example, consisted of 504 pages. Advertisements were charged at a rate of 25 cents a line, higher than prevailing newspaper rates. It was estimated that the Ring received $68,000 in profits for that issue alone. The Christmas number for that year was a special: a double extra of 1000 pages, all advertisements, for which double rates were charged. It appeared to one newspaper that the Ring paid for its Christmas presents out of the public till.[36] The profits, then, made by the three companies of the Ring which corralled city printing reached a grand total over a three-year period of $2,641,828.30, of which nine-tenths was pure profit.[37]

As Boss Blossom Brick said, "Give the people plenty of taffy and the newspapers plenty of advertising—then help yourself to anything that's lying around loose." [38] Funneling the taxpayers' dollars through the *Transcript* was a way to finance Tweed's mansion on Fifth Avenue and his palatial estate in Greenwich, Connecticut, but there was another method of using city advertising which ensured, for a few years at least, that gracious living could be enjoyed. The Tweed Ring found that the best way to protect itself against newspaper criticism was to distribute city advertising as a token of peace. It became a kind of hush money which bound the press to silence. Until the storm broke, in 1871, probably no New York political regime ever enjoyed less newspaper criticism than the Tweed Ring, and only when the evidence became painfully obvious and practically overwhelming did the press join the crusade against evil begun by the *New York Times* and *Harper's Weekly*. Before the storm, there had been some criticism, but it was spotty and half-hearted. The *Tribune* might thunder for a while, the *Sun* became nasty—as was its style—but a general grant of advertising had the same effect as placing alum on the tongue.

By law, the city corporation was limited to nine daily and eight weekly papers in which to advertise. But the Tweed Ring, with its usual disregard for procedure, extended delicious morsels of city advertising to twenty-six daily and forty-four weekly newspapers in the city alone, and seventeen weekly journals outside the city, making a total of eighty-seven organs.[39] Probably no political regime in the history of New York City had exerted so much influence on the press.

When the Aldermen investigated the Tweed Ring years later in 1877, Tweed explained that most papers were subsidized with advertisements, but some were given cash, like the *Albany Evening Journal*. S. C. Hutchings, a representative of this paper, a Republican journal, would come to Tweed with strong articles against the Ring, "containing some things we wouldn't very much care to have made public," and Tweed would be forced to pay blackmail money.

> "Well, now, you say you paid money; did you pay any large sums of money?"
>
> "Oh, sometimes $5000, sometimes $1000, and sometimes $500. It was a general dribble all the time."
>
> As for the *Albany Argus*, "I never gave any money to the *Argus*, but we were always ready to help the *Argus* in any way.

We helped them by inserting items in the tax-levy, called the budget—their bills for printing, advertising, etc."

"Were those items *bona fide* items?"

"We didn't inquire about that." [40]

The question of subsidies was often brought out into the open by the newspapers themselves. Both the *Herald* and *Tribune* at various times accused the *Times* of launching its crusade against the Ring because Connolly had refused to honor its claim for over $13,000 of advertising.[41] The *New York World*, which briefly supported a rival faction of Tammany in a fight over a new city charter, came forward with high-mindedness to shame the *Herald's* acceptance of subsidies. But once the Ring crushed the faction, the *World* made hurried return to its arms.

Not content with the method of using advertising, the Ring also won the hearts of City Hall reporters by giving them $200 gifts at Christmas. This practice had started as early as 1862, under the administration of Mayor George Opdyke (who disapproved), but the Ring elaborated on the scheme. It also subsidized six to eight reporters on nearly all the city papers with fees of $2000 to $2500 to exercise the proper discretion when it came to writing about politics. There was the reward of patronage for the especially deserving: Stephen Hayes, on the *Herald* staff during the high days of the Ring, was rewarded with a sinecure in the Marine Court ($2500 a year), and Michael Kelly, also of the *Herald*, received positions in both the Fire Department and the Department of Public Works. Moreover, reporters from various newspapers of the country, from a Cleveland newspaper to the *Mobile Register*, were hired to write favorable notices of the Democratic administration in New York.[42] And if a firm went too far and tried to print a pamphlet exposing the Ring, it might find its offices broken into by the Ring's men and the type altered to present a glowing account of the Ring's activities—as did the printing company of Stone, Jordan and Thomson.[43]

At the time the Ring was breaking up, the City found itself confronted with claims amounting to over a million and a half dollars negotiated between newspapers and the Ring, some fraudulent and some not, for not all journals which received city advertising did so on the basis of a conspiracy with the Ring. But enough of them did to ensure the complacency and the apathy which seemed to grip many during the Ring's rule.

The Ring needed complacency and apathy when it came to operations behind the opening, widening, and improving of the city streets. With the city's enormous growth came a legitimate demand for new streets and the improvement of old ones. It became one of the Ring's most lucrative forms of graft. It was, indeed, a democratic form of graft—laborers got work; City Hall clerks were able to supplement their incomes; political debts were paid off in commissionerships; judges no longer had to rely entirely on their salaries; Ring members and friends prospered from the assessments involved and the excitement of "gambling" in real estate. As in the case of Recorder and Street Commissioner Hackett, the key factor was the appointment of reliable Commissioners by the Ring judges, upon the suggestion of Corporation Counsel O'Gorman. From then on a pattern emerged: Tammany favorites and members of the Ring's families constantly appeared as Commissioners; awards for damages were exorbitantly high; Commissioners charged "from ten to one hundred times as much as the law allowed" for their services and expenses, despite the fact that the Commissioners as employees of the city were disqualified by law from receiving any pay.[44]

To "open" a new street did not mean to begin construction work. It was a legal term signifying that the land had been bought and was now officially "opened." Announcements of the transaction were published, and those property owners involved were invited to declare any objections to the Commissioners. The clerk drew up a report and the thing was done. Actually it usually amounted to a mere formality.

The cost for this activity under the Tweed Ring, however, would seem to indicate that an enormous amount of work went into it. What usually happened was that the surveyor reproduced a map of the street from maps made in 1811, when Manhattan island, except for a small area at its northern end, was surveyed so well that the maps were still adequate in post-Civil War New York. On the borders of the copy made by the surveyor, the clerk wrote the names of the owners of the lots on both sides of the street, copying his information from the tax books. Then the fun began. "The surveyor charges as though he had made original surveys and drawn original maps. The clerk charges as though his reports were the result of original searchers and researchers. The commissioners charge as though the opening had been the tardy fruit of actual negotiations."[45] For the year ending in June 1866, it was estimated that the cost for "opening" twenty-five streets was $257,192.12. Of this cost, $4433 was charged for rent of an office, which ordinarily rented for $300 a year; "disbursements and postage-stamps" cost $950; and one surveyor's bill alone accounted for an astounding $54,000.[46]

The Broadway widening "job" was a good example of the Ring in action. On May 17, 1869, the State legislature passed an act providing for the widening of Broadway between Thirty-fourth and Fifty-ninth streets, whereupon the Ring seized control of the legal machinery that decided assessments and damages to the property involved. With the friendly judge Albert Cardozo presiding, and two of the three Commissioners good Ring men, the Ring and a selected few began to buy property. Two of them paid $24,500 for a lot for which the Commissioners generously awarded them damages of $25,100. The new front was worth $10,000 more. Another lot sold for $27,500, but this payment was absorbed by a $30,355 award in damages.[47] It was the resale value of the property, however, where the profit was made, and lots on Broadway were worth thousands. With tactics of this sort, the Ring managed to purchase some of the most valuable property in New York City.[48]

With minor variations, the Broadway widening scheme was repeated in the Madison Avenue extension, the Church Street extension, the opening of Lexington Avenue through Stuyvesant

Park, the Park Place widening, and the so-called "Fifth Avenue raid," where the Ring profited from the widening, extending, and "improvement" of that street. To one writer, who greatly exaggerated, it seemed that streets were opened "which no mortal had seen, no foot had trod; and they appeared only on the city map as spaces between imaginary lines leading from No-where to No-place." [49] To a New York citizen in 1871 who examined the New York State *Senate Journal* of 1869, it might have seemed that the State legislature had gone No-where. On page 61 was an act entitled, "An act to afford relief against frauds and irregularities in assessments for local improvements in the city of New York."

Whether the source of graft was street openings, real estate speculation, city advertising, padded contractor's bills, juggled city records and bond issues fat with graft, a simple but imaginative profit on the City Directory, or a straightforward attack on the city treasury by supplying printing and stationery goods, the Tweed Ring explored the various paths to civic dishonesty. The roads to graft, however, were paved by the very interests the Ring exploited. The financial community, consumed in its own self-interests, stood to gain from the massive pump-priming in city improvements. The "open door" policy of state and city welfare deadened the voice of religious and philanthropic organizations; the newspapers, split by political partisanship and competitive self-interest, were softened by the morsels of political handouts; and the "people" were indifferent. The Tweed Ring thrived on the lack of civic conscience, and the result was graft. But the worst was yet to come.

12

"PECULATION TRIUMPHANT"

They just seen their opportunities and took them.

George Washington Plunkitt,
Plunkitt of Tammany Hall

THE LOVE AFFAIR between the Tweed Ring and the treasury of the City and County of New York, a courtship lasting five years from 1866 to 1871, was a series of illicit, passionate seductions. What distinguished the Tweed Ring was not merely the millions it made in graft. It was the Ring's keen sense in exploiting every opportunity, high or low, big or little, that suggested a chance for plunder. What might have escaped the attention of less artistic thieves, was made into a bountiful harvest by the Ring. The so-called "armory raid" is a good case in point.

In a shabby neighborhood on Hester Street, the Fifth Regiment of the National Guard had an armory on the floor above a saloon. The armory was a tiny, dirty room for which the city paid $10,000 a year rent, a larger sum than the entire block would rent for.[1] The Ninety-sixth Regiment was about to move to a new armory. Before they moved, James Ingersoll, the Ring's contractor, came into the armory and removed the furniture, carpets, desks, armracks, gas-fixtures, and even the water-closets, even though the armory had been furnished only a short time before at the cost of several thousand dollars to the city.[2] On the fifth story of a building on the corner of Green and Houston was the meeting room for the Seventy-ninth Regiment. It was reached only after a somewhat harrowing walk through dark, dingy halls and up filthy stairs. The regiment, which had a fine war record, nearly broke up because of the wretched accommodations. Yet the city paid $8000 rent for the armory. Peter Sweeny and Hugh Smith bought the entire block between Thirty-third and Thirty-fourth Streets and immediately leased a hall in the block as an armory. They received $30,000 a year for a hall not worth more than $3000. Moreover, they predated the lease eighteen months, and got $45,000 for use of a hall they did not yet own, and at which time the city did not use.[3]

While there were only twelve regiments and two companies in the city, the city leased twenty-four armories at an annual rent of $281,000. Of this number, ten were stables, and these were sublet to the county as armories at a rent of $85,000 per year. In thirty months alone, the city paid out $2,940,473.70 for rent and upkeep of its armories.[4] (It was never known, however, whether Connolly charged this to "Armory Relief Funds," or to "City Contingencies.")

If rents were slightly swollen, repairs—dollar for dollar—were preposterous. Between 1869 and October 1871 a total of $3,200,000 was spent on armory repairs, and the *New York Times* estimated that twelve out of every thirteen dollars were stolen.[5] The gang of Ring contractors had a field day: Andrew Garvey ($197,330.24 for plastering), John H. Keyser ($142,329.71 for plumbing), George S. Miller ("the lucky carpenter," $431,064.31), James H. Ingersoll (furniture and accessories, $170,729.60). For just ten armories the repair bills were run up to $941,453.86.[6] This included work done on the top floor of Tammany Hall, which also rented its rooms as an armory. In fact, in one day, March 14, 1870, four men received $163,992.66 for repair work alone.[7]

The armory raid represented, among other things, the breakdown of the system to protect the city against fraudulent contracts.

In theory, the city seemed amply guarded by a law that required that all business done with the city in excess of $600 had to be awarded to the lowest bidder. In practice, the Tweed Ring's power was so extensive that it could almost cavalierly evade the law. The law that guided the Ring was the law of political favoritism; contracts were awarded to pay off a political debt or to reap a corrupt profit—or both. A number of techniques accomplished these ends. Either phony bids were submitted or the lowest bidder, after receiving the contract, was persuaded to alter his bid by padding it. Often the Ring simply "forgot" the legal statute that required the city government to announce publicly that it would entertain bids for future work. Instead, the job went to a friendly contractor who presented a fat bid, while respectable business firms, who might have done the work more cheaply and efficiently, were totally unaware of the job or the transaction. The end result was not only political corruption but also a menace to public safety. Political hacks, not qualified businessmen or skilled engineers, were in charge of much of the city's construction work. For example, the contract for building "a very costly bridge over a wide river" was awarded not to a recognized engineering firm, but to a pork-butcher.[8]

Unlike the decade of the 1850's and the later reigns of Kelly, Croker, and Murphy, the Ring was not able to profit as much on city transportation. It was not, however, for lack of trying. Public transportation in the city of New York during the Tweed era was a shambles. In a city of more than 700,000 people, there was a desperate need for efficient and more rapid transportation. The streets were jammed with people, pushcarts, and overloaded streetcars and omnibuses drawn by huge, plodding six-horse teams. Traffic was so heavy that it often took an hour to go a hundred yards. One wag defined martyrdom as riding in a New York omnibus.[9] Something had to be done, a solution had to be found. It was. In February 1870 began a battle over New York's first subway, what the later boss of New York, Richard Croker, once ridiculed as "that hole in the ground." It was a battle that could have resulted in an almost unbelievable exercise in graft—millions upon millions that would have made previous feats of the Tweed Ring paltry indeed, if fate and a bad press had not intervened.

It actually began two years earlier in 1868, with a genius and a vision. Alfred Ely Beach was an extraordinary human being in mind and body. A short, fragile creature with a long, rapier-like nose matched by a long, thin, upper lip, he had moved with restless energy from one venture to another as an inventor, publisher, and patent attorney. He not only held a host of patents (he created the "literary piano," the first workable typewriter), but also had advised Samuel F. B. Morse on his "talking machine," R. J. Gatling, inventor of the machine-gun, and Captain John Ericsson, who launched the *Monitor*. At nineteen Beach took over a floundering scientific journal, the *Scientific American*, and made it into one of the most influential publications for both the nineteenth and twentieth centuries. Forty-two years old in 1868, Alfred Ely Beach prepared for his greatest performance in imagination, his wonderful pneumatic underground railway.

Beach laid his plans carefully. He realized that the Tweed Ring was the critical roadblock to his solution to New York's transportation problem. The subway could be a threat to the Ring's control over the existing public transit, from which they exacted tribute. The Ring could destroy his idea initially in the State legislature in a fight for a charter, by mustering the Black Horse Cavalry, the Ring's group of corrupt legislators. Or it might possibly wrest control of the subway from him as the price for building it. Therefore, Beach introduced a rather innocuous charter asking for a postal dispatch system whereby the mails could be distributed underground via cylinders whisked through underground pneumatic tubes. Sensing little opportunity for plunder, the Ring's Black Horse Cavalry permitted the charter to be granted. And then Beach went to work.

For the next two years, working in absolute secrecy, at night,

Beach poured $350,000 of his money into what later would be a subway system—a hole and a tunnel. In February 1870 he revealed his marvelous creation, and the astonished *Herald* startled New York with the headline, "A FASHIONABLE RECEPTION HELD IN THE BOWELS OF THE EARTH!" For the next year, 400,000 incredulous tourists visited the Beach Pneumatic Subway. It consisted of a waiting room, an elegant place with a grand piano, a water fountain, a goldfish tank, and frescoed walls. More astonishing was a track laid in a tube stretching some 312 feet under the center of Broadway. But most spectacular of all was the subway itself, whose only power was air! The subway car, seating twenty-two people, was propelled by a huge blowing machine which shot the car down the track at a tingling speed of ten miles an hour. When the car reached the end of the track it tripped a wire causing the fan to reverse itself. The car was now caught up in a sucking wind and sent sailing back down the track. To Beach, air power was the only answer. The gasoline and electric engines had not yet been invented, and steam engines seemed woefully inadequate. They were filthy monsters, belching soot and cinders, and since they were always exploding, subway travelers might face death by scalding.

If Beach seemed to have conquered the bowels of the earth, his problems had only begun on the surface, where the Tweed Ring was perched for the kill. Beach presented his Beach Transit Bill. This legislation would have run a five-mile subway line up to Central Park, carrying, Beach argued, 20,000 persons a day. It would cost just over five million dollars, and the beauty of it was that it would cost the City and State nothing. The money would be raised privately. Moreover, the public had had a year to be dazzled by Beach's initial experiment, and the bill seemed to have overwhelming popular approval.

Faced with this challenge, the Ring responded with a bill of its own, the so-called Viaduct Plan. It was a bill of double-barreled mischief. The Viaduct Plan would at once scotch Beach's plan for an underground subway, and at the same time meet the public's craving for rapid transit, by creating an operation that would return to the Ring millions of dollars of graft. The plan, in fact, would have cost the city from $50 to $65 million. It proposed a viaduct railroad running the length of Manhattan, supported by huge stone arches at least forty feet high. The graft involved in the construction of the railway alone would have been enormous, but it was further enhanced by the provision that everything under the railway be condemned and razed and that the streets along the course of the railway be widened and graded. The Viaduct Railroad Company was not only to be given the privilege of exemption from taxes and assessments, but it was also to be given the right to build other lines of railways in any part of the city, thus virtually enabling the Ring to put a railroad in every street of the city.[10] To start the project the city would be compelled to buy five million dollars of stock issued by Comptroller Connolly. This would have been only a starter, an appetizer as it were, for the Ring would have followed up by asking for more money from the legislature when the five million had been squandered. The final move of the Ring was a masterful stroke. Touting the venture as a great city improvement, harnessing civic pride, they disguised the true intent of the scheme by having some of the most distinguished men in the community act as incorporators of the Viaduct Railroad: John Jacob Astor, Horace Greeley, Oswald Ottendorfer, Peter Cooper, August Belmont, Charles A. Lamont, Levi P. Morton, Charles L. Tiffany, John T. Agnew, Simeon B. Chittenden, and James Gordon Bennett, Jr. No wonder Gustavus Myers called this "an almost unparalleled steal."

New Yorkers waited with acute apprehension as both bills were presented to the State legislature. The Beach Transit Bill, introduced in January 1871, with its hearty public support, easily passed both houses of the legislature, as did the Tweed Ring's Viaduct Plan, with its hearty support from the Ring's Black Horse Cavalry. Both reached the desk of Governor John Hoffman in March 1871.

It was now Hoffman's choice: New York's first subway and rapid, efficient transportation, or the overhead railway and massive corruption. It was not an agonizing decision. Hoffman acted with dispatch when it came to Ring legislation. He vetoed the subway and approved the Viaduct Plan. Many New Yorkers were outraged, charging that since the bills had reached him scarcely twenty-four hours before his decision, Hoffman scarcely had time to read them.

The game little inventor had a flinty edge on his courage. He tried again the following year. Again Hoffman vetoed. He tried again in 1873, pouring the last of his fortune into lobbying fees. Then he received perhaps the cruelest blow. The bill more than handily passed the legislature and was accepted by the Governor, John A. Dix, but just a few months later Dix was forced to withdraw the charter because of the depression of 1873. New York would have a few more years to wait for its first subway.

Nor did the Tweed Ring's Viaduct Plan fare any better. The Ring exposures in the summer of 1871 and Tammany's disaster in the fall election were more than enough to discredit the Viaduct Plan, and New York was spared one of the greatest swindles of all time. An epitaph to the genius of Alfred Ely Beach still exists today. In the BMT's City Hall Station, the site of the wonderful pneumatic underground railway, there is a plaque which commemorates Beach as the founder of the New York subway system.

If the Ring never capitalized on the need for rapid transit, it timed its recognition of New York's need for more water perfectly. The Tammany journal, the *Leader,* for which Mayor Hall contributed many a literary criticism and peppery political observation, had long campaigned for more water, hinting darkly that the city was on the verge of a water famine. Boss Tweed, his civic pride aroused, purchased lakes in Putnam and Westchester counties. A bill was introduced in the State legislature authorizing the city to acquire upstate water rights. It was an outrageous bill in the Ring's eyes because it limited expenditure to just one million dollars. This was soon adjusted by defeating the bill and introducing another which would place no limitation on the Comptroller's large talents in issuing stocks and bonds to finance the project. Not only was expenditure unlimited, but the Commissioner of Public Works, W. M. Tweed, was also given the authority to issue the requisitions. The well-meaning Peter Cooper, who had made a fortune manufacturing glue and iron, went to Tweed and complained about the bill. Tweed, apparently sensing that the Ring in its eagerness had overplayed its hand, gracefully backed down. While certain features of the bill remained, like the right to acquire title to all areas and property deemed necessary to the water project, and rights to build roads and viaducts, Tweed showed remarkable restraint by introducing an amendment limiting expenditure to just five million dollars.[11]

The Ring's seemingly occult power in anticipating the needs of city and state was again demonstrated when the State decided to purchase arms for the National Guard. Almost overnight, a company with the imposing title of the United States Regulation Firearms Company sprang into existence. The company had no gunsmiths, no factory, not even a workshop. But it did have as president Boss Tweed's great friend James H. Ingersoll; Charles H. Green, an agent for Peter Sweeny, was the company's general agent; and its major shareholder was William Marcy Tweed. It also had the patent rights to an ancient and obsolete breechloader, called the Allin gun, long superseded by better weapons, and once condemned for army use by General Sherman himself. At the 1870 legislative session, a clause was tacked onto an Assembly bill, "by some mysterious process," appropriating $350,000 out of the state treasury for supplying the National Guard with the Allin gun. Governor Hoffman, faced by an indignant public, was forced to veto it. But soon thereafter, a provision was inserted in the General Appropriation bill, assigning $250,000 for firearms; again the brand was the Allin gun. This time Hoffman did not veto. He appointed a commission of experts to examine all different models of weapons and gave them the authority to choose the best weapon. By some mysterious process they chose the Allin gun.[12]

The Ring was able to control big business in several ways. Corporations could be threatened with regulatory bills; to obtain public franchises, businessmen were forced to pay tribute to the Ring, which Gustavus Myers estimated, netted the Ring a million dollars a year.[13] These facts about the Tweed Ring are generally known, but what is little known, however, is the fact that tribute and extortions were levied on the small businessman. Here the bible of graft was the bulky volume of over 900 pages of city ordinances. The Ring used it to harass, blackmail, and demand illegitimate fees. A merchant, stable-keeper, hotel owner, saloon-keeper, inn-keeper, contractor, or any owner of real estate who fell under the ban of Tammany Hall could be given an object lesson in city government, chapter and verse, from the book of ordinances. A livery stable owner who was indiscreet enough to make himself conspicuous by being an "antisnapper"—an opponent of Tammany—might be visited by a Health Inspector who would fine him, by citing an ancient ordinance passed fifty or more years earlier that showed his manure pile to be in the wrong place. A hotel owner might find his plumbing was always out of order, from a Tammany point of view, or his fire escapes insufficient. A merchant who did not pay an election-day tribute might find that his signs or awnings were contrary to a city ordinance, or he was causing an obstruction of the streets by having wagons in front of his shop.

City ordinances offered many opportunities for graft, one of the most profitable sources being the public markets. Two public markets alone were defrauded of half a million dollars.[14] In the Washington Market, as Thomas DeVoe pointed out, "there is hardly a stand in the five hundred and twenty-eight, or in the West Washington Market, that has not heretofore paid *somebody* a bonus of from $500 to $5000, which sums it was never thought proper to pay into the City Treasury." [15] The methods of graft were many, from blackmail and illegal interference, to petty annoyance. For example, all market vendors were subject to high assessments and had to pay for a "permit" to operate. If the owner of a stand opposed Tammany, he might find his permit suddenly revoked. Moreover, city officials concerned with the markets took their jobs seriously. One industrious superintendent collected as much as $40,000 to roof the markets, which he split with the Ring. The fees for just remodeling or relocating a business were enormous; they varied from between $100 to $500, and netted the Ring over $200,000 during its reign.[16] On July 31, 1871, the *New York Times* published an angry letter written by H. G. Swimer, a hapless New York merchant, who complained about a special permit of $10 levied on merchants for the temporary use of sidewalks and the privilege of putting up signs. (This was additional to the regular $10 tax which permitted the passage of goods in and out of a store.) The permit in question required the consent of the Alderman of the merchant's ward. "It is not a pleasant thing," wrote Swimer, "to hunt through a score of rum-mills to find the Alderman, and then pay him $10 to pass your case." Most of the merchants, he said, went to the Mayor, "where some scamp can be found who will sign the name of the Alderman, Assistant Alderman, and Mayor for $10."

Blackmail money was paid to the Ring by merchants who deliberately broke the law requiring sanitation and the proper care of foods. Thus many sheep and lambs were already "dying a natural death" when they were slaughtered for public consumption—

> and the same may be said of pork, which is often from hogs smothered in rail cars, especially in cold weather, and in, or nearly in, a dying condition when slaughtered. Chickens and fowls, too, are often spoiled, or become stale and musty from long carriage and sudden change of weather, when the process of washing with a preparation to make them appear fresh is resorted to. Game, either in a putrid state, or having died of starvation in consequence of deep snows, is often picked up and sent here for

our especial epicures . . . often found hanging on stalls for sale, with stale fish, oysters, clams, lobsters.[17]

The black brain behind market graft was a tough, burly, square-jawed man who worked in the office of the Superintendent of Market Rents and Fees. Once the leader of the famed Tunnel Mob, he led a "wheel within a wheel" known as the Market Ring. Later he became one of the great city bosses of New York. He may be introduced by this notice that appeared in the *Times:*

> On last Tuesday evening, September 5 about 8:45 P.M., ex-Alderman Richard Croker, of the Twenty-first Ward, who is the leader of the St. Patrick's Alliance [a Connolly organization] with the assistance of another individual, . . . assaulted a man named James Moore with a sling-shot, knocking him down and then kicking him, at the corner of Thirty-first Street and Third Avenue.[18]

Nor were the saloons exempt from paying tribute to the Ring. "If a student of history were reviewing the gloomy lists of the evils which have most cursed mankind, which have wasted households, stained the hands of man with his fellow's blood, sown quarrels and hatreds, broken women's hearts, and ruined children in their earliest years, bred poverty and crime, he would place next to the bloody name of War, the black word—INTEMPERANCE."[19] The moralist who penned this outburst would hardly be in sympathy with saloon-keepers who were forced to pay, like harassed medieval peasants, tribute to the barons of the Ring. There were at least 10,000 saloons in New York during the Tweed Ring reign, and despite the profound convictions of the reformers to the contrary, not all saloon proprietors were supporters of the Tammany Hall Democracy. For this they paid a price, like many merchants and public market vendors. One blatant but effective device of extortion was entrusted to the head of an auxiliary department within Tweed's Public Works Department, Water Register Charles Cornell. It was his duty to collect revenue derived from the sale and use of Croton water by saloon-keepers and others. One saloon-keeper, an "antisnapper," received an enormous water bill. His saloon had no water faucet. He complained about the bill to the Water Register, saying that he supplied his place with water brought from his own house. He was promptly notified that this was not a good reason, and unless he paid his bill the water at his home would be shut off.[20]

The most effective form of extortion against recalcitrant saloons, however, was to evoke the Sunday closing laws. Despite the legislative enactment against the sale of liquor on Sunday, saloons continued in full blast on Sundays. The Germans deeply resented this interference with their lager beer, and the Irish liked their whisky. A saloon closed on Sunday by civic-minded police would lose a great deal of business. Probably the law was only upheld to exert discipline and to exact a fee from saloons on the wrong side of the political tracks. Unlike middle class merchants, few saloon-keepers tried to defy the Ring. More than a majority of saloon-keepers were deeply committed to the Tammany cause; they were, in fact, unheralded heroes of the Tammany organization. On this subject, the high-minded reformer, E. L. Godkin, had the same perception as a Tammany ward-heeler.

> The fuss that is made by the Anti-Tammany people about the number of Irish liquor-dealers who are found on the Tammany General Committee, and whom it nominates for office, is another illustration of their imperfect comprehension of the nature of the situation. Liquor-dealers are the medium, and the only medium, through which political preaching or control can reach a very large body of the voters of this city. The liquor-dealer is their guide, philosopher, and creditor. He sees them more frequently and familiarly than anybody else, and is more trusted by them than anybody else, and is the person through whom the news and meaning of what passes in the upper regions of city politics reach them. The selection of such men as the Boss's advisers and

> lieutenants, the captains of hundreds and fifties, is therefore not only expedient but necessary. They are the natural administrators of Boss government. The notion that city missionaries or Republican philanthropists, or scholars and gentlemen from Fifth Avenue, can be substituted for them is absurd. Neither the Republican party nor any reform party has at its command any agents or propagandists who can compete with them.[21]

The saloon, then, was not only the Elysium of the workingman, but it was also a rendezvous where politicians could recruit followers, hold meetings, and gossip about the great game of politics. Places favored by Tammany, such as the bistro of "Christ" Johnson and the Burnt Rag, openly flouted the Sunday closing laws.

Aside from such large-scale operations, the Ring also engaged in a good deal of petty graft, or perhaps, misdemeanors—in terms of the Tweed Ring at least. James Bridge, an employee of the Ring's plumbing tycoon, John Keyser, gave an example. He testified at the Tweed investigation that Keyser had done work on the homes of many of New York's leading politicians, including the Tweed Ring and friends.

> "Did you receive any instructions from Keyser when you did the work?"
>
> "Yes, sir," said Bridge, "I received instructions to do it as lightly as possible."
>
> "Why?"
>
> "He would say that he would not get paid for it. . . ."
>
> "Did you understand that these jobs would be charged against anybody at all except the city?"
>
> "I supposed it was going to be charged in some way but it was always considered that they were 'thankee' jobs."[22]

At the same investigation, Andrew Garvey, the enterprising plasterer, said he had done "some superficial repairing" to Connolly's house and charged it off against the city treasury. Asked how much it cost, Garvey said it was about $40,000. It was found, in fact, that Connolly's beautiful mansion was built at the city's expense and the bills were so raised as to pay all commissions on fraudulent bills to other Ring members. As one investigating Alderman put it, "He got his house for nothing and 20 per cent besides for allowing the city to build it for him." [23]

There were other kinds of petty graft which Connolly probably filed under "City Contingencies." There was the water meter swindle, where the Ring forced merchants to use a meter that never had been properly tested or formally approved and was almost worthless. Worth around $18, it cost merchants $60; a super-political sales campaign sold some 20,000 meters, and the Ring had some $840,000 profit to use as petty cash.[24] Nor did the Ring's imagination end here. It suddenly became urgent for the city to have more safes. J. McBride Davidson, a favorite tradesman of the Ring, received a contract to supply city departments with $31,780.15 worth of safes. William Marcy Tweed received $3640 worth of safes and sent an additional $8775 worth to his family. However, the clerk of the Fourth District Civil Court, a Mr. Smalley, who was protected only by glass doors and was compelled to furnish a $10,000 bond to cover the safe-keeping of important books and papers in his office, thought at last he would get a safe. He made repeated requests, but was refused.[25]

In 1931 Chicago's Big Bill Thompson ended his political career largely because he allowed graft in the public school system; fifteen years later, in the same city, Edward J. Kelly's long rule was tottering for the same reason; but in the years of the Tweed Ring, school boards were packed with political appointees. There was fraud behind the city's generous supplies of school materials, and teachers often bribed the school trustees to get a job. John R. Hennessy, a canny politician but insufficiently tutored in the three R's, was nonetheless appointed a school trustee. However, soon thereafter he was fired for "immoral and disgraceful conduct" in taking a bribe of $100 from a Mary Cannon for finding her a job in the Seventeenth Ward.

Nathaniel Sands was a key member in the so-called Education Ring, and also a key member in the reform group, the Citizens' Association—not a contradiction if one considers Mr. Sands's character. He was a black-eyed, stout, ruddy man, with a massive forehead, "a wealth of highly moral white hair," whose appearance of inward spiritual grace was compromised by "a peculiar craftiness of general manner that was warning to the visitor at once that this was a peculiarly tough lemon to squeeze."[26] The *Times* said he had patriarchal pretensions: he always seemed to be on the point of stretching out his arms and blessing the multitude, after the manner of earlier patriarchs.[27] As an important member of the Board of Education (although he had painful difficulty in speaking the language grammatically), he tried on two occasions to divert attention from educational graft by posing as an educational reformer. On the first occasion, he published a pamphlet against the study of Latin for Americans, on the ground that it was the language of an Empire, and would certainly undermine the republican principles of American youth. On the second, he published a seemingly distinguished and learned study of classical education. Actually, it was later found to be a massive plagiarization of John Stuart Mill and Herbert Spencer.[28]

All these operations in the business of graft, large or petty, did not go entirely to fatten the personal fortunes of the Tweed Ring. Vast amounts of political booty had to be plowed back into the Ring's organization, for its overhead was enormous. Indeed, graft became the crude gas that ran the Ring's political machine: elections had to be financed, State and City legislators had to be rewarded for voting correctly; loans were made to ensure friendship; raffles, picnics, and Tammany balls had to be financed, and so on. As Tweed himself said, "the money, of course, was distributed around in every way, to everybody, and paid for everything, and was scattered throughout the community."[29] In 1877, the Aldermen who investigated the career of the Tweed Ring tried to find out how the Boss had spent some of his plunder. They asked him how much he had given to the Democratic party alone. "I think," said Tweed, "it would frighten me if I told." [30]

He was not frightened when he told about the building of the New York County Courthouse. Of all the Ring's achievements in what could be called graftsmanship, this yielded over $9 million in graft. It was the Tweed Ring's masterpiece.

13

"THE HOUSE THAT TWEED BUILT"

This is
BOSS TWEED
The Tammany Atlas who all sustains,
(A Tammany Samson perhaps for his pains),
Who rules the City where Oakey reigns,
The master of Woodward and Ingersoll
And all of the gang on the City Roll,
And formerly lord of "slippery Dick,"
Who *con*troll'd the plastering laid on so thick
By the comptroller's plasterer, Garvey by name,
The Garvey whose fame is the little game
Of laying on plaster and knowing the trick
Of charging as if he himself were a brick
Of the well-plaster'd House
That TWEED built.

"The House that Tweed Built"

TODAY AMONG THE SLEEK, soaring municipal buildings of downtown Manhattan huddles a shabby, squat pile of Massachusetts marble. It is the old County Courthouse, a sad, forlorn, almost forgotten little building. A small, chunky, three-story structure, barely reaching a hundred feet, it is dwarfed by surrounding buildings and shunted aside from the main legal traffic in New York. Behind its dirty gray walls only a few offices are now used. There is nothing in this ancient and rather grotesque relic of little old New York to suggest a raucous past, or even the slightest hint of scandal. But in its old rooms and long corridors there is a whisper of history, like the sound of the sea in shells.

The courthouse was designed with great expectations. By the time the Tweed Ring finished with it, however, it looked more like a cross between Middle Tweed and Late Sweeny. It exceeded by more than four times the cost for the Houses of Parliament.[1] It cost nearly twice as much as the whole of Alaska.

The house that Tweed built was actually begun years before the Tweed Ring was formed. In 1858, the distinguished architect John Kellum (who had designed the *New York Herald* building) completed the designs for the new Courthouse. Here was to be a Corinthian marvel signifying the greatness of New York and the sanctity of the law. Except for providing for the site in City Hall Park, little was done until 1862 when, by no coincidence, William Tweed became president of the Board of Supervisors. There had been a legal wrangle over who should appropriate funds for the new building: the State, by a Board of Commissioners, or the City, by the Board of Supervisors. It was Tweed's artful persuasion that won the case for the City. Thereafter appropriations became particularly brisk.

The enactment law of 1858 stated specifically that the building, with all its furnishings, should not cost more that $250,000. But this was hardly enough, argued Tweed, to build a fitting tribute to the city and to the law. The city fathers complied, and $1,000,000 more was authorized. In 1864 an additional $800,000 was granted. But even this was not enough. In 1865, $300,000 more was appropriated, yet the very next year still more money was needed, and Tweed lobbied successfully for an additional $300,000.[2]

When a further half million dollars was granted in 1866, a reform group became suspicious. It seemed a bit odd that millions of the taxpayers' dollars had produced a courthouse that was still not finished, except for one corner occupied for only a few weeks during the year by the Court of Appeals. The reformers indignantly demanded an investigation. The statesmen of the City and County of New York were obliging, but their feelings were somewhat ruffled. They pointed out that the Board of Supervisors had already set up a committee to investigate the courthouse contracts.

Nevertheless, to serve justice, they established another committee, christening it the Special Committee to Investigate the Courthouse. This committee was to investigate the investigating Committee of Supervisors who were investigating the courthouse.

The Special Committee took a remarkably short time to declare that the investigating committee, the contracts, and the courthouse were free from fraud. The reformers were appalled, but what was acutely exasperating was that the Special Committee had taken this opportunity to investigate its own chances for graft. For just *twelve* days' work, the Special Committee submitted this bill of expenses: $2938 for a clerk and stenographer; $900 for legal counsel; $6389 to the *Transcript* (a journal owned by Boss Tweed) for publishing the report of the original investigating committee, the Committee on Investigation; $205 to one George W. Roome, for "meals furnished"; and $7718.75 to the New York Printing Company (owned by Boss Tweed) for printing 5000 copies of its own investigation report, making a grand total, for what was now called the Notorious Investigating Committee, of $18,460.35.[3] The Mayor of New York, John Hoffman, had little to say. After this slight interruption, business went on as usual.

The tempo now increased as the Tweed Ring expanded its power in the city and state. The State legislature authorized the Board of Supervisors to spend more money. But this was not enough, and the City donated $6,997,893.24 more.[4] "Just imagine," said a newspaper, "the untiring industry, the wear and tear of muscle, the anxiety of mind, the weary days and sleepless nights, that it must have cost the 'Boss' to procure all these sums of money."[5] Thus from 1858 to 1871 the courthouse had suffered awesome growing pains. In thirteen years, more than $13 million had been spent—and it still was not finished.

When New Yorkers realized in 1871 that their courthouse had been the instrument for graft, one of their first questions was, how was this incredible swindle managed? What astonished, angered, and perhaps embarrassed New Yorkers was that the Ring, confident of its power, contemptuous of detection, had employed tactics so simple that they were conspicuously brazen.

The scheme hinged upon each Ringman's playing his role according to his particular talent and position. Boss Tweed was left free of dreary administrative detail to operate on the higher levels of decision-making and to exercise his charm—always enhanced by a bulging pocketbook—among his colleagues in the city and in the State legislature. To assist him in the subtle art of political persuasion, Tweed, like most successful executives, was able to call upon a resourceful and imaginative aide—Peter Barr Sweeny.

The scheme was launched when Tweed and Sweeny made arrangements with businessmen of easy conscience, the contractors of the courthouse. The operation then swung into the bailiwick of Richard Connolly, the City Comptroller, and his right-hand man, the ex-convict James Watson, the County Auditor. It was Connolly's job as the Ring's bookkeeper and financial expert to supervise the assault on the soft underbelly of the city treasury.

The contractor submitted a bill for his work, so ill-disguised that the most untutored could recognize it as being padded to its final decimal point. Connolly made sure that the Ring received 65 per cent as its commission, with 35 per cent going to the contractor. He then drew up payments, or warrants, which he and Watson approved. Boss Tweed, in turn, "persuaded" the Board of Supervisors to give its official approval to the warrants. When in 1870 this authority was shifted to a Board of Courthouse Commissioners as a reform move, the Boss was equal to the occasion. Using his position in the State legislature, Tweed made sure that appointive power lay with the Mayor, and the congenial Oakey Hall thereby packed the Board with four Tammany buffs: Mike Norton, James Ingersoll, Thomas Coman, and John J. Walsh. At first there was unexpected trouble. The Commissioners were not agreeable to certifying bills for the current courthouse appropriation of $600,000. Watson, the paymaster, was as canny as Connolly was slippery. He immediately made up $600,000 worth of vouchers and expedited them before the Commissioners took office. It was not long before two of the Commissioners—Walsh and Norton—changed their minds and agreed to take a cut of 5 per cent.[6]

The operation then reached its final stage, as the fraudulent warrants were placed under the authority of the Mayor of New York, Abraham Oakey Hall. When he, as the highest officer in city government, signed the padded courthouse warrants, the deed was done.

What made the building of the County Courthouse a classic in the annals of American graft was the way in which money was spent. As Robert Roosevelt, one of the reformers, put it, the bills rendered by the Ring's contractors were "not merely monstrous, they are manifestly fabulous."[7] For example, for just three tables and forty chairs, the city paid to the penny, $179,729.60.[8] Roscoe Conkling, a Republican leader in New York state, complained that more money was spent for furnishings than it cost the Grant Administration to run the United States mail service, as much as the yearly cost of collecting the customs revenue, and nearly three times as much as the entire diplomatic expenses for two years.[9] Conkling was referring to expenses for furniture, carpets, and shades supplied by the James Ingersoll Company, a faithful tool of the Tweed Ring. The total expense was "the rather startling sum" of $5,691,144.26. Fascinated by the charge of $350,000 for carpets alone, the *New York Times* asked Ingersoll for an explanation. "There is one thing you people down in the *Times* don't seem to take into account," was the angry reply, "the carpets in these public buildings need to be changed a great deal oftener than in private houses." The *Times* concluded that the city had been overcharged $336,821.31.[10]

John Keyser, the plumber, surpassed the fees of even his highly paid colleagues of today. He received nearly a million and a half dollars for "plumbing and gas light fixtures." It was estimated that in one year alone, Keyser made over a million dollars.[11]

Compared to Ingersoll and Keyser, Tweed's carpenter, "Lucky"

George S. Miller, submitted puny expenses. Lumber not worth more than $48,000 cost the city $460,000. Miller, who kept a fine, large lithograph of Boss Tweed in his office, was apparently a fast worker. He was paid $360,747.61 for one month's work.[12] All this was rather odd because little carpentry was needed, as the building was made primarily of iron and marble. As for the marble, it was supplied by a quarry owned by the Boss, and the *New York Times* claimed it cost more to quarry marble than it cost to build the entire courthouse in Brooklyn.

The prices for safes and awnings suggested an obsession with security and shade. J. McBride Davidson, who maintained a private bar in his office for select politicians, charged over $400,000 for safes (door locks cost $2676.75). James W. Smith charged $150 apiece for 160 awnings. Considering this, plus the charge for carpentry, a newspaper calculated each courthouse window was costing an astounding $8000.[13] Smith defended himself by saying his charge for awnings including taking them down in the fall, putting them up again in the summer, and repairing them, and therefore he was entitled to every cent he charged. Another manufacturer said, however, the awnings were worth not more than $12.50 apiece.[14]

When a person is building a house he does not expect the architect to send him a huge bill for repairs. Yet the house that Tweed built cost the taxpayers of New York nearly two million dollars in repairs before the building was ever finished. In one year Garvey, the "Prince of Plasterers," charged the city $500,000 for plastering, and a million dollars for repairing the same work.[15] His bill for a three-year plastering job on an iron and marble building was $2,870,464.06—the *Times* suggested the six cents be donated to charity—and of this $1,294,685.13 went for repairs![16] It was estimated that an honest plasterer could have done the job for $20,000.[17] For "repairing and altering wood work," Tweed's carpenter George Miller was paid nearly $800,000.

For all the shocking displays of greed, there was sprinkled throughout the Ring's secret account books evidence of good humor, a certain dash, a feeling that here were men who really enjoyed their work. For example, two checks dated December 28, 1869, and December 31, 1869, were made out to Fillippo Donaruma. The first check was endorsed by "Philip F. Dummey," the second by "Fillip Dummin." Together the checks amounted to over $66,000.[18] Another check was made out to T. C. Cash for $64,000. And wedged in among columns of massive figures was this masterpiece of understatement: "Brooms, etc.,... $41,190.95."[19] A devil-may-care attitude, or just plain sloppiness, was displayed when in no less than thirteen instances the day upon which large fraudulent payments were made was Sunday.[20]

Then there was the astonishing charge for thermometers. Tweed bought eleven thermometers for the new courthouse, each five feet in length and one foot in breadth and encased in heavily carved frames. The faces were made of inexpensive paper, highly varnished and badly painted. Everything about them was cheap. The taxpayers paid for those eleven thermometers exactly $7500. A reporter asked a reputable thermometer manufacturer what he could supply with this amount. "For $7500," he said, "I could line the courthouse."[21]

The New York Printing Company's charge of $186,000 for stationery was unique. Since it included the printing of all the reams of contractors' bills—and repair bills—it does have a ring of honesty to it.

While the Boss busily built and rebuilt New York's Corinthian marvel, he did not overlook the opportunity to use the courthouse as a rich patronage mine. The courthouse became another way to woo the immigrant by giving him a job as well as to reward the political faithful. Thus Jim "Maneater" Cusick, a prize-fighter, was graduated from Sing Sing to become a Court Clerk. William Long, alias Pudding Long, was made a court "Interpreter." He could neither read nor write. But no one seemed to mind. He spent most of his time looking after Boss Tweed's valuable kennel. M. E. Flanagan, Thomas Connor, James Carty, Thomas Pender, and William Runnett were on the payroll. They were all dead—

but mysteriously their pay went on. As the *New York Times* said, "What's in a name?"

The basement of the new courthouse was so crowded with political appointees that it must have resembled the Black Hole of Calcutta. For just one job, the maintenance of the heating apparatus, thirty-two men were employed as engineers, firemen, secretaries, clerks, messengers, and inspectors. For this the city paid $42,000 in wages. But even this veritable army could not do the job. A basement engineer complained to Tweed that his contractors were sending him boilers of such poor quality that not one could produce more than 50 pounds of pressure![22]

When the Tweed Ring was exposed in 1871, it became a game to calculate how far, placed end to end, the chairs, carpets, awnings, shades, etc., would reach. An historian of Tammany Hall said that some mathematicians got as far as China before they finished. One newspaper reckoned that the 122,222 square yards of carpeting would reach nearly from New York to New Haven, or halfway to Albany, or from Albany to Oswego, or four times from the Battery to Yonkers.[23]

The exposures also inspired several New Yorkers to visit their new courthouse. Although they realized that corruption had been at work, they expected to see some kind of magnificence for their thirteen million dollars. Instead they found a waste of masonry, a gloomy maze of dirty rooms, dark halls, and ugly walls, resembling more an ancient ruin than a new, unfinished building. In 1871, after thirteen years of construction work, one of the largest rooms, the Bureau of Arrears of Taxes, had no roof. The County Clerk's office, Sheriff's office, and office of the Surrogate were not carpeted but were covered with oilcloth and grimy matting. The walls were filthy, and in many places large chunks of plaster had peeled off, leaving ugly blotches—a fitting tribute to Garvey and his repair bills.[24] The *New York Times* concluded that a stranger visiting the courthouse would think the city officials were the most economical, indeed, the most miserly of men. Charles Nordhoff expected to find something of a mansion, since he had heard that

Ingersoll had made Tweed's stable a marvel of fine wood and expensive furniture and that the mighty plasterer, Andrew Garvey, had once worked on Vassar College. Instead, he found that only the old City Hall was dirtier and more dilapidated than the new courthouse.[25]

The prominent reformer George C. Barrett made his pilgrimage and came away shocked. His impression left no doubt that the city must long endure a reminder of the most audacious swindle in its history. "It might be considered," he said, "that the cornerstone of the temple was conceived in sin, and its dome, if ever finished, will be glazed all over with iniquity. The whole atmosphere is corrupt. You look up at its ceilings and find gaudy decorations; you wonder which is the greatest, the vulgarity or the corruptness of the place." [26]

A few months after Barrett made his observation, the Tweed Ring was smashed, and Tammany braves scattered. But the courthouse remained. As the years went by, the scandals of the Tweed Ring softened into just another memory of old New York, but this was one which Tweed had made certain would not be forgotten. The shabby little building in City Hall Park, the house that Tweed built, was as unforgettable a memorial as a statue in Times Square. And Tweed had provided his own epitaph. When he arrived at prison to begin his sentence, the warden asked him what his profession was. The Boss, in a clear, strong voice, answered, "Statesman!" [27]

14

THE BLACK HORSE CAVALRY

Election day, it's up to me
To vote as often as can be,
And, if I fail to land the bluff,
I get a lemon sure enough.

The guy that hasn't lots of dough,
On eats and drinks and smokes to blow,
He's got the double cross for sure,
Or else his politics is pure.

Oliver Herford

THE YEAR 1868 was a turning point in the history of the Tweed Ring. It now extended its activities to the State legislature. Elected the previous year to the State Senate, Tweed began his term in 1868 and, aided by the wily strategy of Peter Barr Sweeny, was soon in control of the main sources of the legislature's power. For example, the Ring seized control of the so-called Black Horse Cavalry, a band of political buccaneers of both parties who made bribery a business by selling their votes. The Ring made an alliance with another potent group, the professional lobbyists or "Third" House. As the leader of the powerful block of city Democrats in the State legislature, the Ring occupied an important role in determining policy for the state Democratic party at Albany, as well as having a voice in placing their own men in key legislative posts. All this added up to power: power to propose legislation that could consolidate and maintain its influence in both city and state politics;

power to better finance its operations through means such as "cinch" bills or legislation involving tax levies.

Also in 1868, A. Oakey Hall became Mayor of New York City and John Hoffman the Governor of New York, and with the sweeping Democratic victory in city and state the following year, the Ring had its men placed in the highest executive and legislative posts from the Governor's chair to City Hall, from the Assembly and Senate to the City Comptroller's office. And, finally, in 1868 began the first rumbling of a revolt against Ring rule, which culminated in 1870 in the so-called War of the Rings, a civil war within Tammany Hall in which the Ring fought for its political life. The catalyst for all this was the election of 1868, one of the best examples of the power behind the organization built by the Tweed Ring.

Election day was Judgment Day for the city boss. The machine, power, graft, all depended for their existence upon the verdict at the polls, and any means justified the end of winning, even if it meant rigging the verdict. In times of crises, from South of the Slot in San Francisco to the Strip in Pittsburgh, from the North Side in Kansas City to the South Side in Chicago, when an election promised to be close, or the city machine was threatened by a reform movement, political bosses of both parties tried to protect themselves. Corrupt election officials were appointed; election laws were violated; politically controlled police were prepared to protect the machine from the enemy; friendly judges were instructed to be lenient to the pleas of partisans who broke election laws; and, with an imagination that was breathtaking, the registration lists were padded with phony names and addresses. Names of persons in jail, in hospitals, in cemeteries, or simply of the nonexistent were added with abandon.

Repeaters were recruited to vote early and often (as Boss Curley of Boston once put it, "Do others before they do you"). On the eve of election, the boss and his ward leaders collected an army of the party faithful, the unemployed, the underworld, the flotsam and jetsam of the slums—the bums, frowsy, bleary-eyed, and ragged—and entertained them royally at the saloons, where votes were openly bought and sold.

And on election day itself, the hired mercenaries of the bosses, armed with slingshots, brass knuckles, clubs, and sometimes guns, poured from the saloons, dives, flophouses, and gambling dens, to go to the polls and vote again, and again, and again; to stuff ballot boxes, destroy the opposition's polling places—and each other. As one politician recalled the hectic elections of the good old days, "Elections nowadays are sissy affairs. Nobody gets killed any more and the ambulances and patrol wagons stay in their garages. . . . It was wonderful to see my men slug the opposition to preserve the sanctity of the ballot and stop the corruption of Tammany Hall." [1]

Most of these techniques were employed by the Tweed Ring in the election of 1868. Each ward was responsible for organizing its own electorate and making it aware of its democratic duties in exercising the ballot. By law, each citizen had to have a permanent residence in order to vote, but the Ring circumvented this by the old tactic of padding the registration lists. Scores of men were provided with false residences; for example, six men were registered from Tweed's home, thirty from Senator Michael Norton's, and twenty from Alderman Isaac Robinson's.[2] Perhaps anticipating accusations of fraud, election officers protected themselves morally by being sworn in not upon the Bible but on Ollendorf's "New Method of Learning To Read, Write and Speak French." [3] On election day they swarmed to the polls to vote for Tammany Hall and, of course, good government. From the alleys and cellars of Tweed's Town came the added support of muscle—the raiding parties of Tammany braves. Supplied with five dollars, fictitious names, names of the dead, and plenty of liquor, which gave a certain resonance to their political war whoops, they swooped down on the election booths, voting each time with enthusiasm, terrorizing the opposition, browbeating Election Inspectors, and returning in triumph to the wigwam.

Some men voted eighteen to twenty times.[4] On one occasion an Irishman came in to vote. The Inspector asked his name.

> "Michael Murray, sir."
>
> "Michael Murray?" said the Inspector. "No such name on the list. There's a Michael Murphy."
>
> "Hould on, gintlemen, hould on, gintlemen," said the voter as he pulled a piece of paper from his pocket. "Sure and it *is* Michael Murphy, instid of Michael Murray!"[5]

Another repeater identified himself as "William Croswell Doane," a prominent Episcopal clergyman.

> "Come off," said the election official, "You ain't Bishop Doane."
>
> "The hell I ain't, you ———," said the voter.[6]

Some repeaters thought it was necessary to change hats and coats and adopt various disguises to avoid recognition. "Big Tim" Sullivan, a tough Tammany Hall buff also known as "Dry Dollar" Sullivan (he was once found drying off a revenue stamp from a brewery keg under the impression it was a dollar), argued that repeaters had to have whiskers:

> When you've voted 'em with their whiskers on, you take 'em to a barber and scrape off the chin fringe. Then you vote 'em again with the side lilacs and a mustache. Then to a barber again, off comes the sides and you vote 'em a third time with the mustache. If that ain't enough and the box can stand a few more ballots, clean off the mustache and vote 'em plain face. That makes every one of 'em good for four votes.[7]

The immigrant was a vital factor because he often held the balance of power. Consequently Tammany men played like virtuosos on the immigrant's ignorance of political issues and on their old-world prejudices. Tim Campbell, who had learned his politics in the Tweed days, made this clear in a speech in his Irish district in the 1890's when he was running against an Italian.

"There is two bills before the country—the Mills bill and the McKinley bill," Campbell declared. "The Mills bill is for free trade with everything free; the McKinley bill is for protection with nothing free. Do you want everything free or do you want to pay for everything?

"Having thus disposed of the national issue, I will now devote myself to the local issue, which is the Dago Rinaldo. He is from Italy. I am from Ireland. Are you in favor of Italy or Ireland?

"Having thus disposed of the local issue and thanking you for your attention, I will now retire." [8]

Thus in the election of 1868, along with repeating and sleight-of-hand techniques in stuffing the ballot boxes—"a very beautiful operation," said reformer Robert Roosevelt, "an exquisitely simple process"—the Ring called upon Judges McCunn and Barnard to convert aliens into citizens for the coming election. Their courts literally became naturalization mills, sometimes grinding out a thousand new American citizens a day. Foreigners became Americans, as the *Tribune* put it, "with no more solemnity than the converting of swine into pork in a Cincinnati packing house." [9] To understand the extent of this conversion, there had been 70,604 naturalizations in the twelve previous years. In 1868 alone, some 41,112 aliens were naturalized; on one day, October 14, 1868, Judge McCunn's Superior Court alone naturalized in "indecent haste" some 2109, sometimes averaging three a minute. Of the naturalizations, only 10,000 were legitimate.[10] The New York Printing Company (William Tweed, president) printed 105,000 applications for citizenship and 69,000 certificates of naturalization. Batches of applications were given to Judges Barnard and McCunn, and they, seldom examining one properly, placed their initials on the certificates. The proceedings were not made public. Some immigrants who received certificates of naturalization, did not bother to appear in court. Witnesses were hired to confirm an applicant's qualifications. James Goff, for example, attested to the "good moral character" of 669 applicants. Forty-eight hours later, he was arrested for stealing a gold watch and two diamond rings.[11]

Fraud during election hours was one thing, but it did not end with the closing of the polls. The Ring pulled an old Republican trick—in reverse. Hall sent out a letter to all Democratic State Committee members throughout the state asking them to telegraph William Tweed, before election results were officially announced, all information regarding the election in their district. The telegram should read, said Hall:

> "This town will show a Democratic gain (or loss) over last year —(number)." Or this one, if sufficiently certain: "This town will give a Republican (or Democratic) majority of . . ." [12]

The letter, however, was not signed by A. Oakey Hall. Instead, the name of the chairman of the State Committee, Samuel J. Tilden, was forged. Hall received over 200 answers to this letter, and early in the evening of election day about one-third of the state's vote had been heard from. With this information, the Ring was able to manipulate the vote in the city to offset the returns from heavily Republican upstate New York. To prevent the Republicans from learning how the vote was going in the city, the Ring ordered a delay in counting the votes, while Tammany braves descended on the telegraph offices and tied up the wires by sending hundreds of telegrams. Tweed later testified they were prepared to telegraph the entire Bible if it were necessary.[13]

The art of manipulating the vote was a fairly simple one. As the reformer Robert Roosevelt explained it, one canvasser counted the ballots while the other recorded them. When the first had counted five votes, he sang out "tally" and his companion recorded the five ballots as *ten*. "In one instance," said Roosevelt in a speech, "this was done so enthusiastically that the Tammany candidate had received fifty 'tallies,' or five hundred votes, and had a large quantity yet uncounted, when the poll-clerk felt it advisable to inform the canvassers that there were only 450 names on the registry." Years later after the downfall of the Ring, Boss Tweed shed more light on how to stifle the voice of the people.

Q. What were they [Tammny Hall] to do, in case you wanted a particular man elected over another?
A. Count the ballots in bulk, or without counting them announce the result in bulk, or change from one to the other, as the case may have been.
Q. Then these elections really were no elections at all? The ballots were made to bring about any result that you determined upon beforehand?
A. The ballots made no result; the counters made the result.[14]

With these methods the Democrats carried Seymour and Blair in the presidential contest, and Hoffman, Tweed's compliant aristocrat, in the gubernatorial race. No one knew precisely how many fraudulent votes had been cast. During the Tweed investigation, an Alderman naïvely asked Tweed if he had ever given directions to any persons to falsify or change the result of the actual *bona fide* ballots cast. Tweed said it was more of a request than a direction. Asked if he knew how many fraudulent votes were cast, Tweed said, "It would need a man higher up in arithmetic than I am to do that." [15] Despite Oakey Hall's pious assurance that no fraud had occurred, it was estimated that the vote cast in New York City was 8 per cent in excess of its entire population and that illegal votes exceeded 50,000.[16] The election was so colossally fraudulent that it attracted national attention. The federal government, in fact, through the House of Representatives, set up a special committee to investigate it, but the investigation never went far enough to endanger the Tweed Ring, which was now firmly in power.

For the Ring, the corruption of 1868 was a necessary and practical expedient. The State legislature, under Republican auspices, had long since sapped away much of the city's authority. There were opportunities aplenty in the city for graft, but real power existed in Albany. It was simple political mathematics: control of city plus control of the state equaled complete dominance, with possible national implications. The building of a city organization and the election of Tweed to the State Senate was the first step;

the 1868 election the turning point; and the success of the 1869 elections opened an unlimited future.

The contrast between Tweed the Congressman and Tweed the State Senator was striking. At Washington he had been an obscure and unnoticed member devoid of influence; at Albany he was a political magnifico. For a weekly rent of $500 he occupied a luxurious suite of seven rooms on the second floor of Delevan House, elegantly furnished from the best of carpets to the best of liquor. And above the desk, "Mr. Tweed is inspired to all high and noble aims, by the contemplation of personal beauty and innocence as embedded in a photograph of himself."[17] Through these portals for business and pleasure came such robber barons as Jay Gould, Jim Fisk, and Daniel Drew, as well as statesmen like Peter Sweeny, and prominent lobbyists and legislators. Tweed lived like a prince. He traveled in regal style from New York to Albany in a Wagner parlor car. For large parties, to impress the local statesmen and newspapermen, he entertained lavishly at Albany's House of Mirth and the Tub of Blood. George W. Curtis of *Harper's Weekly* remembers Tweed striding into the great dining room of Delevan House at dinner time, surveying all the members of the legislature and the Third House:

> He had a benignant, paternal expression, as of a patriarch pleased to see his retainers happy. It was a magnificent rendering of Fagin and his pupils. You could imagine him trotting up and down in the character of an unsuspicious old gentleman with his handkerchief hanging out of his pocket, so that his scholars might show their skill in prigging a wipe. He knew which of that cheerful company was the Artful Dodger. . . . And he never doubted that he could buy every man in the room if he were willing to pay the price.[18]

Curtis's portrait was not far from being accurate. From 1868 to 1871, Tweed made the influence of the Ring one of the most potent political forces in State politics. This was achieved by a persistent campaign to make his power felt in every possible branch of the legislative process. He began by assuming leadership of two of the

Senate's most powerful committees, Finance and Internal Affairs. His influence there was such that when appropriations time arrived, the legislators were forced to court the Boss directly. Shrewdly he ingratiated himself with the rural members of the legislature, who traditionally feared and despised city politicians. He helped them pass pet measures for their farming districts, saw to it that they received a fair share of the state budget, often without exacting an honorarium—a true stroke of statesmanship. He commanded the purchasable members, the Black Horse Cavalry, a group of about thirty Democrats and Republicans. Carefully and profitably he cultivated two of the most important men in Albany, the lobbyists Hugh Hastings and A. D. Barber.

Hastings has been described as the most intellectual and popular man, second only to the famous Thurlow Weed, in the Albany lobby, a lobbyist's lobbyist, "the truest of friends and the bitterest of enemies." [19] He rated the title of "intellectual" from his book, which had the quaint title of *Ancient American Politics*. A. D. Barber, another polished and talented successor of Weed, was known as the King of the Lobby. As there was only one Bismarck, said Matthew Breen, there was in the history of the Albany lobby only one Barber. "He could pass or kill a bill quicker than any man in his time or line. He generally preferred killing bills to passing them, however, because he found 'Nay' votes cheaper than 'Yea' votes, and easier to get." [20]

Tweed assumed the leadership of the New York delegation of five Senators and twenty-one Assemblymen—one-sixth of the entire representation in the legislature—although this body was often a recalcitrant group. As a counterbalance, Tweed, with the aid of Sweeny, who was a constant visitor to Albany but always in the background, handled the Republicans in ways that even won the begrudging admiration of Samuel Tilden. Knowing that the success of their own legislation would often depend on Republican support, they never sought to incur needlessly the wrath of the opposition. When differences arose they were artful in compromise. They wooed the Republicans by marshaling Democratic support for some of their pet projects. Political debts were piled up as grateful small-town or farmer Republicans got the support of city Democrats for a new road, a new bridge, or a new appointment. Tweed and Sweeny were adept in probing for the weak points in the Republican ranks, the members who would co-operate for a bribe. Tilden said that Tweed was never so supreme as in his control over nearly the whole body of the Republican members. With their aid the Ring could suppress and punish a Democratic revolt. "The combination," said Tilden, "had such control over the Republicans at Albany and in this city, that a revolution in the Republican party was necessary to create an opposition; and, without an opposition, dissenting Democrats were powerless." [21]

Not all of this power was exercised from the Senate. One of the Ring's first victories was to gain control of the Speaker of the Assembly. The speaker actually had more power over the making of laws than the Governor. He appointed the committees of the Assembly, which spread the tentacles of Ring power deep into the Assembly. In the election of 1867, the Democrats won the Assembly for the first time in years, and it precipitated the first fight in the open between Tilden and Tweed for control. When the legislature met in 1868, Tweed forced the issue, a daring move against Tilden, the powerful chairman of the Democratic State Committee and one of the most influential Democrats in the party. Tilden backed John L. Flagg for the speakership, a man who had distinguished himself as Mayor of Troy. Flagg had an M.A. degree from Harvard, and it followed that he was "highly esteemed for his gentlemanly qualities." [22] Tweed supported William ("Billy") Hitchman, "of long features . . . and bold development of the head." He was a self-made man, that is, a Tweed-made political hack from the upper East Side. As his official biographers put it, he "carved" his way from carriage-painter, fireman, policeman, to the Tammany General Committee and the Assembly. To the two men who wrote short biographies about the members of the legislature, Billy Hitchman illustrates this lofty ideal: "It is the genius of our institutions that young men, born with noble impulses and honorable ambitions, as they press energetically on to the goal of their hopes, find the way opening clearer and brighter before them."[23] The way did indeed open clearer and brighter before Hitchman and the Ring. In the contest for the speakership, Tweed, "slipping around like a porpoise among the small fishes of the Assembly, varying the performance, now and then, by reverently raising his hands and blessing his dearly beloved Democratic children," won a smashing victory over Tilden.[24] For Tweed it meant control over one of the most influential figures in state government. He had managed the victory by winning over long-time supporters of Tilden, the upstate rural Democrats.[25] For Tilden, it was a humiliating defeat. In 1870 Tweed repeated his triumph by having Hitchman re-elected Speaker.

Behind a rock-like nose, determined lower lip, a languid mustache, Governor John T. Hoffman was a compliant tool to the Ring. He made an excellent Tammany figurehead. His Teutonic ancestry gave him a strong appeal to the Germans, while his wealth and noted family, linked by marriage to the Kissams and the Livingstons, gave him a measure of respectability in the eyes of the gentry. He was one of the silk-stocking members of the Tammany hierarchy. When he was Recorder, his stern action against the draft-rioters during the Civil War helped considerably to make him Mayor, with an added boost from Tweed and friends in 1866. While it has never been proved that he ever profited monetarily from the booty of the Tweed Ring, Hoffman was an intensely ambitious man who could turn his head at the right time. Thus with apparent good conscience he signed a raft of Ring legislation, such as the Erie Railroad bill, the Harlem Court House bill, the Jefferson Market Court bill, preposterous tax levies, and vetoed the reform measure to abolish separate bureaus in the county offices.[26] On one occasion, after a riot on Ward's Island, he indignantly demanded an investigation, calling for reform. But when the investigating committee of State legislators presented an enormous bill, covering their consumption of cigars and liquor, Hoffman seemed to lose his tongue.[27] Later, when the Ring started falling apart, Hoffman found a rare sense of independence, and uttered one of the few things he said worth remembering, "Save me from my friends." [28]

The Ring operated in the State legislature with the same boldness as it did in the city. "Sweeny and Hall scanned every measure introduced in either house to prevent enactment of innocent-appearing bills containing valuable grants of public property or a delegation of power for which a price had not been paid." [29] The lobbyists did business as usual. As one explained:

> When we get to Albany, we make out our lists, and, after studying them and comparing notes, we *classify* members, and make an estimate of what it is going to cost to get our bills through. We find out about how much each man expects, and who is running him. Then we arrange the thing in New York with certain people, whose consent is necessary. The price for a vote ranges from fifty dollars to five hundred, unless it is that of the chairman of a committee. *He* wants more because he has to appear on the record as originating the measure.[30]

Tweed paid men to vote for bills when they came up on the floor, or when this might embarrass the voters, as with the Republicans, they were paid to give their support in the Committee on the Whole.[31] Tweed explained another method:

> There were a great many bills granting charters, etc.; charters for a savings bank, or for a railroad, for which members were bought by their friends. Smith would stick in Brown's name as stockholder, and then Brown would get the bill passed for Smith; and after that, if there was anything in it, Brown would sell his share out.[32]

The Ring made some of its greatest profits, however, out of its partnership with the notorious James Fisk and Jay Gould and the ensuing Erie Railroad scandal. In 1864 the two speculators, Cornelius Vanderbilt and Daniel Drew, were on the eve of their famous battle for the control of the Erie Railroad. At that time, Gould was a pupil of Vanderbilt, and Fisk a pupil of Drew. By

1868 the positions were reversed, and the pupils were engaged with their mentors in a historic battle of corruption. Never before had the members of the New York legislature had such sums of money handed to them in the form of bribes. In the legislature of 1868, Tweed was one of Vanderbilt's agents on the floor of the Senate, and through Tweed's direction, Judge Barnard plagued Fisk and Gould with court injunctions that confounded their moves. Fisk and Gould soon saw that co-operation was to their advantage, and won Tweed and his Black Horse Cavalry over to their side. Tweed, Sweeny, and John Bradley, Sweeny's brother-in-law, were all made directors in the Erie Railroad. From stocks and other bonuses, Tweed in just three months realized profits of $650,000 from the Erie.[33] Sweeny, for acting as a receiver of the railroad for just forty-eight hours, received a fee of $150,000. In bribes to the legislature, the Erie spent nearly a million and a half dollars; Gould dispensed $586,000 of it; Tweed, more than $105,000; Sweeny, $150,000; and Fisk, more than $193,000.[34] Once asked if Gould suggested the names of the legislators to be bribed, Tweed replied, "I don't think he did. I was pretty well up on that myself." [35] For a period of three years, the Tweed Ring used its influence in the legislature and its control over the courts to act as companionable allies to the so-called Erie Ring. Of all the measures the Ring pushed through Albany, the most notorious was the Erie Classification bill, which legalized the Erie's fraudulent stock. For New York legislators it meant half a million dollars in bribes.[36] Ironically the least fraudulent claim was the $20,000 in "legal services" awarded to that erstwhile reformer, Samuel Tilden.[37] Tilden never lived this down. It plagued him throughout his political career and was particularly harmful when he ran for the Presidency.

While the alliance with Fisk and Gould increased the personal fortunes of the Ring, what interested it most in Albany were various financial measures, especially the annual tax levies. The first bill Tweed supported as a State Senator was the Adjusted Claims Act. An act carefully calculated for Connolly's talents, it not only empowered the Comptroller to adjust claims against the city, it also gave him the authority to raise money by bond issues. Thus the Adjusted Claims Act became a profitable source of graft: of the $3,300,000 in claims between July 1868 and November 1869, 55 to 65 per cent of it was divided among the Ring.[38]

The tax levies were handled in a special way. The Comptroller made up two budgets, one for the city and one for the county; these were submitted to the Speaker of the Assembly, who, in turn, referred them to the Committee on Affairs of Cities, a committee loaded heavily in favor of Tammany. There the budgets remained, as one writer said, to hatch more eggs. Many additions were made to them, fraudulent "jobs" of all kinds. It was not until the end of the session that the budgets returned to the desk of the Speaker. At this time the legislators, weary from the grind of state politics, were looking forward to leaving Albany and returning home. They were too impatient to check the authenticity of the hundred or more paragraphs of dreary financial prose and statistics; they generally forwarded this responsibility to the Governor. He approved the measures, and legislators voted with the New York members and passed the bills.[39]

Even when the tax levy bills passed both houses, this by no means meant an end to tinkering with the budget. Tweed's secretary was always present at budget time, especially when subcommittees from both houses met to compromise disagreements about the levies. He made it a point to obtain the last handling of the bills before they were passed on to the Governor.

> And rumor stated that this sly manipulator would adroitly slip into the officially endorsed coverings of the bills that had been before the Legislature, exact duplicates of the amended Tax Levies, with such new additions as were required to carry out the purposes of the Ring, and as the records of both Houses would show no objections to these additions (for they had never been read in either body) the bills would go to the Governor as if these additions had been ratified by both Houses and they would thus receive his approval.[40]

During an investigation, Thomas Jefferson Creamer, an old hand at tax levies, was questioned about them.

> "You said that some of them showed items that were excessive?"
>
> "Yes, sir; I don't suppose that there ever was an appropriation asked for of $500,000 that they had not to spend $150,000 to get it through." [41]

The fitting climax to the Tweed Ring's capture of the State legislature came with the 1869 elections, which enhanced Democratic power in Albany to an unprecedented degree. For the first time in twenty-four years, Democratic majorities were elected to the State legislature. Not since 1845 had the Democrats carried both the Senate and the Assembly. Of course, on election day there were a few incidents—fights at the polls, stuffed ballot boxes. Judge McCunn, for example, dismissed twenty-two repeaters on the ground that the arresting officer had detained them unnecessarily at the station house.[42] But as the *Times* said: "Generally the day was quiet."

The Tweed Ring now seemed invulnerable in both city and state. The new Democratic majorities swelled the ranks of the Black Horse Cavalry. The Ring controlled the key committees in both houses. Governor Hoffman, his ambitions aroused, looked forward to the coming election in the fall of 1870. If he could win re-election, he and many others thought he might have a chance for the Presidency. If this giddy dream came true, rumor had it the English might be treated to the spectacle of the bulky figure of William Marcy Tweed strolling into the Court of St. James's as the American Ambassador to England![43] Preposterous as this may sound, nothing seemed impossible for the Ring when the legislature convened in 1870.

15

THE WAR OF THE RINGS

'Tis the voice of the croaker—I hear him complain
Those Tammany boys, they are at it again.

John G. Saxe, "Old Tammany"

ONE OF THE BEST IRONIES in politics is that success often sows the seeds of disaster. The power of the Tweed Ring in city and state by 1870 seemed to many to have all the elements of a dictatorship, although in fact it never was. The final and ultimate basis of the Ring's leadership rested not on coercion but on co-operation. Like any other ruling group in the history of Tammany Hall, the Tweed Ring's political life depended upon the support of powerful ward leaders. But by the spring of 1870, co-operation fizzled into a major revolt against the Tweed clique. The Ring, ironically, had become too successful.

Success bred jealousy, resentment, and ambition among the ward leaders. Success created more patronage but also more mouths to feed, and there was less to go around, at least not enough to satisfy the voracious appetite of the leaders of the Twelfth and Eighth Wards. Success demanded more discipline, but there were Tammany leaders who, having been disciplined, eagerly awaited revenge. Success meant booty, and the ward chiefs gazed with envious eyes at the gaudy mansions of the Ring along Fifth Avenue. To compound it all, there was intense resentment at Sweeny's ultimatum that seemed to strike at their independence. He decreed that all the New York City delegation in both houses of the State legislature must promise not to introduce a bill of any kind without the consent of a majority in secret caucus. The ward leaders, in effect, resembled those medieval feudal barons who saw in the growing power of the king an usurpation of their former, long-enjoyed independence and authority.

The revolt began with the dissatisfactions of three local leaders: Henry "Prince Hal" Genet of the Twelfth Ward; Mike Norton of the Eighth; and Thomas Jefferson Creamer, who dreamed of being Mayor. Dissatisfaction begat dissension which begat the sin of independence from party authority. Independence demanded discipline. The Ring threatened to destroy them if they attempted to run for re-election as State Senators in 1869. Only after humiliating reassurances that their previous acts of independence and lack of teamwork had been dreadful mistakes were they permitted to run.

After being re-elected in 1869, the three leaders immediately struck back and sought recruits for a revolt. They found John Fox, powerful on the waterfront, who thought the Ring blocked his chances of being Sheriff; Jimmy O'Brien, the ex-Sheriff, who presented a claim of a third of a million dollars against the city, only to be refused payment by the Ring; Joseph Ledwith, an unhappy ward leader and Police Justice; John Morrissey, the politician-gambler, who had served the Ring well as a repeater but who had not been served well in his ambitions to become Chamberlain; Jimmy Hayes, who had fallen out with Tweed; Lawrence D. Kiernan, an honest Assemblyman who thought the rebels sincerely wanted reform; George H. Purser, who felt slighted when the booty was passed around; Peter Mitchell, an ambitious and tough leader in the lower wards; and the firm of Jones and Company, who financed the revolt in revenge for being squeezed out of supplying the city's printing and stationery. Through Samuel Tilden, the services of Manton Marble, editor of the *New York World*, were obtained, and the *New York Sun*, which loved a fight, also joined. There were many others, also, who saw in the toppling of the Ring's power an enhancement of their own political fortunes.

This group, composed mainly of seasoned politicians, sprinkled with a few well-meaning reformers and rookie malcontents—"a dashing and gritty set of fellows," as the *Sun* called them—banded together, chose Apollo Hall as their headquarters, and gave themselves the compelling and innocent name of the Young Democracy.

The Young Democracy, old in the ways of political infighting, began a noisy campaign, styling themselves reformers, opponents of the insidious Tweed Ring, who would redeem New York's political virtue. While the *Sun* and the *World* leveled their heavy guns on the Ring with such headlines as "Tweed Must Walk the Plank," "Honest Democracy's Contest with Traitors," "The Ring Has No Strength Whatever in the State; It's a Dead-Duck," members of "ye fierce Democracie" unfurled a banner across Apollo Hall reading, DEATH TO THE TWEED AND SWEENY RING, THE PEOPLE SHALL BE EMANCIPATED. On the steps of Apollo Hall, the sonorous Tammany maverick Henry Clinton promised: "Whatever may be our political future—through sunshine and storm—through prosperity and adversity—come weal or woe, sink or swim, survive or perish, we will never relax our efforts, until this corrupt, infamous and damnable Ring is broken, destroyed and utterly exterminated." [1] The Young Democracy made such a parade of its virtue, said one unconvinced newspaper, that it reminded one of a certain lady who "doth protest too much." [2]

Unlike other great Tammany brawls, before and after this period, the battle was not fought in the voting booths and saloons on election day. The Democrats had come into office riding on the promise that they would give New York a restoration of local powers. For a generation New Yorkers had been clamoring for more independence. Home rule continued down to La Guardia's time, Arthur Mann has said, as "an article of faith, a religious tenet." [3] The Tweed Ring, acutely aware of the demand for more home rule and just as aware that some of the most formidable men of Tammany had joined the Young Democracy's revolt, presented a solution for both problems. On February 3, 1870, Alexander

Frear, a Tweed henchman, presented on the floor of the Assembly a new charter for New York, officially known as "An Act to Reorganize the Government of New York." It was one of the most ingenious, imaginative, and effective schemes ever concocted by the Ring. The Tweed charter, as it came to be called, was remarkable in that it could accomplish several things with one stroke. First, restore some autonomy to New York, but not enough to incur the wrath of the Republicans. Second, incorporate many of the changes which reformers had for years been demanding. Third, reorganize the government of New York so that those in the Young Democracy who held official positions would soon be put out of office. And last but not least important, provide new opportunities for graft. The Tweed charter was, indeed, a remarkable document, and it was not long before the Young Democracy introduced one very near like it. The War of the Rings, therefore, was fought in the State Assembly and the Senate. It was a battle of city charters, and political control of New York was to be the victors' spoils.

New York government suffered from a lack of direct responsibility and from confusing and overlapping jurisdictions. The Tweed charter met the problem of responsibility in a manner ahead of its time in many ways. Government power was consolidated in the hands of the Mayor. Responsibility was sharpened by giving the Mayor the power to appoint department heads, who in turn had to report to and were responsible to the Mayor. Department heads were given clear lines of responsibility and were free from interference from the old and often corrupt Common Council. In a clause tacked on the tax levy, which followed the charter, the Mayor was given powers of appointment and removal of all court attendants. The powers by which the Governor and other state authorities could appoint or remove city officials were abolished, such officers being appointed by the Mayor. The Mayor must bring to trial any official accused of malfeasance, and the Board of Aldermen could bring the Mayor to trial for the same charge. The Board of Aldermen could appropriate money only by a three-fourths vote of all the members. Those on the two boards of Aldermen who had joined the Young Democracy were taken care of in a clause that practically legislated them out of office—a new election was called for the next May. Many of the overlapping jurisdictions between departments were swept away. The Commissions of Police, Fire, and Health were withdrawn from their extended Metropolitan jurisdiction and resolved into local departments without the loss of any power in respect to the city. The Department of Finance was placed under the Comptroller; confusion on the docks was resolved by the creation of a Department of Docks; the Departments of Streets and the Croton Aqueduct were absorbed by a new Department of Public Works.

In other measures introduced with the charter, the Board of Supervisors, long a breeding place for corruption (and a legislative branch effectively invaded by the Young Democracy), was abolished. The tax levy contained a clause establishing a Board of Special Audit, composed of the Mayor, Comptroller, Commissioner of Public Works, and President of the Park Department, who were authorized to manage the financial affairs of the city government. Final power over the tax levies still remained, however, with the State legislature. The Board of Special Audit was similar to the later Boards of Apportionment and Estimate.

There were, of course, a few loopholes. The Commissioner of Public Works could be removed only after being convicted by all six judges of the Court of Common Pleas. The absence of a single judge would prevent removal. Control over the Board of Audit allowed the Ring to cover up what had already been stolen and also gave it new chances for plunder. The plan of making appointees of the Mayor serve longer terms than the Mayor was an obvious device to maintain some of Hall's appointments in office in the event a reform Mayor was elected.[4]

The architects of this plan were Hall and Sweeny, although Hall never admitted it. Once asked who drew up the charter, the Board of Supervisors' bill, and the special clause in the tax levy, Hall answered with characteristic flippancy. "Mike Norton, on account of his legal lore; General Pratt, because he's modest; and the Honorable Mr. Faulkner, late Temperance candidate for the Assembly, on account of his familiarity with the Rum business." [5]

Tweed could hardly conceal his glee at the prospect of his charter's routing the Young Democracy rascals. "All veteran office holders," he said, "in the abolished departments must give way. They must be removed. Old abuses will be wiped out, and a new order of things will spring up, which in their operation will be necessarily healthful." [6]

The charter of the Young Democracy differed only in a few details.[7] Hungry for patronage, the rebels wanted to abolish the Central Park Commission, while the Tweed charter kept it intact but allowed the Mayor appointive powers which could rid it of any undesirable member. The Young Democracy also introduced a Supervisors' bill, the same as the Ring's, but went one step farther with a Police bill which literally would have made the force a political machine.

After the Tweed Ring exposures, there was almost unanimous indignation about the insidiousness of the charter. At the time it was being debated and passed, however, those who later scorned it were its most ardent supporters. The leading reform group in the city, the Citizens' Association, gave it full and enthusiastic backing. Indeed, the charter contained almost point by point what this group had been clamoring for since 1866.[8] Some of the most prominent men in the city, like Moses Taylor, H. B. Claflin, C. L. Tiffany, Andrew Gilsey, as well as W. and J. Sloane and Company, petitioned the Senate for its passage.[9] While Horace Greeley had some reservations—he was more interested in reform of the election laws—he did say the charter had "many excellent advances." [10] The Union League Club, dominated by Republicans, protested its passage, but only by a small majority and after a tough contest. The real basis of the League's unhappiness was that it was a Democratic measure which had stolen the League's thunder. For years the League had been demanding many of the changes incorporated in the charter, such as more concentration of power in the Mayor, more appointive offices, and a separate docks department.[11] Even the leading anti-Ring organ, the *New York Times*, at first showing good Republican skepticism, changed its mind and made the extraordinary statement that "Senator Tweed is in a fair way to distinguish himself as a reformer."[12]

Considering the abuse later heaped upon it, the Tweed charter—created ironically by the most notorious political thieves in the city's history—was a reform measure. The city paid two-fifths of the state's taxes; its population was one-fourth of the entire state population; its seaport, its geographical position, its creaking governmental structure, gave the city the right for more autonomy and administrative reform. The experience of later years has shown, said James Bryce, that the Tweed charter and the accompanying legislation "were for the most part sound and wise, according to principle and the most advanced modern theory of municipal administration. [The Ring] tended to give the city greater power over its own local affairs, to simplify its extremely complex administrative institutions, and to center the responsibility for the administration of local business in very few hands." The charter's only fault was that "these hands were at the moment unclean and grasping hands."[13] Other scholars have agreed with this appraisal.[14]

The War of the Rings drew first blood on the Tweed charter itself. No sooner had it been introduced than Senator Genet opened fire with a fusilade of amendments, and the charter staggered back wounded into the Committee of Cities, a rear-line bivouac of the Ring. The Young Democracy showed surprising strength, and the Ring was forced to bide its time. The rebels' charter fared no better. A newspaper said it was "like a child of sin; it has been 'toted' about from city to city, and from house to house, and laid on every man's doorstep, with the humble request . . . that somebody would take it up and adopt it."[15] For a long time the contest was a parliamentarian stalemate, as each side introduced measures and countermeasures. The legislature became so involved with the battle of the charters, Police bills versus Supervisors' bills, that nothing was accomplished. It reminded one journal of the time Queen Elizabeth asked a politician what had recently been passed in Parliament. "May it please your Majesty," he said, "six weeks!" [16]

That the Young Democracy could maintain such resistance in the face of the Ring's known strength in the legislature seemed to indicate that the Ring was weakening. The *World* said it heard the death knell of the Ring. The politicians' uncanny instinct for self-preservation was aroused, and several on the Tammany General Committee wavered and then joined forces with the rebels. Even Judge Cardozo tentatively switched sides. Most of the pundits had expected an early and decisive victory for the Ring, and its apparent inability to overcome this resistance made it appear that the Young Democracy might be replacing it.

But Tweed, Sweeny, Hall, and Connolly had not been standing idly by. While the rebels were counting on the rural Democrats to carry the breach, the Ring wooed the enemy, the Republicans. The Democrats had won a majority in the 1869 elections, but only a slim one—seven in the Assembly and one in the Senate. The support of enough Republicans could break the deadlock. Accordingly, the Ring quietly built a war-chest: plunder from many graft operations was siphoned into Albany. Ring contractors were forced to contribute a total of $200,000 for the cause. Senator William Woodin, who represented the honest yeomen from Cayuga and Wayne counties, was given $200,000 to distribute among five Republicans.[17] As the official biographers of the legislators said about Woodin, "few Senators have been more influential in shaping legislation." [18] Patronage in the new Department of Public Works was promised the Republicans. And many others were tempted by bribes. Hugh Hastings and A. D. Barber were given $20,000 and $112,550 respectively as "lobby commissions." [19] William M. Graham had his income increased. As Tweed later explained, "I was giving him money all the time. It was $1000 today, $500 tomorrow, $10,000 the next day...." [20] Republican Senator Benjamin Wood kept complaining about how poor he was and asked

Tweed if he would take an interest in a rectifying distillery. Teetotaler Tweed, who was more interested in a charter than whisky, gave Wood $40,000 to vote the right way and told him to forget about the distillery.[21] And on it went until the Ring distributed $600,000 in bribes. As Andrew Garvey said, "The prices charged were very high in those days."[22] To make matters legal, as it were, Tweed promised the Republicans to support their new election law, an excellent piece of legislation—if it could be enforced.

That "dashing and gritty set of fellows" was unaware of these negotiations. The Young Democracy scheduled March 22 as the day for the assault, confident the Ring was ripe for plucking. All went well at first. Three bills of the Young Democracy—the charter, Police bill, and Supervisors' bill—passed through the Committee of the Whole and were seemingly safe for adoption. With apparent victory within their reach, Assemblyman Dennis Burns, an ardent Tweed supporter, moved that all three be sent back to committee with power to strike out the enacting clause. There were enough Republican votes to carry the measure. Suddenly and decisively, the rebels' cause seemed lost. Tom Fields, flushed and plump, waddled to a chair and sat down with a sigh. Daniel Murphy strolled to his chair, "his jocund face," said the *Herald*, "not showing a single St. Patrick's Day wrinkle"; George Washington Plunkitt walked around as if he had "come out of the same bonnet box and fresh from the hands of the same Albanian Fibaro."[23]

Staggered but not defeated, the Young Democracy rallied to counter with two effective moves. George McLean, the Street Commissioner, was persuaded to dismiss his deputy, Bill Tweed, from the department. Following this flanking action, the rebels moved in from the rear. Taking advantage of the by-laws of the Tammany Society, they called for a meeting of the Tammany General Committee to entertain a motion to depose Tweed and elect one of their own number in his place as chairman of the

Democratic County Committee. More than half the General Committee was persuaded that the dismissal of Tweed as Grand Sachem would crush the Ring and renew the chance for another attempt to pass the Young Democracy's charter, and so they signed a petition for a convening of the meeting. Tweed was by the law of the society forced to comply. It was a brilliant move. On the threshold of defeat the Young Democracy had renewed the battle; their goal was to capture Tammany Hall itself. The meeting, set for March 28, aroused the whole city. Tweed, now vulnerable on both flanks, from Albany and the city, was forced to leave the State capital with the charter fight still undecided, and return to New York to fight for his political life.

The *Sun* announced triumphantly the "Tweed Ring's Waterloo," and for spite's sake followed it up with an interview with the Boss himself.

> "Do you anticipate a hot time tomorrow night?" asked the reporter.
>
> "Mark my words," said Tweed, "they are desperate men. They will seize upon the least pretext for assassination. For instance, supposing one of their gang should call me a damned liar, and one of my hotheaded friends should resent it and punch his head. A general fight would be the result. Pistols would be drawn, and somebody might get hurt."[24]

The Boss told a *Tribune* reporter that Tammany was aware of "its moral strength" and did not intend to allow the rough-and-ready element to capture the organization.[25] New Yorkers were prepared for a Donnybrook.

What occurred instead was just a smoothly executed Tammany massacre without bloodshed. A crowd of expectant citizens waited outside Tammany Hall. The General Committee arrived and was prevented from entering the building. Five hundred policemen surrounded Tammany Hall with drawn clubs. In a fit of civic passion, the Grand Sachem Tweed had alerted the Police Commissioners to a possible riot in Tammany Hall. The Commissioners Henry Smith and Benjamin Franklin Manierre, both good Tammany Republicans, responded to the crisis. It was announced solemnly that a riot might endanger the lives of innocent citizens in Bryant's Minstrel Hall next door to Tammany. Obviously there was only one thing to do: the police must stop the meeting of the General Committee. The meeting was stopped—and the Tweed Ring scored another triumph.[26] Tweed returned in triumph to Albany buttressed by his *coup* in New York to resume the fight for a new charter.

The *New York Sun*, sensing disaster and scurrying back into the good graces of the Ring, announced not a "Barefaced Outrage," but "The Most Stupendous Political Joke of the Century—The Gathering of the Tribes at the Wigwam, but the Wigwam Closed against the Braves—The Camp-fires Guarded by a Regiment of Henry Smith's Policemen—The Grand Sachem Outflanks the Enemy—The Howlings of the Savages." The Young Democracy retreated to Irving Hall, howled, and made mighty speeches—Henry Genet proclaimed that the Ring had shown the white feather.

The Boss was a gentleman about the whole thing. Asked if he felt sorry Tammany Hall was closed against him, he answered, "Yes, it has worried me considerable. I can't account for their action. It astonished me. Why, the last thing I did was to give my friends of the *World* seven entrance tickets to Tammany Hall. I suppose they will give me a bitter dose tomorrow morning." Several friends came to interrupt the interview. "Why Mr. Tweed," said one, "you have become thin. What's the matter with you?" "Grief," answered a Tweed henchman. "That's what's the matter with the boss. He is so sorry that he was locked out of Tammany Hall tonight. It ain't serving an old Democrat right to lock him out of his home."[27]

The revolt which had been so formidable collapsed. The Young Democracy retreated, said the *Times*, to the lower reaches of

Irving Hall "to wail their monstrous melody to the moon."[28] Back in Albany, Tweed sensed victory. "I have declared," said Tweed, "by the Almighty that I will press this bill [the charter] to a vote by all the energy and ability that I possess." Replied Henry Genet, who fought to the bitter end, "I don't see any necessity to call upon the Almighty about it."[29]

On April 4 the charter came before the Senate Committee on Cities for public debate; William Marcy Tweed was chairman. The dynamic reformer Samuel J. Tilden delivered an insipid speech against it. Directing his remarks to Tweed, he said: "I come here, sir, to aid no party of men; I come here simply to contribute what I may be able, however little, to a result in which you, I, and all of us have a great interest. . . . And let me say here, that if I know my own heart, I have no feeling of unkindness to any human being. To yourself, Mr. Chairman—." Tweed interrupted, angrily: "I am sick of the discussion of this question."

Tilden continued maintaining his poise, ". . . or to anybody else, I am unconscious of ever having done an unkind act or entertained an unkind feeling." Tilden went on to say that the Ring had capitalized on home rule, and concluded: "Mr. Chairman, I am not afraid of the stormy sea of popular liberty. I still trust the people," and left the room, according to his biographer, "ashy white," and revealing "suppressed rage."[30] Tilden's criticisms had no effect. Horace Greeley entertained mild objections. The Citizens' Association representative, Joseph F. Daly, eulogized the charter, and it passed out of committee with no amendments. The next day the charter passed the Senate with only two dissenting votes from Henry Genet and the Honorable Francis S. Thayer, an honest Republican from Troy. The Ring's Supervisors' bill and Tax Levy bill passed soon after. To pass these bills and the charter, the Tweed Ring paid an estimated million dollars in bribes.[31]

The Young Democracy was smashed. In the fashion of Tammany revolts, and as a measure of the Ring's acuity, some were punished, some allowed to return to the fold. The Ring negotiated not a Carthaginian peace but a truce according to John Milton's couplet:

While the lamp holds out to burn
The vilest sinner may return.

John Morrissey, James Hayes, and James O'Brien were sent into the wilderness (to return another day); Edmund Jones and Company never collected their claims; Judge Cardozo was forgiven—he scratched his name off the list of dissenting General Committeemen at the last minute—and lesser figures in the offices of Aldermen, Supervisors, and Street Commissioner were punished. But the rebel Ring leaders were placated. The Ring learned its lesson, and the barons of the most powerful wards were forgiven. Creamer and Norton were bribed and given patronage to give their votes to the Tweed charter, and this move of conciliation took the final resistance from the Young Democracy. Even Genet for all his aggressiveness was given the commissionership to the Harlem Court House. All three thereafter were faithful and loyal to the Ring to the end. One writer provided an epitaph for the War of the Rings.

O, children, you should never let
Your angry passions rise;
Your little hands were never made
To scratch out each other's eyes.[32]

The final delicious taste of victory for the Ring came on April 19, 1870, when Boss Tweed was re-elected Grand Sachem, and the rebellious General Committeemen were replaced by the Ring's candidates with an overwhelming vote of 242 to 23. The casualties included Tilden, Morrissey, and Fox.[33]

With the charter struggle settled, the Boss returned again to New York and the whole East Side turned out to greet him in Tweed Plaza. Chinese lanterns surrounded the area. Cannons boomed a welcome. Fink's Washington Band played the *Star-*

Spangled Banner as a torchlight parade poured into the area. The "Young Men's Democratic William M. Tweed Club" carried an illuminated banner with the Boss's picture. Speeches were made, the band played, and balloons crowded the sky. The crowd eagerly awaited the Boss, but he never appeared. Tweed knew his limitations as a speechmaker, and instead of coming sent this letter:

> The generous confidence and unwavering friendship of constituents toward a public servant is his highest praise. Duties of an urgent public character compel me to be absent; they, of course, are superior to political pleasure, or the pleasant society of friends.
>
> In political contests as in military battles, the person happening to be at the head of the forces at the moment of victory obtains the primary credit. . . . Yet there are always among his associates and soldiers those who perhaps deserve more credit. I congratulate you, fellow citizens, upon the restoration of municipal rights. I trust our victory will, by wise use of its fruits, result in raising our party above the plane of selfish aggrandizement and redound to the harmony and success of our majestic party in this Metropolis and throughout the State and Union.[34]

Now the triumph of the Ring seemed complete. Only high days appeared ahead.

16

HALCYON DAYS

The *Times* has thundered, *Tribune* popped.
These jolly rogues have danced and hopped.
Harper employed the roaring Nast,
To give a thund'rous, trumpet blast;
Tweed asks the newsboys, while they shout,
"Say, what're they goin' t' do about it?"

"The Downfall of Tammany Hall"

The Tweed charter became law on April 6, 1870. In July 1871 the *New York Times* electrified the entire state and country by exposing the Ring frauds. The fifteen months intervening can be called the halcyon days of the Ring. Many of the acts described in previous chapters happened during this period, but there were other events as well.

The Ring immediately made use of the new reorganization of city government. The enlarged powers of the Mayor concentrated city appointments in his hands. Hall handled them with the same dexterity a gambler used in running his game of three-card monte. The *New York Times* was misled, for it found Hall's appointments "far above average" and they "should be satisfactory." [1] Hall, however, merely played the old Tammany trick of appointing several honorable and respectable men who would attract enough public attention to obscure appointments of less honorable and hardly respectable men. Thus the Ring's spokesmen and the newspapers made much out of the fact that such "respectabilities" as George McClellan, the Civil War hero; John T. Agnew, the well-known merchant; the reformer Wilson G. Hunt; Jacob A.

Westervelt, an old Knickerbocker and once Mayor of New York; William Wood, a wealthy banker; honest Andrew Green; and Henry Hilton, "a gentle man . . . a gentleman of culture and refinement," were named to important offices. Less was said about the appointments of a raft of Tammany and Tammany Republican faithful—Billy Hitchman, John J. Bradley, Alexander Frear, James S. Hennessy, Owen W. Brennan, Thomas Fields, Henry Smith, Benjamin Franklin Manierre, and Isaac Bell. City Hall was in fact besieged with office seekers, from the elegant gentleman down to the brawny street laborer, "and streams of water, mud and tobacco juice flowed together into offensive pools upon the floors"; the corridors resounded with swearing, talking, and laughter which drove "the ushers to madness." [2] The chairman of the Liquor Dealers' Association was appointed to the Excise Board. James McGregor, a well-known repeater and "shoulder-hitter," was reappointed Superintendent of Buildings, although a month before he had inspected a building which later collapsed and killed five people, and just a week before his appointment, within hours after he had attested the soundness of another building, it suddenly became a shambles.[3] Peter Barr Sweeny was made head of the Department of Parks. Now a Tammany naturalist, as one wag quipped, he left for Europe to study parks and "culture in rural affairs." One reformer, long accustomed to Ring rule in the city parks, cried, "Ringman, spare that tree!" [4] The most important appointment of all was revealed in this letter from Mayor Hall to Tweed:

> It is an important trust. It will require a man for the place of firmness, decision, and great executive ability coupled with extensive knowledge of the details of the duties. . . . But I cannot resist the impulse to my feelings, as well as of the high sense of justice I mediate toward the public, in now writing to you to say it is my intention to confer on you that important trust of Commissioner of Public Works. . . . I shall ask you to accept it untrammeled and I feel already assured that in your hands, the Department will augment the glory of the city and your fame.[5]

Nor did the Ring slight the opportunity incorporated in the tax levy of 1870, now called variously "the budget for frauds" and "Boss Tweed's Plum Tree." The tax levy not only placed the financial affairs of the city in their hands but also allowed them to adjust all claims made against the city and county prior to the passage of the act. Here was a boon of massive proportions, and, characteristically, the Ring took its opportunities. On May 5, 1870, which Tilden called "a day destined to be famous in our municipal annals," the Board of Audit authorized the payment of $6,312,500 in claims, of which 90 per cent was fraudulent. By 1871 the Board had issued nearly $15,750,000 of fraudulent bills, of which at least $12,250,000 was sheer plunder.[6]

The true measure of the Ring's strength, however, was shown in its control over the state Democratic party. At the Rochester convention in September 1870, the party seemed agreeable to the Ring's every whim and influence. Accompanying Tweed and Sweeny to the convention was a Praetorian guard of hundreds of New York shoulder-hitters, tagged "Tweed's lambs." The Ring wanted the insurance of numbers and those experienced in intimidation in the event of another rebellion like that of the Young Democracy. The lambs, in fact, caused such a disturbance on the trains (free passes provided by the Erie)—stealing, drinking, fighting—that the Mayor of Rochester asked for the trains to be delayed until daylight, to protect local inhabitants against an invasion at night.

The legend of Samuel J. Tilden casts him in the heroic role as the destroyer of the Tweed Ring, which helped him in his campaign for the Presidency in 1876. In October of 1870, at Rochester, however, Tilden appeared to be more of a Tweed lamb than an avenging angel. The State Central Committee, Samuel Tilden chairman, was herded into secret session in Sweeny's room and approved the Ring's program with apparently little revolt from its leader. The Rochester convention could have been the occasion for a sweeping attack against the Tweed Ring. Tilden, enjoying great prestige, could have marshaled the so-called "Hayloft and

Cheese Democracy," the rural Democrats, reformers, and dissident city politicians. As the one who gave the convention's opening address, he had an auspicious opportunity to rally an attack. He did none of this. His address was an insipid harangue on the European war, the danger of standing armies, the glories of the American political system, the evils of centralization and dangers from the exponents of this doctrine, the Republicans. He seemed more shocked about King William and Bismarck than about Tweed, Sweeny, Connolly, or Hall. In fact, the Ring was never mentioned.[7]

When the Young Democracy, now under new and more respectable management, with the exception of John Morrissey and James O'Brien, found themselves barred from the convention, Tilden explained lamely that he had given the convention tickets to the regular Tammany delegation and none were left, since several hundred had mysteriously vanished from his room. Instead of contesting delegates, the Young Democracy suffered the humiliation of being admitted as spectators. Where Tilden could have fought over the naming of the temporary chairman, he obligingly nominated William C. De Witt, a Tammany politician from Brooklyn. The nomination was vigorously but unsuccessfully opposed by more than a majority of the delegates from Brooklyn.[8] From that time on the convention went smoothly. Tammany men were nominated for office, Hoffman and Hall were selected to run for re-election, and one William Tweed, Jr., was nominated for Congress. The *Herald* called the convention the "most out-and-out Tammany demonstration ever held in the State of New York."[9] Perhaps the most fitting symbol of the entire affair was that Samuel J. Tilden had his pocket picked and lost his gold watch.

If the convention demonstrated the power of the Tammany Tiger, it also caused deep rumblings from the city. The Ring's power was seen to be effectively awesome; for over a year the *Times* and *Harper's Weekly* had been crying "foul," but with little concrete evidence to back it up. It was near election time, and

Republican papers which were normally quiet toward the Ring at other times came alive. More and more ugly rumors circulated about city corruption. To quiet the rising discontent, the Ring selected as its spokesman the "classic and eloquent" Richard O'Gorman, a silver-tongued Irishman with a bag of oratorical tricks. O'Gorman made a speech for the Tammany General Committee that was widely circulated for publication. It was the most remarkable speech ever delivered in behalf of the Tweed Ring. O'Gorman reminded the public of Mayor Hall's notable appointments to city government; he soothed their suspicions about the rising debt, reminding them of the Democrats' provisions for charities and schools; he attacked the Republicans. "We appeal to no passion; we raise from the grave no dead facts. We are the party of the present." The ruling Democrats, he said, wanted taxes reduced, honest use of public money, the poor relieved of their burden, "honest industry" for all. Then he moved to the crux of the message:

> Now, fellow citizens, what is the meaning of this word "Ring"? A Ring I take to be a collection of men united for some common object. If the object be bad, it is a bad Ring—if good, it is a good Ring. . . . There is the Whiskey Ring, the Land Grabbing Ring, and the Gold Ring, and the Bessemer-steel Ring, and all the other Rings in which the Republicans in Congress have been disporting themselves. These are the "bad" Rings, for they are conspiracies to plunder and defraud and dishonor the American people. . . . But if the Ring referred to means a body of men in the City of New York directing, organizing, guiding and governing the Democratic Party in this City, and governing it so that the effect and history of the Party expresses strong success, then I say that a "Ring" is a necessity; it is a good "Ring," and I, for one, am in favor of it. (Enthusiastic applause.) If instead of the present Ring composed, if you will, of Mr. Tweed, Mr. Sweeny and Mr. Hall—if, instead of that, there is to be a Ring composed of any other men I have ever heard named in what is called the "Young Democratic Party," I for one will stand by the old Ring, because I believe it

has more sagacity, more power, more intelligence, more political skill, and more promise of success than the other.[10]

But even O'Gorman's comforting words and plump clichés did not stem a rising dissension. The attack on the Ring, which had been scattered and generalized, now centered specifically on the Comptroller's books. If these were examined, it was said, vast schemes and dark deeds would be revealed to the public. Shrilly and persistently, reformers, Republicans, and rebel Democrats demanded an investigation; tension from some quarters and glee from others mounted over the expected explosion. And trouble for the Tweed Ring seemed imminent, indeed, when Hall, forced to bow before public pressure, called upon the patriarch of the House of Astor to head a blue-ribbon investigating committee composed of some of the most respectable and distinguished men in New York City: Moses Taylor, Marshall O. Roberts, George K. Sistaire, Edward Schell, E. D. Brown; John Jacob Astor, chairman. It was a brilliant move on the part of the reformers. The timing was perfect. The Astor Committee would reveal massive evidence of corruption just before the election; the public would be shocked, and with one burst of righteous indignation it would go to the polls and vote Tammany and the Tweed Ring out of office. While the committee toiled over the records of Comptroller Connolly, the city waited with great expectations, and the reformers, nearly bursting with self-confidence, planned for the great day of redemption. On the very eve of the November election the committee made its report. It would be difficult to find in the annals of American urban history a greater example of political whitewash. The businessmen of the committee feared the retaliatory power of the Ring more than they hoped for reform, and shamefully put their own interests ahead of the public interest. The Astor Committee certified that the account books were "faithfully kept, that we have personally examined the securities of the department and sinking fund and found them correct." The financial affairs of the city under the charge of Richard Connolly "are administered in a

Three Blind Mice! See how they Run!
The *Times* cut off their Tails with a Carving-Knife.

Cartoon by Thomas Nast ridiculing the Astor Committee's whitewashing of the Tweed Ring; courtesy of the New-York Historical Society, New York City

correct and faithful manner." The committee gave the city the reassurances that, if the present rate of redemption was maintained, the total debt would be extinguished in less than twelve years.

Later, but not in time for the November elections, an investigation discovered that the committee had not examined the books in a manner befitting their high position in the financial community. They had underestimated the city debt by thirty million dollars![11] They missed the fact that a check for $35,000 had been raised by the receiver to $135,000. The "slightest examination," said one writer, "would have disclosed payment of more that $15 million in fraudulent claims in the first few months of the year."[12]

The *World* and the *Sun*, friendly to the Ring, said it only showed the character, capacity, experience, and energy to govern the city—all was well. Infuriated, the *Times* said it was easier for a camel to pass through the eye of a needle than for a rich man to commit a wrong.[13] And George Templeton Strong noted in his diary that he went through the "farce" of registering as a voter merely from a sense of duty.[14]

The whitewash from the Astor committee, and its "perfect" timing, was another *coup* on the part of the Tweed Ring. The committee's report instantly dispersed the dark suspicions of corruption and lulled the public once again into complacency. Tammany celebrated with one of the largest and gayest election demonstrations in its history. To remind the voters of registration day, Tammany warriors fired at daybreak several hundred twenty-inch shells. Unhappily, one went out of range and sunk a ship in the East River. There was a giant torchlight parade of 50,000 red-shirted Democratic faithful. A rally brought together on the same platform Horatio Seymour, James Fisk, August Belmont, Samuel J. Tilden, John Hoffman, and William Marcy Tweed ("I will only say a few golden words—go home early, work industriously . . ."). James Fisk, "the improbable rascal," arrayed in gaudy evening clothes, mentioned his friendship with Tweed, Sweeny, "and all the great Indians of this lodge." He spoke of the Federal troops sent by that black Republican Grant to guard the ballot boxes, saying he was not afraid of soldiers and it was "high time I should take a hand with you . . . if I find an opportunity I shall vote three times a day. I have got fired up with Democracy."[15]

It was another quiet election day. The rum-set prowled the streets, "men with red noses and other signs of bibulous tendencies." J. K. Murphy, a bartender working for Tammany, labored so hard at supplying repeaters with whisky that he himself collapsed from it. A newspaper reporter saw a Tammany politician—"with a greasy exterior, a leering expression, and his head covered with knotted and combined locks"—give a man $5.00 to change his vote from Thomas Ledwith to A. Oakey Hall. A United States marshal, attempting to arrest a ballot stuffer, had a revolver shoved in his mouth, but was miraculously rescued in time. The marshal's assailant was released after he explained to Judge John McCunn that "it was done in fun."[16]

The election confirmed the power of the Tweed Ring. All Tammany candidates for Congress were elected. Hall won with a majority of 24,645 votes, defeating Thomas A. Ledwith, a Democratic maverick, whose support from reformers and Republicans was not enough. The Ring added new officers to their already bulging list: the Sheriff, all the Coroners, the County Clerk, and nineteen out of twenty-two School Trustees. Combined with Tammany's victory in the Alderman's election of May 1870, the Ring seemed more than firmly entrenched in the city. For the State legislature the results were equally impressive. Hoffman was re-elected Governor handily over the Republican candidate, General Stewart L. Woodford. As testimony to the efficiency of the Ring's election organization, New York City gave him a majority of 52,089 votes.[17] To the State assembly the Ring sent a delegation of men, nearly all of them faithful to the dictates of Tammany, and their loyalty further confirmed by awards of city jobs, which could be taken away in the event of unfaithfulness.

Considering that the Tweed Ring was basically a city organization, its influence in the State legislature from 1868 to 1870 was an impressive demonstration of power. Control of the legislature of

1871, however, was the high point in the halcyon days of their domination over Albany. Unlike the previous year, there was not a rebellion to deal with. There was, however, an embarrassment which, for a moment, halted the onslaught of their special legislation.

Assemblyman James Irving, a plug-ugly from New York's lower wards, drunk and belligerent, struck down Smith M. Weed, Republican from Clinton county, on the floor of the Assembly. Even the Ring was powerless in face of public indignation. Irving was forced to resign. This created an obstacle in the Ring's control of the Assembly, since the body was so evenly divided, 65 Democrats to 63 Republicans, that the Ring had a bare constitutional majority of 65 to pass a measure. With Irving gone, the majority control was gone. The Ring, however, was able to cope with the situation in a characteristic manner. The day after Irving's resignation, the Honorable Orange S. Winans, a Republican from Chautauqua county, was given $75,000 in cash by Boss Tweed and promised a job with the Erie Railroad for at least five years at $5000 a year, if he would vote for Democratic legislation.[18] The scheme was so blatant, with Winans suddenly voting the straight Democratic ticket on every piece of legislation, that it attracted national newspaper attention, from the *Detroit Post* to the *Baltimore American*.[19] And the *New York Tribune* ran this editorial:

> For Sale or To Let for Business Purposes—a Member of Assembly. Rent, for the season, $100,000, or will be sold cheap for cash. Possession as soon as the Tax Levy and Election Bills are passed, the present lessee having no further use for the property. Inquire of William M. Tweed, Albany, or O. S. Winans, on the premises.[20]

With this difficulty settled, the Ring resumed the smooth flow of legislation into law. A Board of Apportionment was created for the city, ending the old and often injurious control of the legislature over the tax levy, but also enhancing the Ring powers, since the Ring named themselves as members of the Board. The so-called Two Per Cent Bill, attached to this bill, authorized the Board of Apportionment to raise money for the expenses of the city and county to an amount not exceeding 2 per cent of the assessed value of taxable property. After paying the interest on the city debt and providing for the sinking fund, the Board was to distribute the money among city departments.[21] While Peter Cooper and his Citizens' Association backed this measure, the *New York Times* in vain pointed out the joker: It was thought that the 2 per cent would be on specific valuation, when, in reality, it was on aggregate valuation. The aggregate might be swelled to enormous figures by assessing nontaxable and nonexisting property.[22] Thus the Ring had another source of income, as they had with the tax levy itself, which gave the city a budget of $48 million to be raised by taxation, loans, fees, licenses, etc. And Connolly wasted little time in trying to raise $3 million in foreign loans.[23]

While Tweed held honorable intentions in regard to the election law he passed for the Republicans while they backed the Ring's charter in 1870, he tinkered with the registry law sufficiently to take the strength out of the election law. An amendment was attached to the registry law extending the time in which voters could register before the election, and preventing the rigid inspection of names and detection of repeaters. The law also allowed a person not registered at all to vote if he made an affidavit before any notary or before any Inspector of Election.[24] And there were other bills: an amendment to the city charter to increase the patronage of the Ring, by redistricting of the State to add to Democratic representation in Congress; $880,000 to provide for charity and schools; and an appeal to the immigrant by reducing the entrance fee on newcomers arriving at the port of New York from $2.00 to $1.50. And there was a raft of "cinch" bills designed to force various businesses to pay to stop their passage through the legislature. With its usual finesse, the Ring presented both good and bad bills.

Matthew Breen introduced another side of the Ring while at the height of its power.

> One of the most suave, sleek and oleaginous persons on earth is the New York professional politician, when things are going his way. . . . Had there been any doubt of his identity, it might have been easily determined by the size of his diamond and the conspicuous position it occupied upon his person. . . . The politician who had not got a diamond on his bosom was of little account among his fellows, and was looked upon as having neglected his opportunities. . . . But the days of the politicians' diamond glory are well nigh gone. . . . They went out with Boss Tweed, who set the political fashion, and who wore the most brilliant diamond of all.[25]

Like other prominent men in the community, the Ring and their executives indulged themselves in high living and conspicuous consumption. Diamonds were their badge and, in a sense, their union card. The thirst for status equaled their appetite for booty. Important Tammany politicians of the Tweed era went beyond diamonds to luxurious houses, sleek trotting horses, social clubs, and proper weddings for their children. In regard to ethics and honesty, only a thin line separated a Sweeny from a Vanderbilt, a Connolly from an Astor, and no line at all separated Colonel Jim Fisk and Bill Tweed. But the chasm of social recognition that divided them yawned wide. All the important Tammany politicians sought in one way or another to cross that chasm—Watson with his trotting horses, Woodward with a home in Connecticut; Connolly, Corson, Frear, Ingersoll, Keyser, with their brownstone houses in New York. Only Sweeny was content to live elegantly but not on public display. All forgot (if they ever read) Montaigne's admonition: "Political philosophy lays this down as a fundamental and incontestable maxim, that all the most flourishing states owed their ruin, sooner or later, to the effects of luxury."

The most conspicuous consumer of them all was, appropriately, the Boss himself. Like Connolly, Tweed had a mansion on Fifth Avenue, estimated at some $350,000. Unlike Connolly, Tweed extended his extravagances to the country. A reporter once sought out the Boss's home in Greenwich, Connecticut. He passed by the village and the old Stone Church and came before a mansion with two dogs in front. Apprehensive, he asked a boy if the dogs would bite, and the boy answered with a grin, "No, cos they can't; them's iron dogs." [26] Beyond the dogs was a beautiful green lawn reaching to a handsome rambling house, and replicas of famous pieces of statuary. The story is told, undoubtedly a tall tale, that Andrew Garvey was responsible for decorating the grounds with statues. While he was placing them, so the story goes, Tweed appeared and asked what each represented. Garvey named each one and when he came to a flying Mercury, Tweed is supposed to have asked, "Who the hell is that?" "That," replied Garvey, "is Mercury the god of merchants and thieves." "Good! that's bully!" said Tweed, "put him over the front door." [27] At the side of the house were the most publicized stables in New York State, estimated to have cost over $122,000. The *Times* said, "It is better to be one of Mr. Tweed's horses than a poor taxpayer of this city." [28]

The history of the Tweed Ring is not merely the story of politics and graft; it had its social side as well. The monument to Tammany's prosperity and sociability was the Americus Club. It rested on a cliff overlooking Long Island Sound at Indian Harbor, Connecticut, not far from Tweed's Greenwich home. The clubhouse, a magnificent three-storied L-shaped building, was topped with a Mansard roof. It was called by a historian of New York Clubs the finest summer accommodation in the country.[29] For former Bowery Boys and "shoulder-hitters" of the Sixth Ward who had risen high in Tammany ranks, the Americus Club provided a life and surroundings as sumptuous as found in New York's or Philadelphia's clubs for the gentry. For a Democrat's bed there were aristocratic sheets of blue silk and white lace; there were mantels of black Italian marble ornamented with imported bronzes, a huge reception room ("Tweed's Room"), an elegantly frescoed *salon*, a library furnished with plush armchairs and finely bound books, "which do not betray the marks of much use," a barbershop (with bathrooms), sleeping rooms, billiard rooms, poolrooms, and a well-stocked bar.[30] In the summer there were a hundred servants on hand to attend to the members. Dinner time always began with the pop of champagne corks, and the meals were prepared by French chefs. This parody of a Tammany feed could well describe an Americus Club feast:

> Thin all sat down, and the soup wint roun, and
> The fish and mate and the Irish stew,
> And the fruits and paste for to whet the taste, or
> To build foundayshun for something new.
> Wid Roman punch, and the nuts to crunch and
> Jellies from Spain and ices Greek;
> Wid Clarit oldin and Sherries goldin,
> Tha sint a glow to the drinker's cheek.[31]

In the harbor there were boats for the Democrats' pleasure, prominent among them the greatest status symbol, a steam yacht, "The Wm. M. Tweed," a floating palace equipped with Oriental rugs, a library, monogrammed linens, sterling silver, a crew of twelve, and for large parties—an orchestra.[32]

The Americus Club was strictly limited to one hundred members, to wit, the key executives of the Tweed Ring organization. Since these included Republicans, like Isaac K. Oliver, Owen W. Brennan, and Henry Smith (vice president), Boss Tweed (president and secretary) argued—with little persuasion—that the club was strictly a social organization of genial gentlemen who found pleasure in each other's company. The initiation fee was $1000, monthly dues $250. A special badge denoted membership: a tiger's head made of gold on a relief of blue enamel. Tweed and the more affluent members wore tigers' heads whose eyes were set with rubies, which cost $2000. As in any gentlemen's club, rules were made and a fine imposed for violation. Meals must be taken at regular hours; any member destroying another's property was held personally responsible; no unnecessary noise or disturbance could be made between midnight and five in the morning. Particularly important, the club uniform must be worn at all times—blue navy pantaloons with a gold cord running down the sides; blue navy coat; white vest, and a white navy cap.

All was proper and decorous at the Americus Club, but to many New Yorkers it was a robbers' retreat, a pale and pitiful imitation of respectability at which all proper people sneered. It was one thing for Tammany politicians to buy aristocratic symbols from proceeds from the city treasury and ape the clubs of the gentry; it was quite another for a professional politician of questionable habits to invade the bailiwick of New York society itself. The hit of the social season of 1871, in fact the most dazzling and spectacular event New York society had seen in years, came not from the Belmonts, Astors, or Taylors, but from William Marcy Tweed, late of Cherry Street. If there was one event symbolic of the height reached by Tweed and his associates, it was the wedding of Tweed's daughter, Mary Amelia Tweed, to Ambrose Maginnis of the famous New Orleans family. New York was agog, and the newspapers stumbled over their adjectives describing it.

The wedding took place on May 31, 1871, at Trinity Chapel. A huge crowd was controlled only by a strong detachment of police. The chapel "was crowded with a richly dressed audience," awaiting "in speechless expectation." As E. A. Gilbert, "the fine musician," played Mendelssohn's Wedding March, father and daughter entered. The bride was wearing "white corded silk, décolleté, with demi-sleeves, an immense court train [with] . . . an abundance of *point aiguille* lace." The Tweed family seemed to be a Christmas tree of diamonds. The Boss wore his familiar diamond-planet on his shirt front, and Miss Tweed sparkled from top to toe—diamonds on her ears and arms, diamonds on her bosom and neck, and tiny, twinkling diamond buttons on her white satin shoes.

The reception was held at Tweed's home, a mansion on the corner of Fifth Avenue and Forty-third Street. The house "was ablaze with light." The parlor, said the *Sun*, was so magnificent it "beggared description." "Imagine all this," said an overwhelmed reporter, "lighted up with the utmost brilliancy, and hundreds of ladies and gentlemen in all the gorgeousness of full dress and flashing with diamonds, listening to the delicious strains of the band and inhaling in spirit the sweet perfume which filled the atmosphere, and some inadequate notion can be formed of the magnificence of the scene." [33] Everybody was there: Peter Sweeny, Richard Connolly, Judges Daly, Bosworth, Barnard, and Hogan; Colonel James Fisk, Jr. (in blue coat and brass buttons), Congressman S. S. Cox, Sheriff Brennan, Superintendent of Police Kelso, Mr. Andrew Garvey, and among others, curiously, the reformer Chauncey Depew.

What made the wedding so outstanding was the wedding presents. James Gordon Bennett of the *Herald* said the gifts surpassed the "celebrated Oviedo diamond wedding," as well as the recent wedding of a daughter of the Khedive of Egypt. "There were, for instance, 40 sets of sterling silver, one of which contained 240 separate pieces. James Fisk, Jr., sent a huge frosted silver iceberg, intended for ice cream... Superintendent Kelso, of the Police, sent an exact duplicate of Jim Fisk's contribution." Peter Sweeny gave diamond bracelets of "fabulous magnificence." One gift of jewelry alone was valued at $45,000. The total cost of the wedding presents was something of a record in New York marriages and a fitting tribute to the Boss—"Seven hundred thousand dollars!" gasped the *Herald*.[34]

After all these displays of extravagance, the only thing that seemed lacking was a monument. And that is exactly what was proposed! The *Sun*, with tongue in cheek, started the marble rolling by suggesting that the Ring followers should show their gratitude by building a monument to the Boss. Vanderbilt had one on the railroad station on Houston Street, why not Tweed? The *Sun* suggested a nautical pose, exhibiting the Boss as a bold mariner in the fury of a hurricane, splicing the foretop gallant shrouds of his steam yacht.[35] Tammany men, however, took the suggestion seriously. A Tweed Testimonial Association of the City of New York was quickly formed. At the city's expense, an elegant circular was printed and distributed calling upon all to donate to the "erection of a statue of the Honorable William M. Tweed in consideration of his services to the Commonwealth of New York." Subscriptions poured in not only from professional politicians but also from men prominent in the professions and society "who, having once opposed him, sought this opportunity of ingratiating themselves in his favor." [36] The newspapers, even those friendly to the Ring, had a field day. The *Herald* suggested that the Grand Sachem could be cast, it said, as a huge Indian, slouched in an armchair, holding in one hand the scroll of the new city charter, and in the other a peace pipe. A sign on the armchair would read: "I love it, I love it, and who shall dare / To chide me for loving this old arm chair."

The *Times* suggested that the statue of Washington be torn down and be replaced by one of Tweed to show how history had changed. And one wag objected to a proposed design of Tweed in a Roman toga as "it made him look too much as if he were going to take a bath." By March 13, 1871, after $7973 had been collected, Tweed realized that the monument was becoming an object of ridicule and asked his followers to abandon the idea. "Statues are not erected to living men. . . . I claim to be a live man, and hope (Divine Providence permitting) to survive in all my vigor, politically and physically, some years to come." [37]

Tweed was to survive, politically, for only a few more months. The sprees and extravagances of the halcyon days did more than the tongue-clucking and finger-wagging of the reformers to convince the public that a tight little aristocracy of Tammany politicians was living too high and too well. New York must be delivered, said Horace Greeley, from the thralldom of the Hall family. "It is wearied of Tammany Hall, Mozart Hall, all the political halls, Oakey Hall, and alcohol."

17

THE CRUSADE AGAINST THE TWEED RING

I thank my God the sun and moon
Are both stuck up so high
That no presumptuous hand can stretch
And pluck them from the sky.
If they were not, I do believe
That some reforming ass
Would recommend to take them down
And light the world with gas.

Judge James T. Brady

For five years the Tweed Ring had led a great treasury raid. The power of the Ring, like the tentacles of an octopus, encircled city government, the courts, the police, the underworld, and the State Legislature. The command centers of political power from the Governor to the Board of Aldermen were controlled by the Ring and its lieutenants. The Ring ruled over an empire of patronage with thousands of the faithful on the city payrolls. Tammany Hall had been remodeled into an awesome political machine, supported by the immigrant and the native poor, and sustained on election day by a horde of Tammany warriors, repeaters, and corrupt election officials who made a mockery out of the power of the ballot. No wonder Boss Tweed could ask the reformer, "What are you going to do about it?"

Seldom have the forces of "good" government faced such a formidable opponent as they did in July 1871. Yet five months later the Tweed Ring was destroyed. Most accounts of this campaign emphasize the Ring's sensational thefts. But few questions have been raised about the crusade itself; few attempts have been made to understand the anatomy of a reform movement on a local, grass-roots level. For example, how was the crusade conducted? What was the impact of the Tweed Ring upon the reformer's imagination and in what way did the Ring reveal his attitudes toward reform, corruption, and political institutions? If the rascals were such capital rogues, why did it take so long to destroy them?

By the fall of 1871, when damning evidence was being unearthed and New York echoed from the cries of one reform rally after another, most of the press, a multitude of reform groups, and politicians from both parties were noisily scrambling after the scalps of the Tammany Ring braves. Now that the Ring was disintegrating, all vied for the heroic role of redeemer. Samuel Tilden almost reached the Presidency on the claim that he destroyed the Ring. But Tilden was a hero of last moments. A skillful general when the enemy was in retreat, he was the soul of indecision, procrastination, and lost opportunities when the Ring was in power. In those quiet days before the great uprising, only two led the crusade against the Tweed Ring: Thomas Nast of *Harper's Weekly*, and the *New York Times*. *Harper's Weekly* began in 1868 to print Thomas Nast's brilliant political cartoons, and his talent with the poisoned-pen portrait, which could at once inspire fear and ridicule, has led many to think he was the chief wrecker of the Ring. Tweed himself thoroughly recognized Nast's artistry in making a cartoon a deadly political weapon. "I don't care a straw for your newspaper articles, my constituents don't know how to read, but they can't help seeing them damned pictures." [1]

A picture may say a thousand words, but it still took many a thousand words to excite and motivate the indignation of New Yorkers. It was the *New York Times* which published the first evidence of corruption, helped to raise the crusade to the heights of near hysteria, and therefore deserves the mantle of champion opponent of the Tweed Ring. The role played by the *Times* is a kind of case study of the enormous difficulties and stubborn persistence involved in arousing a sometimes confused and often apathetic public.

Prior to September 1870, the fight against corruption was represented by a series of angry but irregular outbursts from reform groups and newspapers. These in turn were thwarted by grand juries vulnerable to the persuasion of hard cash and lack of evidence. The Citizens' Association and the Union League, both eminent bodies of "respectabilities," had long fished in the murky waters of New York politics with only occasional luck.[2] While the reformers suspected that something was desperately wrong, the rub was in proving it. Although the Ring was organized as early as 1866, there was little awareness by reformers of either a centralized city machine or of how politics operated at the level of the ward and precinct. Instead, there was talk of a host of "rings" but uncertainty as to who were the ringleaders.

Apathy, a lack of civic conscience, and fear—which permeated every level of society—also accounted for the reformers' failure to get an audience. An absence of consensus, generated by party partisanship, divided the press and the gentry, the two groups who might have sounded the alarm and carried the fight. While the business community furnished several leaders to the reform groups, other businessmen were either afraid of the retaliatory power of Tammany Hall or they benefited from the Ring's operations, while others, too interested in making money, simply did not care.

The Tweed Ring exploited these conditions and reinforced complacency by giving something to everyone: city advertising to the press, special favors to businessmen, state aid to charitable and religious organizations, jobs and food to the poor. Tweed through his business connections and Hall through his clubs ingratiated themselves in the upper branches of society, while Sweeny and Connolly, seasoned ward leaders, were effective in the rank and file. And then there was the Astor Committee and its whitewash of the Comptroller's records, which contributed as much as any event to creating complacency.

Into this atmosphere, the champion of reform, the *New York Times*, made its "auspicious" beginning in the winter of 1870, by announcing that Messrs. Sweeny, Hall, and Hoffman were busily engaged in bringing good government to New York![3] One delicious irony was topped by another when the *Times* gave its first (and last) cheer for the Boss himself.

> Senator Tweed is in a fair way to distinguish himself as a reformer. . . . From beginning to end the Tweed party has not manifested the slightest disposition to evade or prevaricate. . . . As a whole, the appointments of the heads of the various departments of the City Government . . . are far above the average in point of personal fitness, and should be satisfactory.[4]

The *Times*'s course, however, was radically altered by the summer of 1870. Ugly rumors of corruption were once again abroad, and George Jones, the *Times* publisher, apparently feeling hoodwinked and humiliated, angrily turned on the charter and its creators. An Englishman, Louis Jennings, was imported as editor. Jennings's zest for a good fight, his acerbic prose, coupled with Nast's cartoons in *Harper's Weekly*, infused the campaign with a pitch and tempo of almost evangelical fervor. For over a year, from September 20, 1870, on, there was not a day that the *Times* did not, with furious and heroic invective, assault the Tweed Ring, its organization, and allies. The *Times* begged, cajoled, scolded, and demanded that the electorate rout the rascals; nevertheless, the public, including some of the "best people," seemed to sink deeper in its apathy, and the Ring got stronger. What was wrong? Was it entirely public indifference, the usual scapegoat for corruption, or did the trouble lay partly in the nature of the crusade itself?

Two elements are necessary in any successful campaign against civil corruption: moral indignation and facts. Until July 1871, the *Times*'s attack was a grand crusade conducted without fear and without facts; it was long on denunciation, short on documentation. The slack in legal evidence was taken up in an amazing exercise of invective, the central theme of which was the wickedness of the Tweed Ring, a theme with a hundred variations on the words "thief," "rogue," and "scamp." The crusade had persistence. It had gusto. It had all the subtlety of a sledge hammer. It was literary alchemy using the crudest of alloys. There was none of the humor or painful ridicule of a Nast cartoon, none of the dash of the *New York Herald* or the deft sarcasm of Dana's *Sun* when those two papers finally joined the bandwagon later in 1871. It was just a juggernaut of epithets, taking the edge off the crusade by dulling the reader's senses with a repetitive cry of "wolf." E. L. Godkin of *The Nation*, although admiring the newspaper's spirit, found its denunciation "tiresome." [5] Even the *Times* admitted that its readers were probably bone-tired from the constant accusations.[6] And while the *Times* spewed platitudes about political sin, the elegant Mayor of New York quipped, "Who's going to sue?" [7]

Nor was abuse heaped solely on the Ring, for the public in general, and the rich, the workingman, and the church in particular, came within the *Times*'s range as it sharpened its aim at iniquity. One major strategic device of the crusade was to arouse a feeling of guilt and shame. The public had failed its civic responsibilities. There should be a moment of self-castigation coupled with redeeming political New Year's resolutions to sweep away the apathy that allowed the monstrosities of the Tweed Ring. The rich were scorned for their complacency, hypocrisy, and lack of action.[8] They were "cowardly and effeminate," refusing to leave the comfort of their libraries for the "unpleasant smells" of the political arena.

The policy of the Ring, in fact, was to drive the honest, decent middle class out of the city and leave it to the very rich and the very poor—"the one too lazy to oppose them, and the other too ignorant." [9] It the workingman understood the elementary principles of political economy, he would not be grateful for the jobs the

Ring gave him on the streets and in the parks. He should realize that the robbery of the rich was the robbery of the poor. Labor actually took the full brunt of the Ring's adventures in graft through raised rents, increased taxes, and higher priced goods.[10] As for the church, the *Times* said, at most it applauds while others fight. If only the church acted with responsibility, the public conscience would be inflamed, and the sores on the body politic would be burned out, "as if by fire." [11]

With these tactics of shock, blame, and invective, the *Times* seemed to be searching for some way to shatter the complacency of the public. An attempt was made, in a pedestrian Jeffersonian vein, to exploit the chasm between town and country, the fear—and fascination—of the city. The "hay-loft and cheese-press Democrats" were told of the moral quagmire of the Sodom-by-the-Hudson, its city-slicker politicians, its crime, its cancerous effect on the Democratic party.[12] The trouble with that approach was that upstate politicos well knew that the success of the party depended on the city Democrats' delivering a large bloc of votes, and the Tweed Ring had time and again shown it could deliver.

Perhaps an appeal to the citizens' pocketbook would help, for here lay men's hearts—"touch them there and they will wince and exhibit more sensitiveness than they will show to even the strongest appeals made to their sympathies," as the *Times* said.[13] The newspaper became choked with figures demonstrating the Ring's damage to property owners. But most of the electorate did not own real property. Columns were devoted to an awkward analysis of city finances. But the average voter would have difficulty making sense of them. As the *Times* executed its complicated sums, apathy seemed to increase.

One reason why the crusade raged on for so long amid apparent indifference from the rest of the New York press was that the Democratic press, from the *World* on down—"or rather up, for you cannot get lower than the *World*"—(as the *Times* remarked)—were infuriated over the profound Republican partisanship of Nast and the *Times*. The *Times* was fond of repeating the adage that every Democrat was not a horse-thief, but that every horse-thief was a Democrat. Moreover, according to the *Times*, "all" Democrats were corrupt; the party had "never" undertaken a "genuine" reform.[14] Righteous moral indignation was rudely compromised when the *Times* condemned city Democrats and blithely whitewashed the Grant administration.[15]

Skepticism (and perhaps jealousy) also influenced the press. The *Times* motto should read, said one newspaper, "Print everything you please, without regard to whether it is true or false, but refuse to prove anything." [16] Horace Greeley, who puffed hot and cold throughout the campaign, even suggested that the Ring sue the *Times* for libel.[17] The *New York World*, after a brief flirtation with the Young Democracy, returned to revolve around Tammany Hall; it stoutly defended the Ring, calling the crusade as "stupid and absurd as it is wicked," and designed to introduce "a reign of anarchy." [18] Moreover, both the *Herald* and the *World* liked Oakey Hall. James Gordon Bennett of the *Herald* once said approvingly of Tweed's left-hand man, "He calls a spade a spade and Horace Greeley a humbug." [19]

Thus when Tammany wildly celebrated on July 4, 1871, it seemed that Nast's cartoons and the *Times*'s river of rhetoric had produced a crusade without followers, a cause apparently lost to corruption and apathy. All had not been lost, however, for it prepared New Yorkers for what was to follow. This was made possible not by any renewed moral gusto from Tammany's "unloyal" opposition, but by a quirk of fate and an emotion common in politics—the hankering for revenge.

The first real step in the Ring's fall to disaster came on January 21, 1871, when James Watson, the trusty County Auditor and Ring bookkeeper, was killed in a sleighing accident. The Ring was to learn how indispensable he was, for the door was now open for espionage. Matthew O'Rourke was appointed County Auditor, but was not taken into the Ring's confidence. It was a fatal appointment —"a dirty traitor and a fraud," Tammany's *Leader* cried later. O'Rourke was not a happy man. He once had a claim against the city which the Ring had seen fit not to pay. A disgruntled claim-seeker could be as vicious as a woman scorned. With the patience and accuracy of a good bookkeeper, O'Rourke copied the explosive facts and figures of corruption from the Ring's account books and passed them on to the *Times*.[20]

Acting independently, Jimmy O'Brien, one of the leaders of the rebel Young Democracy, assumed the role of a political Judas. He had managed to ingratiate himself back into the good graces of the Ring, by abandoning the Young Democracy and acting as an enthusiastic trustee for the Tweed monument association. But beneath his ruddy Irish complexion, he smouldered with resentment over the Ring's refusal to pay him $300,000 in claims he collected while Sheriff. O'Brien persuaded Connolly to give one William Copeland a job in the Comptroller's office. Copeland was, in fact, O'Brien's spy, sent to obtain information to use as blackmail to get O'Brien's claims. With Watson dead, Copeland found the voucher records loosely guarded. Lush accounts, such as "County Liabilities," furnished him with a wealth of information, which he copied for O'Brien. Confronted with this political dynamite, Tweed began to pay blackmail. He paid O'Brien over $20,000 with the promise that $130,000 would be forthcoming in mortgages on prime property. O'Brien coolly pocketed the cash and turned his information over to the *Times*.[21]

The breakthrough in the crusade had come. Publisher Jones began his attack with uncommon good sense. He bought up a large block of *Times* stock, fearful the Ring might retaliate by a stock raid. And then on Saturday, July 22, 1871, the *Times* opened up with its first front-page blast: "The Secret Accounts: Proofs of Undoubted Frauds Brought to Light." Slowly and deliciously, as if opening a long-awaited Christmas package, Jones released his figures—on the armories, the courthouse, padded payrolls, judicial indiscretion—topping one horror with another.[22] On the 29th the *Times* printed a special supplement in English and German of statistics on the armory and courthouse swindles; 200,000 copies of the first printing were quickly sold out. It was not only a sensation in New York, but it also attracted immediate national attention. For the next four months Jones never let up; front page and editorial page boiled with journalistic frenzy—and Nast drew his cartoons with even greater venom.

Now as the facts were exposed, New York stirred, rumbled, and awoke—shocked, frightened, angry. It was now time for the reformers to take more decisive action. The massive reform rally on September 4 at Cooper Union, the first of many, registered the impact of the *Times*'s exposures: the temper was explosive, the spirit was that of a back-country revival meeting. The rally was sponsored by the Committee of Seventy, whose roster bulged with some of the most distinguished names in New York, such as William F. Havemeyer, Judge James Emott, Robert Roosevelt, Charles Richard O'Conor, and Joseph H. Choate, who presented the Committee's resolutions against the Tweed Ring with the battle cry, "This is what *we* are going to do about it!"[23]

A rostrum of distinguished speakers aroused the audience to a passionate fervor: "We shall get at them. The wicked shall not always rule"; "Pitch into the boss, give it to him, he deserves it"; "There is no power like the power of the people armed, aroused, and kindled with the enthusiasm of a righteous wrath"; "What are we going to do about it?"—"Hang them," cried the voices from the audience.[24] The *Times* said afterward that if the Ring had heard the curses, hisses, and denunciations heaped on them they would have felt "too mean to live."[25]

It was evident that New York had awakened from its apathy. The Citizens' Association, the New York Council of Political Reform, and the Union League threw their weight into the crusade, and they were followed by a host of reform groups—the Young Men's Municipal Reform Association, the Apollo Hall Democracy, the Young Democracy, the German Reform Organization, the Democratic Reform Association, and the Ward Councils of Political Reform. The press joined the chorus. Prominent businessmen and attorneys like R. A. Hunter, George W. Benster, and James Whitten met and considered forming a Vigilance Committee, but cooler heads prevailed. And Samuel Tilden entered on his somewhat gray charger. It was now expedient for him to be a reformer. The crusade reached a new dimension. It was no longer the concern of two but an issue that attracted many New Yorkers.

The impact of the Tweed Ring upon the reformer's imagination once again demonstrated the American capacity to create a morality play out of politics. Here was a drama of good versus evil. The principal characters were so wonderfully wicked that little embellishment seemed necessary. But embellished they were. While the reformers' responses were varied and often contradictory, certain dominant themes emerged.

The beginning theme, which Thomas Nast did more than anyone else to fix, was the image of the city boss, a portrait of evil. Tweed was pictured as gross, vicious, lowborn, colossally corrupt. Sweeny was the man with the black brains; Connolly was dark and oily; and Nast's favorite target, Oakey Hall, was the buffoon. These "beastly rascals" were also seen not as an indigenous product of the American urban political system, but as something sinister and alien. The corruption of the Ring was compared to the treachery of a Judas Iscariot, to the cunning of a Robespierre, the slothful greed of Oriental potentates; in tyranny and insolence they "would put their Roman predecessors to the blush." [26]

But the Boss and his ministers were only mirrors in larger size and more evil proportions of those who flocked to their support—the Irish-Catholic immigrants. One of the most significant responses to the Tweed Ring, one which rounded out the image of evil by adding fear to it, was the revival of nativism in New York. On July 12, 1871, Protestant and Catholic Irish engaged in a bloody riot which shocked New York and revived the Know-Nothing attitudes of the 1850's and nativist fears of the 1863 draft riots. The Ring was vehemently denounced for trying to prevent the annual parade for the Orangemen, which precipitated the riot, as pacifying the Catholic Irish. When the parade was allowed, the Ring was accused of protecting the Catholic rioters. No other single event so well illustrated the tie between Tammany Hall and the Irish-Catholic voter. The cry for "clean government" now emitted the voice of nativism. There was a papal conspiracy as "Irish Catholic despotism rules the City of New York, the Metropolis of free America." [27] Letters poured into the *Times* office calling for a revival of the Native American party.[28] The Citizens' Association announced that the city had become a "common sewer" for the "dregs" of Europe; an army of ignorance was being led to the polls by the Tweed Ring.[29]

Nativism, in turn, elicited another response. The reformers, for the most part of the middle and upper class—professional men, bankers, merchants, journalists, the "better" politicians—felt a distinct loss of status since their old position of leadership had been captured by the wicked and the mob. Prior to the reign of Fernando Wood, political factions were controlled by men belonging to the upper or middle class, to whom the emoluments of office, while desirable, were not always essential. From the days of Tweed's Forty Thieves through the Civil War, a change was occurring in New York politics, gradually, not completely, not easy to recognize; like the grin of the Cheshire Cat, sometimes it was seen, sometimes it was not. The old ruling groups, even the august Albany Regency, were being slowly displaced by a group not new, but different in numbers and the ranks from which it came—the lower-middle class, and the bottom of the social heap, the immigrant and native poor. The old ruling groups had to begin to move over and make a place for a new group, the Irish. This change found its source in the city, its growth, the changing composition of its population, the nature of its government. But the old middle- and upper-class elite, especially the reformers, who largely came from these groups, never completely understood this change and felt only bitterness toward the new and not always "respectable" elite. Republican institutions under the Tweed Ring, the reformers declared, were safe only in the "rightful" hands of the educated, the wealthy, and the virtuous. Now power had shifted to those at the bottom of society, their morals decayed, their religion Romanist, their Alma Mater the corner saloon.[30] The *Times* echoed the reformer's fears: We exist over a volcano, a vast, explosive mass of the poor and ignorant—"the dangerous classes," who "care nothing for our liberty and civilization."[31] E. L. Godkin traced the phenomenon back to the excessive democratization of the 1846 New York State Constitution.[32] Others saw it compounded by another insidious development, the rise of a new political breed, the professional politician.

As New York itself grew, politics became more centralized, more disciplined, more professionalized. While the professional politician had long been on the scene in New York politics, the impact of the Tweed Ring seemed to wipe out that memory and fix the emergence and the novelty of the professional as coinciding with the Tweed era. The *Times*, in fact, wrote of the "new profession" as if it were just making its appearance.[33] The reformer gave the professional little credit for skill in handling men or for artful political techniques at the "low" level of the ward or precinct, or for his sometimes masterful sense of organization. The reformer generally was little interested in the rude day-by-day operations of politics. His middle and upper class sensibilities were congenial to ideals and principles, not to the often rough, dreary, but necessary work of the primaries. The professional, in the reformer's eyes, was not a Robin Hood to the needy, but rather a Robin the Hood to the degenerate, wasting the taxpayers' money by giving jobs to the immigrant, bailing the drunkard out of jail, and corrupting the unemployed by giving them food and cigars—a parasite undermining the Protestant ethic of civic responsibility. The New York Council of Political Reform summed it all up. It was a contest between two forces: one made up of ruffians and desperadoes, and the other of "the delicately reared, the moral, humane, and the peace loving."[34]

Thus his sense of lost status, his contempt and fear of the masses, his nativism, his reaction to the city boss as rogue and professional politician—all indicate that the reformer's response to the Tweed Ring was more than simple moralizing about political sin. But if there was one response, a dynamic one which gave cohesion and direction to his other reactions and provided the most powerful stimulus to reform, it was the fear that civil liberties were in danger, which to a certain degree was true. This response finally gave to the crusade a sense of genuine crisis, its *raison d'être*. The capital crime, then, was not merely the plundering of the treasury, nor the danger to the taxpayer's pocketbook; it was something more sinister than that. It was that a gang of rogues and its vicious brood, an organization alien to American life, was threatening the very bases of republican institutions—the ballot box, the schools, the church, the freedom of speech and press. "This wholesale filching and slaughter of the suffrage is a deadly thrust at the very source and fountain of our liberties... [we must] recover our mutilated liberties and vindicate our civil rights," shouted Joseph Choate at Cooper Union.[35] The danger to civil liberties was one of the most persistent themes of the *New York Times*.[36] Judge James Emott, Henry Clinton, Henry G. Stebbins, William Evarts, and others, all repeated the same theme: the Tweed Ring had threatened "the existence of free institutions," republicanism was "poisoned," "the glories of liberty are in danger." [37] The threat was felt even outside New York. "Democratic principles can no more carry this curse of Tammany upon them than virtue can thrive in a brothel," said the *Chicago Times*.[38]

If these fears seem exaggerated, it was because the reformers of the Tweed era were faced with their first city boss and his well-organized machine. There had been corruption in the past, but no precedent of modern city bosses to temper the reformer's idealism and sharpen his realism.

Although there were differences among the reformers, and their schemes often overlapped, there were broadly two schools of thought on how best to cleanse New York City. The largest school believed that the Ring was not a natural product of American municipal government but a political disease alien to New World representative democracy. The cure, therefore, was relatively simple. Rout the rascals, lance the boil on the body politic, and the organism would be healthy again. This prognosis reflected an implicit faith in the efficacy of American institutions. The defeat of the Tweed Ring meant the vindication of republicanism, not the questioning of it. There were, of course, minor wounds to be treated: the charter needed patching up, there were too many appointive offices, and a tight little bureaucracy should replace the Ring's bloated monster. If the Ring discredited any institution, it was the political party. Partisanship, therefore, should be replaced by efficiency, honesty, and the methods of business. "The government of a city," declared the Union League, "is altogether more a matter of business, than of statesmanship." The party system led only to "lawlessness, disorganization, pillage and anarchy." [39]

For these reformers, the cause of corruption could be the cure of corruption. The absence of the "best people" in government had allowed the wicked to rule. Thus the call was for the return to power of men with substantial wealth, education, and virtue. "The Ring could not keep its own for a day in the teeth of a combined and vigorous opposition from the men of large property." [40] New York was choked with foreigners, "many of them not possessed of virtue and intelligence sufficient for self-government." [41] Therefore, what was needed, said the New York City Council of Political Reform, under the heading of "The Effectual Remedy," was for the "right-minded" to enter "into a covenant with each other... and the work is done." [42] If this sounded like the voice of the happy ending, it was also the voice of elitism. By implication, the "right-minded" were always the old ruling elite. It represented government of the people, for the people, *by* the "best people."

The second group of reformers did not share the extravagant optimism of the first. Corruption had forced them to re-examine the efficacy of democratic institutions and in so doing they found them wanting. Patchwork will not answer, wrote James Parton. The ship of state needed an overhaul from keel to taffrail, and perhaps it was necessary to "abandon the vessel and build a new one." [43] There must be some "profound defect," said C. C. P. Clark, in the American system which produced the horrors of the Tweed Ring.[44] The defect these reformers saw was one of the hallowed tenets of the American dream, universal suffrage. The comments of E. L. Godkin best illustrate this position. It was nonsense to talk about the Ring as a novelty to the American scene; it was the inevitable result of a "process of evolution," and other great cities have their "mute, inglorious Tweeds" waiting for their opportunity.[45] The curse of the city, "the great city problem," *is* the "people"—or about half of them who constitute the poor, "that huge body of ignorant and corrupt voters." The poor have no conception of self-government and choose only to live off the rich. The blight of universal suffrage is the secret to the Ring's power because it gave them an army. There can be, then, only two cures: first, suffrage should be limited, because only the propertied class, those who have a stake in society, should rule, for "we must somehow put the government into the hands of men who pay taxes." And second, the municipality should be converted into a business, stripped of political influence.[46] This program did not go far enough for Francis Leiber, James Parton, and Isaac Butts. They wanted to impose a literacy test on all New York voters.[47] It was a fine irony that those who felt their civil liberties in danger should seek to curtail the liberties of others.

From whence had come these dreams for a reformed New York? Not from the reformer's own time, for which he expressed a withering indictment. The reformer turned away from his own era, which spawned chaos and upheaval, looked back over his shoulder and found his solutions in a remembrance of things past—or what he *thought* had passed. He reached back for a lost innocence, the simplicity of an older era, the chaste republican order of a golden yesteryear. When he called for the return of the "best people," he thought of past mighties—James Kent, De Witt Clinton, Edward Livingston. His plan for a small, simplified government was the vision of the clean, honest symmetry of the town meeting, which James Welsh fondly recalled as the "natural school of American statesmanship."[48] The concept of limited suffrage, that ideological dog which had had its day, was an image of Order, a responsible aristocracy balancing a rapacious mob. The warmth of reminiscence, however, was an anesthetic to the reformer's memory. For him the Tweed era dated the decline of political virtue. Before that ranged the long years of a paradise to be found again. Forgotten were the gentlemen rogues, Fernando Wood, the Forty Thieves, and Samuel Swartwout. Nostalgia even led the reformer to tidy up the Albany Regency. Now it was remembered as an organization of "culture, integrity, and character." [49] And Thurlow Weed, an able opponent of the old, honest Regency, apparently with straight face, testified that "formerly the *suspicion* of corruption in a member [of the State legislature] would have put him 'into Coventry.'" [50] As one reform pamphlet said, "Pause here, Reader, sadly to drop a tear on the grave of departed Patriotism." [51]

As the crusade accelerated and unified both reformers and the press by early fall of 1871, the Ring, realizing it was in deep trouble, fought back like a trapped tiger and made some clumsy but typical maneuvers. George Jones was offered a bribe of $500,000 to silence the *Times*. He turned it down saying, "I don't think that the devil will ever bid higher for me than that." [52] Perhaps Thomas Nast needed a rest. He was promised $500,000 if he would leave the country and study art in Europe. "Well, I don't think I'll do it," Nast said. "I made up my mind not long ago to put some of those fellows behind the bars, *and I'm going to put them there!*" [53]

For a while Tweed remained cool and calm. A reporter for the *Missouri Republican* asked him if it were true that he had stolen money. Tweed thought a while and said, "This is not a question one gentleman ought to put to another." [54] George Templeton Strong said: "Tweed's impudent serenity is sublime. Were he not a supreme scoundrel, he would be a great man." [55] Finally, on September 8 he lost his composure and declared to a *Sun* reporter:

> The *Times* has been saying all the time I have no brains. Well, I'll show Jones that I have brains. . . . I tell you, sir, if this man Jones had said the things he has said about me, twenty-five years

> ago, he wouldn't be alive now. But, you see, when a man has a wife and children, he can't do such a thing (clenching his fists). I would have killed him.

Nor did Mayor Hall help matters. He became ensnarled in his own contradictory statements and succeeded only in deepening the Ring's guilt. At first Hall cried innocent. The disclosures of the *Times* were "a tempest of ciphers and calumny . . . a second-hand roar about the accounts of the Supervisors and the salaries of extinct sinecures." Then he admitted some frauds were committed by the "old" Supervisors, but not by the Ring. This was interesting, because Tweed was president of the old Board of Supervisors. He said he never signed the alleged fraudulent warrants, and blamed Watson. He retracted this and admitted signing them, but only as a "ministerial act." He then claimed the signatures were forged; then retracted again and said he had signed but had been "hoodwinked." He tried sonorous prose: "When at last the smoke shall clear away, it will be seen where the political sun will clearly shine, that the proudest flag of them all, waving untorn from the highest staff of the victorious army, is that which shall never cease to be borne by Tammany Hall." [56]

And naturally Hall attempted humor. "We are likely to have what befell Adam—an early Fall." [57] In an interview with a newspaper, he showed what the *Times* called "cheek."

> Reporter: "You are looking very well."
>
> Mayor: "Oh yes, I am always cheerful. You know the true philosophy of life is to take things just as they come. How was the clever definition—let me see, I forget his name—of life? What is mind? No matter. What is matter? Never mind. That's my philosophy." [58]

Once more cupidity came to the aid of the reformers. The Committee of Seventy as well as the Citizens' Committee, composed of private citizens and Aldermen, made plans to examine Comptroller Connelly's books for further proofs of the Ring's misdeeds. On Sunday, September 10, the day before this was to happen, Connolly's

Cartoon by Thomas Nast; courtesy of the New-York Historical Society, New York City

office was broken into. From three small cupboards more than 3500 vouchers were stolen. It became a sensation. The Ring had panicked. The *Times* asked sarcastically why the city had spent $404,347.72 on safes and had not given one to the Comptroller. At the same time news came from Washington that Mrs. Connolly had just put one and a half million dollars into government bonds. No longer could the *World, Sun,* and *Herald* spoof the *Times* on its crusade. Even Horace Greeley overcame his jealousy of the *Times* and admitted that a crusade was in order. The theft only intensified Tilden's efforts—he had now committed himself completely to the crusade—to find more proof, which he did when he investigated the accounts at the Ring's Broadway Bank. So careless was the Ring that duplicates of the stolen vouchers were found by Tilden at the bank.

The Ring at best had been untidy. Now all became a shambles. The pressure of the crusade was more than the Ring could endure. The thieves who had traveled so far and so long together quarrelled and split into two enemy camps. Hall and Sweeny, joining forces against Tweed and Connolly, saw a chance for survival with the voucher disaster. On September 12, 1871, Hall asked Connolly to resign. Connolly, with some logic, replied to Hall that such a step would be equal to a confession, and added: "My official acts have been supervised and approved by your superior vigilance. So far as my administration is questioned equal responsibility attaches to yourself." [59]

It was now, as George Templeton Strong put it, "skunk vs. rattlesnake." Connolly, caring little for the role of sacrificial skunk, fled to the reformers. Tilden then performed a master stroke. He persuaded Connolly to step aside for four months, naming in his place Andrew Green as Acting Comptroller. Green was a distinguished public servant, and by no coincidence, a member of the Committee of Seventy.[60] Hall had made himself ridiculous by demanding Connolly's resignation, which he had no authority to do; Connolly refused and imported some of his toughs from the lower wards to guard his office. It was now skunk vs. *coiled* rattlesnake. Hall asked former General George McClellan to take Connolly's post, but McClellan, cautious in peace and war, refused. The press hooted that Hall had failed. In an interview, Hall told reporters, "Gentlemen, some of you yesterday said that I had received a severe check, and *in testimonium veritatis*, I have, so as you see, put on a check suit." [61] Connolly did deputize Green, and so one of the principal bastions of the Ring's stronghold, the Comptroller's office, was captured.

In the meantime, treason developed on the general staff. John Foley, president of one of the ward reform clubs, applied to George Barnard for an injunction to stop the Ring from paying or raising money in any way in the name of or on the credit of the County and City. Barnard, sensing the coming debacle of the Ring, responded with all the agility of a rat leaping from a sinking ship and granted the injunction. The reformers, never expecting this boon, were elated. As Tweed explained it:

> So he put the injunction upon us, and in the straitened condition of our credit, which was so extended on every side, it broke us. You see our patronage had become so enormous and so costly that the injunction, which might not have troubled us at any other time, destroyed all our power to raise money from the banks or elsewhere and left us trapped.[62]

Although the injunction was later modified, government was temporarily brought to a standstill. With the city treasury nearly empty, and no recourse to raise money, city employees went for weeks without wages. Tweed gave $50,000 from his own pocket to help laborers and their families, and the *Star*, one of a few remaining journals kind to the Ring, called on the laborers to start a bread riot.[63] New Yorkers, remembering the horror of the draft riots of 1863, and the bloody Orange Parade riot of July 12, 1870, redoubled their efforts to oust the Ring.

The injunction accomplished its purpose. The main arteries of political power, money, and patronage were suddenly dried up. The thieves were fighting among themselves. With Green ruthlessly chopping off sinecure appointments, the shiny hats, stripped of place and status, were losing faith in their chiefs. With an election coming up, *Harper's* and the *Times* were joined by the rest of the New York press, and the crusade reached fever pitch. The public was daily reminded of Tweed's arrogant, "What are you going to do about it?" The Tweed Ring seemed on the threshold of disaster. But the reformers underestimated the talents of the Boss.

For the leaders of the anti-Tammany Democracy it seemed that victory was in easy grasp. All that was necessary was to control the State nominating convention at Rochester. This did not appear difficult in light of the disasters that had befallen Tweed and company. Then the reformers could elect a reform platform, reveal the further evidence compiled by the investigations of the Committee of Seventy, campaign against the horrors of the Tweed Ring, and ride to victory in the November election. Tilden made elaborate preparations to capture the convention by sending out 26,000 letters to Democratic politicos asking for support with a one-two punch: he put the name of Charles O'Conor in nomination for the attorney-generalship, and disputed the right of the regular Tammany delegates to represent the city in the convention. Thus with belated courage, Tilden arose, rallied the reformers, and denounced the Ring. He realized the Ring's only chance of survival lay in renominating its henchmen for city and state offices, and helping the election of Republicans who had worked with it in past legislatures —but so did the Boss.

The reformers lost some of their confidence when Tweed and his entourage, gangs of New York toughs, arrived in Rochester. Threats of violence were made against anyone who should interfere with the Ring; delegates were warned that the convention would be broken up by force if anti-Tammany delegates were admitted to the floor. The reformers found themselves reliving an old story: once again they were outmaneuvered and outwitted. Crafty as usual, Tweed moved among the delegates and argued that the recent exposures were merely a local issue and that an all-out fight in the convention would undoubtedly split the party and allow the Republicans an easy victory in November. For the sake of party unity he was willing to compromise. If the reform representatives were omitted from the roll of delegates, he would omit the Tammany representatives.

What appeared as a compromise was actually a victory. Even with the Tammany delegation missing, Tweed was able to control the convention, through lack of opposition from the reformers, and with the help of friends won by bribery. Charles O'Conor, who would never have hesitated to throw the entire machinery of the state against the Ring, was defeated for the attorney-generalship by a large majority. A state ticket bulging with names of the Ring's minions was nominated. Tweed turned against the reformers with arrogance. He called Tilden, Horatio Seymour, and Francis Kernan "three troublesome old fools." [64]

Tweed had good reason to gloat. A few days before the convention he was re-elected chairman of the Tammany General Committee, and at the convention he was renominated for State Senator. He returned to New York in triumph. At Walton House he took the platform, removed a little Scotch tweed cap, and told a boisterous audience:

> The newspapers have already indicted, tried, convicted and sentenced and sentenced (roars of laughter), but I feel perfectly free to appeal to a higher tribunal, and have no fear of the result (cheers). I do not come to you, my fellow citizens, in a circuitous way, indicative of the possession of the thought of the necessity of caution engendered by fear, but directly, openly, squarely, as a man to men, and without an appeal for your sympathy other than so far as my family have suffered from the cruel indignities that have been heaped upon them for my political actions (sensation). But asking at your hands the justice and fair play that have been denied me by bitter, unrelenting, unscrupulous, prejudiced and ambitious partisan foes (deafening shouts of approval). . . . [65]

The reformers, who had once gloated, returned to New York shaken and sober. The glitter of their confidence was dulled, but their resolution was firm—even firmer. Tweed's victory at Rochester had robbed them of a valuable tactical weapon, the opportunity to proclaim themselves the regular Democratic organization. The Ring, even though quarreling among themselves, still commanded a powerful election-day army. But failure only reinforced the reformers' determination. What had seemed after the exposures to be an easy victory was now an uphill fight. The reformers were forced to be a rival of the regular organization, and hence a third-party group, with all the difficulties a third party faced. Many of the reformers' leaders were political prima donnas—O'Conor was known for his irascibility, Tilden could be exasperatingly aloof. If thieves fell out, reformers seemed to delight in dissension and to fragment into splinter groups. If the reformers were going to battle the Tweed Ring, they needed unity, organization, and outside support. But the Republicans were notoriously weak and inept. Then, as now, thousands of eligible voters never bothered to go to the polls. There was the danger that the none-too-reputable groups, like Mozart Hall and the Young Democracy, posing as reformers now that the Ring was embarrassed, might capture leadership from the reformers.

If the odds were formidable, the reformers were driven to work together if for no other reason than the fact that election day might be the last chance to destroy the Ring. Public indignation could not be sustained at a high pitch forever. Six days before the election, the Committee of Seventy released the evidence they unearthed from the Broadway Bank accounts. Important Republicans were persuaded to unite in a common cause by voting a straight reform ticket and not to present a separate Republican ticket to complicate matters. Young Men's Reform Associations were organized. The students of New York University, to whom Hall had recently lectured with applause, tore down the Mayor's portrait from their walls. The newspapers maintained a heavy barrage, exhorting voters to register, publicizing the facts behind the Ring's schemes, and explaining all the tactics Tammany might use to defraud the public on election day. Huge express wagons, drawn by six horses, stood ready to convey a reserve police force to any scene of disorder.

Plans were made to take detected repeaters to the armories for custody to avoid the sure chance of their discharge by the courts. With a burst of excitement and energy, the reformers invaded the lower wards, the central nervous system of Tammany Hall, posting signs, passing out pamphlets, haranguing the native and immigrant poor with sidewalk speeches.

The tempo increased as the clergy of New York, pounding their pulpits, spoke out against the Tweed Ring for the first time. Dr Henry D. Northrup of the Presbyterian Church echoed a common theme: there were but two parties, he roared, God's and the devil's. Election day "is a time when every citizen should show himself to be a man and not a sneak." [66]

The reformers who now thought they could win, called several rallies to keep things at a white heat. On November 2, a rally was held to receive the report of the Committee of Seventy. The motto over the president's chair read: "What are we going to do about it?" George Templeton Strong, pessimistic as usual, did not think they were going to do anything. "The disease of this community," he wrote in his diary, "lies too deep to be cured by meetings, resolutions, and committees. We the people are a low set, without moral virility. Our rulers, Tweed and Company, are about good enough for us." [67]

But Strong's pessimism seemed to be shared by few. The cadence of protest from the reformers, the press, the clergy, was picked up in the saloons, the restaurants, the clubs. Apathy had vanished. New York was agog with one topic of conversation, not the recent Chicago fire, not the visit of the Grand Duke Alexis, but the chance—the bare chance, that the reformers might beat the Tweed Ring on November 7th. On the eve of election day, New Yorkers waited with apprehension, and prepared themselves for one of the most important and exciting elections ever held in New York City.

Much to their own astonishment, the reformers gave Tammany Hall one of the worst defeats in its history up to that time. The scandals had finally roused New Yorkers into action. There was an unusually large turn-out, and many who previously had been apathetic, went to the polls and registered their indignation with Tammany. The reformers guarded the polling places well, and were successful in protecting themselves against excessive fraud and repeating. Moreover, several of the repeater gangs sensed the fall of the Ring and withdrew their support. The reformers elected all fifteen Aldermen, thirteen Assistant Aldermen out of twenty-one, and carried fourteen of the twenty Assembly districts. Prominent among the new Assemblymen were ex-Mayor Daniel E. Tiemann and Samuel Tilden. General Franz Siegel effectively wooed the Germans and became State Register. There were impressive upstate gains. The reformers captured four out of five Senatorial seats. The one they failed to win was the sour note. O'Donovan Rossa had once led the Irish against the British but could not do the same against Tweed in New York. The people of the Seventh District stood by the man who had served them so well with patronage and charity, and Tweed won over Rossa by over 10,000 votes. The reformers' broom swept out many of the Ring's important lieutenants. Henry Woltman was defeated by Augustus Weismann, the first German-born man to be elected to the State Senate. Timothy Campbell, Henry Genet, James Irving, and Michael Norton were all defeated. Alexander Frear and Thomas Fields were prevented from taking their seats because of election fraud. The full measure of defeat was revealed a few days later. It was announced that the annual Americus Club ball was postponed.

Once again the *Times* reported a quiet election day. It was a moot point, the newspaper said, whether this resulted from the precautions taken by the reformers or that Tammany was cowed. Of course there were some "altercations and word-combats," and, "heads punched in the good old fashion so dear to the Democracy." Compared to the previous year, the reformers had won away from the regular Democrats almost 75,000 votes in the city and state, "one of the most remarkable political revolutions in the history of the country," said a contemporary, with some exaggeration.[68] The *Times* maintained that the election was won by the strong vote of the so-called neutral population, who seldom voted—"the gentlemen and quiet citizens." [69] But while there was a large registration, there were not enough neutrals to decide the election. Ironically, it was the very people the reformers despised the most, the immigrants and the native poor, who, because of their great numbers, put the reformers into office by splitting their vote between Tammany and the men running on the Democratic reform ticket.[70]

The victory over Tammany was seen as the end of a great crusade. There was much excitement. For most it meant the vindication of popular government, the triumph of the people's voice, a moral struggle where good overwhelmed evil. Under a huge headline, "New York Redeemed," the *Times* said:

> The victory we have won is priceless, not only from what it gives us now, but because it will revive every man's faith in the ultimate triumph of truth and justice—because it will teach scheming politicians that the voice of the people is supreme, and that immortal principles on which this Government is founded, although they may be momentarily stifled by dishonest factions, will constantly rise triumphant, while the men who assailed them will pass away to everlasting infamy.[71]

The reformer George C. Barrett, a successful candidate, said the victory was an answer to those who had scoffed at the success of a republican form of government.[72] *Harper's Weekly* said it was one of the most significant events in the history of free governments.[73]

Only E. L. Godkin pondered whether the great "uprising" was the final and complete triumph over political corruption, whether routing the rascals was only the beginning of reform—real reform.[74]

18

"WHAT ARE YOU GOING TO DO ABOUT IT?"

And put in every hand a whip
To lash the rascals naked through the world.

Shakespeare, *Measure for Measure*

THE ELECTION of 1871 destroyed the Tweed Ring. Glorious as this was to many New Yorkers, it was only a political victory. To make it a complete victory, members of the Ring and their henchmen had to be indicted and sent to jail. On October 17, 1871, the last phase of the crusade began when Charles O'Conor, more dedicated to the complete devastation of the Tweed Ring than any of the other reform leaders, was made Special State Attorney General. He was in charge of the civil suits against the Ring and those who had worked with it. Ten days later, the Committee of Seventy brought criminal charges against the Ring organization by presenting a complaint, signed by Tilden, and its evidence: a huge pile of 190 vouchers demonstrating that the city and county of New York had been defrauded of $6,312,541.37. Henry J. Taintor, appointed special investigator, began his six-year quest for additional incriminating evidence. For the next twenty-four months, reinforced by the findings of Taintor and special investigating groups like the so-called Booth Committee, indictments were issued against all who aided, abetted, and profited from five years of plundering.[1] New York was to be doubly redeemed: civil suits would recover the taxpayers' money, and criminal suits would send the rogues to jail. What the voice of the people and the power of the press had sown, the courts would reap: the end of the Ring's political power and the rebirth of republican institutions in New York.

It soon became apparent that the story of the Tweed Ring might not have the happy ending the reformers expected. If a politician must win an election to become a legislator, the reformer must catch and hold a wrongdoer before he can prosecute him. Stripped of power, patronage, and profit; threatened with the loss of shiny hat and gaudy vest, renegade Tammany braves did not wait for the slow grinding of due process. The Ring organization men scattered. The first to flee were most of those named in the first indictments. They left in October, not even waiting to see if the Ring could win the election and thus stymie the indictments in the courts. E. A. Woodward transferred his property to his wife's name and left for the quiet of the countryside. James Sweeny, the Squire's brother, left hastily for France. He died there four years later, an alcoholic. Police and excited newspapermen made an intense search for James Ingersoll, the millionaire furniture-maker. A reporter interviewed Ingersoll's father.

> "Will you tell me where he has gone?"
> "Well, I think he went East."
> "To Portland, for instance?"
> "Portland! Yes, oh, yes. He went to Portland. Went on Friday."
> "Why did he go?"
> "Why did he go? Why, he had business there, I suppose. Yes, he had business there."
> "His wife went with him, I presume?"
> "His wife! Oh! Yes, his wife! She always goes with him." [2]

If Ingersoll went to Portland, he kept on going. He, like James Sweeny, preferred Paris as a refuge. He returned later and was arrested. Andrew Garvey suddenly retired from the profession of plastering walls. A 240-pound six-footer, he found it difficult to disguise his identity. On a ship traveling to Germany, a vacationing

New Yorker recognized him and dutifully wrote the *Times*. He reported that Mrs. Garvey showed him a gift that Tweed gave her, a gold dollar with the Lord's Prayer engraved on it. He also pointed out that she was carrying a large amount of money concealed in her dress. Garvey, he said, was extremely nervous. At Bremerhaven a German pilot came aboard and Garvey mistook him for a policeman; "like a true son of Tammany," he tried to bribe the man. The pilot, surprised and indignant, threw the money overboard. People laughed. Garvey fled.[3]

After the election the exodus of Tammany politicians increased. The friendly Republican Hank Smith, bank president and Police Commissioner, fled when indicted for fraud in the Bowling Green Bank and for dipping into the Police Fund, a charity for police widows and orphans.[4] George Templeton Strong reported that Mike Norton, Thomas Coman, and James Walsh had vanished. "They were among the minnows whose Triton was Tweed. Their bereaved bailers are seeking them diligently but in vain."[5] James Bradley found he needed a vacation, as did Alexander Frear and Thomas Fields. John Keyser, who had been plagued since July by the *Times* citing his misdeeds, replied to a reporter who asked him if he had anything to say in his own defense, "I have nothing to say except that I am sick, worried out, broken-hearted and hunted down."[6] A few weeks later he vanished. He returned to New York some months later, but he was never sent to jail.

The constantly recurring question, "Have you heard where Genet is?" came to be regarded, said a newspaper, as a joke. Henry Genet held on for two years, befitting the slippery nature of his grand-uncle, Edmond Charles Genêt, Minister of the French Republic to the United States in 1793. He was indicted for fraudulently certifying bills for construction on the Harlem Court House when he was a Commissioner of that project. He was finally arrested, tried, and convicted. Sheriff Matt Brennan, however, dallied in turning him over to Tombs prison after his conviction. One Sunday Genet and his custodian, Deputy Sheriff Shields, celebrated the Sabbath by roaming the bars from Harlem to Astor

House and getting roaring drunk. The next day Brennan was ordered to appear in court with his prisoner. The court was waiting, the attorneys were in their places, the judge was ready, and the Sheriff arrived. At that moment the joke about Genet's whereabouts was born. Brennan explained he had allowed Genet some time to go home and "arrange his affairs," and the dashing Prince Hal had skipped.[7] Brennan got thirty days in Ludlow Street jail and Genet a vacation in Europe.

Not all the associates of the Ring fled. James Irving never had the chance. The former Assemblyman, who was forced to resign for assaulting a colleague, was involved in another brawl on election day. He and two notorious thugs, Owen Geohegan and "Gallows Pat," were arrested for stabbing a policeman six times when he caught them stuffing ballot boxes.[8] Others chose resignation rather than flight. Nathaniel Sands, educator, Tax Assessor, and secretary of the Citizens' Association, for example, resigned all his offices when it was discovered that he had received $75,000 in commissions for helping Connolly to arrange city loans.[9]

The downfall of the Ring had its effect on the business community. The New York Printing Company was sold. The Bowling Green Bank and the Guardian Bank for Savings (William M. Tweed, president), which had swindled its customers and had facilitated various schemes of the Ring, passed into the hands of receivers. The Oriental Savings Bank, fearful that its charter might be repealed, fired one of its trustees—William M. Tweed, Jr. Thirty-seven newspapers, mostly obscure weeklies, died with the Ring. In 1875, instead of paying over a million dollars a year for advertising, the city and county paid only $100,000.[10] Even the *Leader*, long the loudest and most ardent supporter of all things Tammany, passed from the scene. Oakey Hall, as one of its steadiest contributors, could not resist one last pun. "Next year being leap year the *Leader* will leap it." [11]

Thus the first phase of the legal crusade served politics more than justice. The Ring's last political strongholds were overwhelmed. There were many indictments and few casualties. If the smaller fish slipped away, the reformers made plans to hook the biggest fish of all, members of the Ring itself. The evidence against them seemed overwhelming.

The first one got away. Peter Barr Sweeny hated publicity, and being indicted for stealing millions would cause much publicity. He hated courtrooms, especially after his humiliating performance as District Attorney thirteen years earlier. Moreover, he wasn't feeling well. He escaped all these irritations by resigning from the Park Commission, and, complaining of being sick, leaving for Canada to seek his health. The *Times* was furious: Who goes to Canada in the dead of winter when he is sick? it asked.[12] Sweeny later joined his brother in Paris. He would return another day.

Richard B. Connolly was hooked, momentarily. For his co-operation with the reformers by putting Andrew Green in his office, Connolly expected to be treated with leniency. He learned, however, that reformers could play as hard as Tammany Hall. On January 2, 1873, he was arrested. Connolly was flabbergasted to find his bail set at one million dollars. Tilden testified that no double cross was ever intended and that he did not even know Connolly was to be arrested. This was a curious statement, since it was Tilden who signed the complaint that led to Connolly's arrest.[13] The Big Judge's attorneys tried desperately to effect a compromise. Havemeyer would not listen and Tilden suddenly became aloof. As the Police Superintendent said about Genet, Connolly did the only thing a sane man could do. He fled abroad with six million dollars, to spend his days wandering from one country to another. An American tourist reported seeing him much later in Egypt, sitting upon the piazza of his hotel, a lonely, melancholy man, "shunned by everybody, with trembling hands and vacant eyes."[14] He was tried and convicted *in absentia*. But this was an empty gesture, a waste of the taxpayers' money. Slippery Dick Connolly never returned to New York.

No one in the Ring's hierarchy was more elusive and adept at evading the reformers' legal net than the Elegant Oakey Hall. Unlike Connolly or Sweeny, he did not run; he stayed and defended himself on the reformers' own grounds—the courts. From October 1871 to December 1873, he appeared in court four times—for a preliminary hearing before a grand jury, and three trials. Each time the reformers thought they had caught their elegant Mayor, only to see him flip off their line. Hall understood the inherent drama in a criminal trial and played his role as showman to full effect: he could be gay, witty, and charming, or suddenly caustic or tearfully melancholy. He was always the soul of innocence. The one uncertainty in the legal crusade against the Ring was the trial jury itself. While the prosecution paraded its impressive display of evidence, hard facts, and incriminating statistics, Hall posed, pranced, told jokes, and played on the jury's emotions. Each trial became a celebrated affair, the courtroom packed with a motley crowd, from Tammany toughs to silk-stocking gentry. It seemed that the reason for having so many trials was not some legal technicality, but because the public demanded to have an encore of his previous performance.

The first act of the Hall melodrama began in October 1871 when a Grand Jury was called to decide whether Hall should be indicted for malfeasance in office. Hall arrived smart and trim, wearing new kid gloves and a gay tartan cravat, and twirling a light cane. The main outlines of Hall's defense and the contentions of the prosecution were established at this time, and were repeated in every forthcoming trial. The reformers had collected all the vouchers approved by the Board of Audit in 1870, over $6 million of which were fraudulent. Presented with this evidence, Hall acknowledged he had signed them and had approved them only in his "ministerial" capacity. Tweed and Connolly, he argued, were responsible for their incorrectness. Since 39,257 warrants had passed through his office in two and one-half years, Hall claimed he did not have the time to examine each in detail. William Copeland, James O'Brien's busy spy, testified to the effect that even a cursory examination would reveal irregularities.[15] A glance at the names receiving payment should have aroused suspicion, as would the fact that one happy contractor often received ten to twelve warrants in a single day. The prosecution pointed out that signing vouchers without affidavits which certified their authenticity was a misdemeanor in itself.[16] Hall's counsel, his law partner, A. J. Vanderpoel, tried to slough off these embarrassing points by saying that as Hall's law partner he had noticed that his client did not have the talents of a businessman; routine administrative work was just not Oakey Hall's forte; in effect, Hall had "an ineradicable aversion to details." [17] The *Times* wondered how a man with an aversion to details could run the greatest city in the country. And, finally, Tilden contested Hall's major contention. The function of the Board of Audit "was not a ministerial duty," he said, "but a judicial one," therefore the Board had the responsibility of examining the validity of each claim.[18]

District Attorney Garvin, a Tammany Sachem who survived the uprising against the Ring, gave Hall a helping hand when he instructed the Grand Jury on the issues they would have to decide. The question before them was not whether Hall had done wrong, he said, but whether he had done it with a wrong intent. This was an extremely interesting statement for a District Attorney to make, since no one had appeared to testify to Hall's motives. Moreover, it raised a sticky legal question. What if Hall had been arrested for pickpocketing and stealing a watch? According to Garvin's logic, the question would be: Did Hall really *mean* to steal the watch? Were his intentions honorable or dishonorable when he put his hand into the man's pocket? The Grand Jury apparently never pondered these questions. On October 25, 1871, the charge against Hall was dismissed, although the Mayor was scolded for being "careless and negligent" in signing the disreputable warrants. The *Times* was indignant. A. Oakey Hall innocent! "Tell it to the marines!" [19]

The second act began in February 1872 with a new Grand Jury, who did indict the Mayor. Hall seemed undismayed. "A friend," Hall said, "asked if I had given bail. I replied that I did not wish to exert a baleful influence." This was more than Dana could take. The *Sun* replied with a headline: "WILL MAYOR HALL CRACK A

HIDEOUS JOKE AT HIS OWN FUNERAL?"[20] The trial began in February and ended suddenly on March 8. A juror died and a mistrial was declared. The second trial ended with a hung jury. The third and final act of what had now become a farce began on December 22, 1873, and ended two days later. It was a rehash of the evidence and arguments of the grand jury hearing. The prosecution, represented by Wheeler Peckham and Lyman Tremain, concluded its case by insisting that professed ignorance of corruption was no excuse for willful neglect. After two hours of deliberations, the foreman of the jury returned and asked a technical question. Judge Daniels answered it and added with some gusto that if the jury did not find a verdict soon he would lock them in their chambers all night. It was Christmas Eve. Two and a half hours later Hall was acquitted.

Thus another Ring member escaped the law. Hall had managed to retain his office to the end of his term. Four years later, the testimony of Tweed, Garvey, and Woodward in the Tweed investigation added more evidence—as if any were needed—involving Hall in Ring operations.[21] But nothing was done about it. Hall spent his remaining years as a newspaperman and attorney. On March 25, 1898, the former anti-Catholic Know-Nothing was baptized into the Catholic Church. His sponsor: Peter Barr Sweeny. Seven months later Hall was dead. He was elegant to the end.

"Others ran. Others hid. Others could not be found," said John Graham, pointing to his client, Boss Tweed, "but here he is, like a Roman!"[22] It was January 30, 1873, a day many New Yorkers expected to celebrate. In a few hours it seemed inevitable that in the court of Oyer and Terminer a jury would find William Marcy Tweed guilty of all his crimes. If some reserved doubt about this, it might have been because it took more than a year of legal wrangling to get the Boss into a courtroom in the first place.

On December 15, 1871, a month after the Tweed Ring was beaten at the polls, a Grand Jury returned an indictment against Tweed, and he was arrested the next day. He resigned from the

Public Works Department, and a movement was started to prevent him from taking his seat in the State Senate. On December 30, Tammany Hall voted him out of power, and Augustus Schell replaced him as Grand Sachem. The full measure of his defeat, said the *Times,* could only be calculated by finding how much support he still had left among the humble rank and file. A reporter was dispatched. Traveling uptown on a trolley, the reporter asked the conductor how Tweed's fall affected the boys in his district. "We don't know what to be drivin' after," he answered. "I don't keer to drive a coughin' hoss; do you? Yer see, Tweed's gone over if he ain't gone under." The reporter asked if Tweed somehow managed to rise again, would the conductor vote for him. "What'd be the use o' that? I ain't no fool. The man as bosses our district's got to do suthin' for it, and I don't think Tweed's the man now. What's the use o' cryin' after spilt milk? . . . Sir, it's no use. He's bust higher 'n a kite."

Turning from the conductor, the reporter talked to a dockworker, who told him Tweed had done a lot for his kind. "What did he do?" "I've had many a day's work through him. He'd always give a chap something to do. Many of our chaps have lived on him." Asked if there were an election tomorrow, would he vote for Tweed, the dockworker replied: "Me? No. Why, what do you take me for?"

These interviews, plus a number of others the same reporter made, concluded the *Times,* reminded it of a poem that might touch the Boss's heart.

> Where are the friends of my youth?
> Where are those dear ones gone?
> Why have they fallen like the leaf?
> Why have they left me to mourn?[23]

Deserted as he was, Tweed was either too proud, overconfident, or stubborn to run, even though there was more damaging evidence against him than any other member of the Ring. He hired a battery of attorneys, among whom were David Dudley Fields, a wizard at tying up a court in its own technicalities; John Graham, one of the greatest criminal lawyers of his day, whose talents of cross-examination were matched only by his ability to identify his client with mother, mercy, God, and country; and a young, brilliant attorney, later to be Secretary of State under Theodore Roosevelt, Elihu Root. It was a formidable counsel faced with a formidable job.

Ironically, the reformers gave Tweed's attorneys their first opportunity. Charles O'Conor, acting as the Attorney General's deputy, was fearful that if the legal officers of New York City handled the Tweed case, the Boss would be allowed to go free. He therefore demanded that action be brought in the name of the State. Fields immediately seized upon this to argue that the money stolen belonged to the City and County of New York, and that the State could not maintain an action for the theft. This involved the courts in a complex legal battle which lasted more than a year.[24] The Court of Appeals finally settled this dispute by merging the County suits with those of the State. Fields had achieved his goal: a long delay in the hope that time would cool public indignation.

The first trial of Tweed began on January 7, 1873. On January 30, the jury reported it could not reach a verdict. O'Conor, Tilden, and Peckham prepared for another trial, and Tweed took a vacation in California.

There were rumors, never proven, that the jury had been packed and bribed. The quality of the jury aroused this suspicion. One was a "bummer" known to be destitute. Someone gave him a suit of clothes and by "a mysterious process" he was accepted for jury duty. Another was an ex-convict. One said frankly he found serving on juries profitable. Nicholas Muller and Thomas Lynch, known thugs, were seen entertaining jurors at Delmonico's. And Douglas Taylor, Tammany Sachem and friend of the Boss, was Commissioner of the Jury.[25]

The second trial of Tweed began on November 19, 1873, a few weeks before Mayor Hall was acquitted. Warrants were presented totaling over six million fraudulent dollars, made prominent by the scrawl of Tweed's signature. Facts and testimony mounted against Tweed, but he remained calm, trusting in the sonorous outbursts of John Graham. At the end, Graham began his summary, but he never finished. "Overcome by emotion, [he] sank into a chair, and bending forward over a table, with his head between his hands, [he] sobbed convulsively. It was an awful moment," reported Matthew Breen. "Tweed hid his face in his hands and wept." Even the prosecuting attorney, Lyman Tremain, went "pale . . . his lips quivered. There was no man in the Court room that was not visibly moved, but one—Judge Davis on the Bench." [26]

The jury, this time thoroughly screened, delivered a verdict of guilty. The day of sentencing was a scene of "great drama." There was the fearless magistrate on the bench, and the fallen Tweed before him, "his face . . . stolid and his gaze almost vacant. At times his lip quivered, but in the main he was wonderfully calm. . . . When Judge Davis, referring to the audacity of the criminal, brought his hand down upon his desk by way of emphasis, a tremor, faint but still perceptible, ran through the frame of the culprit." [27] Tweed was declared guilty on fifty-one of the fifty-five offenses charged, each offense including four counts, making two hundred and four counts in all. Instead of being sentenced for one charge, as Tweed's counsel expected, Davis gave him a cumulative sentence, punishment for each offense charged. Tweed was sentenced to twelve years in prison and given a $12,750 fine.

The reformers were elated; good had conquered evil. The *Times* congratulated itself for a job well done and added that the City had redeemed itself.[28] George Templeton Strong, in one of his dark moods, was not so sure. "Pity he can't be hanged," he wrote. "But he'll get a new trial, I suppose, and probably get off altogether, the rank, old felonious dog-fox!" [29]

There was a small truth in Strong's prophecy. On January 15, 1875, after one year of prison, Tweed was released and his fine lowered to $250. His attorneys had won release from the Court of Appeals on the ground that a cumulative sentence was improper. The court ruled that while an indictment might contain any number of counts, no punishment in excess of that prescribed for one offense could be inflicted, and the offense for which he had been charged called for a sentence of one year and a $250 fine. Unhappily for Tweed, as soon as he was released he was again arrested and put in Ludlow Street jail. The reformers had anticipated the reversed decision. A civil suit was brought against Tweed in the name of the State. Tweed was held on three million dollars' bail.[30]

The Boss was forced to remain in jail. To have put up his own money for bail would have meant its certain loss in the event his coming trial went against him, and it looked as if it would. But life was gracious at Ludlow. For nearly a year, Warden Dunham and a keeper took him for a drive every afternoon, stopping on the way back at Tweed's home where Mrs. Tweed would have dinner waiting.[31] One evening, while the Boss and his congenial jailers were awaiting dinner at the Tweed mansion, Tweed went upstairs to talk to his wife. Like Connolly, Sweeny, Genet, and others, Tweed became a sane man, and Warden Dunham, like Sheriff Brennan, had to undergo the embarrassment of announcing that his prisoner had escaped. It was December 4, 1875. By a curious coincidence, it was the day before rehearsals began on ex-Mayor Oakey Hall's new play, *The Crucible*, a melodrama vindicating Hall's part in the Tweed Ring, and after it opened and played twenty-two performances, a failure.

Tweed's escape was a sensation. For months rumors circulated about the city as to his whereabouts. He was reported having been seen in North Carolina, Savannah, Havana, Augusta, and one person claimed to have seen him in Canada. Actually, Tweed hid nearby in New Jersey, anxiously awaiting the outcome of his trial, which began on February 7, 1876.[32] If he won the case, he could return to New York. On March 9, 1876, the jury brought in a verdict against Tweed for recovery of $6 million. Tweed was working as a laborer in the Jersey Palisades at the time. He fled to Florida, to Cuba, and finally shipped to Spain as a seaman.

The finest of ironies proved the Boss's undoing: he was recognized through one of Thomas Nast's cartoons! American authorities in Cuba learned that Tweed was en route to Spain, but they did not have a picture for the Spanish police for identification. They did have a copy of *Harper's Weekly,* which they forwarded. Although disguised as a sailor, he was recognized by the police. The Spanish police thought he was an escaped kidnaper, and notified the American authorities that the notorious "kidnaper" had been captured.[33] He was returned to New York on an American ship, arriving November 23, 1876.

In Ludlow Street jail the Warden obligingly rented his own comfortable room to Tweed and allowed the Boss the services of a Negro servant named Luke. Tweed would sit by his window by the hour, where it was reported, perhaps with some exaggeration, "he would call out the names of one of every four persons who passed by during the day, and he could give details of their business, residence, relations, and events in their lives to the few intimates who cared to visit him."[34] In jail Tweed became desperate. Plagued by heart trouble, diabetes, and bronchitis, he saw both his health and his wealth fading. He was faced with a $6 million civil suit and thirteen criminal indictments, ranging from grand larceny to forgery. He contacted Charles Fairchild, the Attorney General, offering to give him a full confession of his criminal activities, checks he had received from many associates, to appear as a witness for the State in any case requested, and to turn over to the State all his real and personal property, in return for his release. According to Tweed's attorney, John Townsend, who later wrote a book on the politics of the Tweed era, Fairchild agreed to the bargain, warning Tweed he must make it a thorough confession, including names, dates, and amounts in connection with all Ring activities. Tweed prepared the document and gave it to Fairchild, with the added condition that if it was used for anything else than the matter on hand, he would be released. It was agreed. Fairchild showed it to his father, Sidney Fairchild, John Bigelow, Tilden, Peckham, and Corporation Counsel William C. Whitney, asking the last two to verify it, which they did, by checking and talking several times thereafter to Tweed.[35] Fairchild, however, according to Townsend, never told his associates that he had promised to release Tweed. And then Peter Barr Sweeny entered the picture.

After Tweed had escaped and was not expected to return, Fairchild had entered into a remarkable agreement with Sweeny. If the Squire would come out of hiding and stand trial, he would be granted complete immunity from further indictment, arrest, and bail while he was awaiting trial and for thirty days after the trial. Sweeny agreed and arrived from Europe on December 19, 1876. For Sweeny, it was a grand opportunity. With Tweed and the rest of his associates gone, and the public indifferent, he ran little risk of being confronted with embarrassing witnesses, and had a good chance of recovering all or part of the $6 million of property the city had attached when he first left.[36] If all went well he might remain in New York; if not, he had thirty days in which to leave. The return of the Boss, however, changed all this entirely. Tweed's testimony could prove extremely damaging.

Meanwhile, Tweed was becoming anxious, not only because Fairchild was keeping his confession for an undue length of time, but also because he heard rumors that Sweeny might be let off for the price of returning some money, whereas he (Tweed) would be tried and sent to prison. On June 8, 1877, this seemed to be true. It was announced that Sweeny had settled with the State for $400,000. The case was closed. Sweeny, the partner in masterminding the sack of New York, went free. The terms of the settlement were such that he deserved to be called, as the *New York Telegram* put it, the Metternich, Talleyrand, and Pitt of the Ring. In the first place, the case was made, not against his name, but his brother's. In the second place, the settlement was made from the estate of his dead brother James, leaving Sweeny's nest egg untouched. Townsend argued with good logic that Sweeny had remained virtuous while transferring his guilt to his brother. Townsend charged that Tweed's confession had been used as a threat against Sweeny, thus breaking the original agreement and, therefore, Tweed should be released.[37]

Four days later, Tweed received a greater shock. Fairchild returned the confession and said it failed to disclose evidence sufficient to justify Tweed's release. There was "a fatal variance," Fairchild said, between Tweed's confession and what he had said to Peckham and Whitney.[38] He never said, however, what the variance was.

Here the crusade against the Ring ended. It was not that the confession and accompanying checks were insufficient evidence, it was that they were too much evidence. The confession involved men high in office, city, state, and town. If Fairchild had completed his bargain, Tweed's confession, the testimony he could have offered in any court action, and other papers he had at his disposal would have blown the roofs off Tammany and the State Capitol because the potential scandal would have been even greater than the Ring exposures themselves. Ironically, at the moment the crusade could be reborn it died, and the responsibility came from those who called themselves reformers. As the *Times* said, "Could even Mr. Tilden afford to have Tweed's story told?"[39] Even Judge Noah Davis, who had sentenced Tweed, condemned the Attorney General and his associates for making the Boss a scapegoat and withholding evidence. The *Tribune* flatly accused Fairchild of suppressing the truth, saying that it would have ruined half the respectable statesmen of both parties![40]

There is strong evidence to support this view, for instance, in the confession itself, a lengthy document, published in full in the *New York Herald*, October 10, 1877. Among other things it contained a description of various swindles and who was involved; a list of twenty-one State Senators who were bribed; a description of how Tweed worked in the legislature; an interesting list of checks, donations, loans, and to whom they were paid; and a list entitled: "Gross Amounts Paid to the Following Persons."

As the confession appeared in the *Herald*, it was unsupported evidence needing corroborative testimony. But the Tweed forces promised such testimony could be produced. Actually, this was only the *beginning* of Tweed's confession, for Tweed had even more incriminating evidence. For example, there were other papers in Tweed's possession, later found in Whitney's papers by his biographer, Mark Hirsch, which promised embarrassment if revealed. There was the interesting information that Samuel Tilden on May 11, 1868, asked a special favor of Boss Tweed. He wanted the Boss to find a job for Samuel Allen, "a very old friend of ours." There was evidence that Daniel Manning, later the Secretary of the Treasury in Cleveland's cabinet, dealt closely with Tweed on New York political matters. There were letters from Peter Cooper and Robert B. Roosevelt, who later joined the anti-Ring crusade. David Bennett Hill, who became governor in 1885, wrote, "Although a week has elapsed I have heard nothing from you in reference to my offer. What do you say?" Moreover, there were indications that the Ring's influence was not entirely confined to New York. Congressman Henry W. Slocum, of Civil War fame, wrote asking for campaign funds, and Samuel S. "Sunset" Cox set up a meeting between Tweed and Congressman Samuel J. Randall, "to know Who's Who." [41]

Many years later, W. E. D. Stokes, a prominent civil engineer, found two trunks of Tweed papers (which subsequently have disappeared) which could have "blown the lid off" New York if Fairchild had not welshed on the agreement. Stokes described the documents in a letter of March 29, 1897, to Mayor William L. Strong. One packet of papers, he said, contained invitations of citizens then prominent for private conferences "to talk over a little profitable business." Stokes did not name the "prominent persons." Another bundle marked "Blackguards, Blackmailers and Thieves," contained letters from men both high and low "on the ladder," who threatened to expose Tweed if not paid. One written on the morning Tweed appeared before the Aldermen's investigating committee implored him not to expose him. There was Tweed's bribe book, a large ledger entitled, "Loan Book." It contained, said Stokes, "photographs of letters of which the originals had been reclaimed by the writers, no one knows at what cost. One public man got the letters of another politician and oh my! and then there are others and others." The most "curious" item of all was a list of monies stolen and the source and individuals involved.[42]

That Fairchild attempted to suppress the full truth about the Tweed Ring seems clear from several letters Whitney wrote to him.

> You have refused to let Tweed out to tell the story of these frauds, and so we must look elsewhere. The same rule does not apply to the clerks and subordinates, as to the ringleaders. . . . Tweed, as you and I know, constantly referred to one man as a person who could corroborate all that he, W. E. King, his deputy Commissioner of Public Works [did] . . . why is King kept away, and why should not he be allowed to come back? . . . if anything is done it must be done quickly. [You] must at least make an effort in this matter and help me out, or the responsibility of the judgment will be too heavy for us. . . .[43]

Fairchild refused to comply.

At the time, $9 million in claims were presented against the City by companies doing business with Tweed, which, when the Ring collapsed, never were able to get their money. There was a strong suspicion that most of the claims were fraudulent. Whitney was particularly concerned over the Baird Water-Meter case, "for which there is nothing to show except some thousands of unused and unusable, little good for nothing machines that have been lying for years in a yard up town."[44] Before Fairchild made his decision, Whitney urged him to accept Tweed's confession. As matters then stood, he said, the City stood to lose one million dollars alone on the water meter case. "Tweed's testimony is to the effect that the making of the contract was the result of a corrupt bargain. . . . We cannot as matters now stand prove it without him . . . it is quite probable that Tweed would save us that amount by telling the truth."[45] As it turned out, Whitney lost his case, and the City lost its million dollars.

There were other letters. Wheeler Peckham, having both studied the confession and having talked to Tweed, wrote that "his testimony would be important and I think with the corroboration we have effective." [46] On May 25, Peckham advised Fairchild that "in my view the trial of the case [Sweeny's] without Tweed gives us less than an even chance for success." [47]

It is unlikely that Fairchild himself was responsible for such an important decision. It was probably made from higher up, most possibly by Tilden, which, if true, would make the suppression of Tweed's evidence wonderfully ironic. However, Tilden's part cannot be proved. It is a matter of historical circumstantial evidence. Fairchild's father, Sidney J. Fairchild, one of the principal attorneys of the New York Central Railroad, was a good friend of Tilden. Charles Fairchild was a Tilden man, owing his position of Attorney General to Tilden's support. John Bigelow was Secretary of State under Tilden. All these men saw the Tweed confession when it was first given to Fairchild. Governor Lucius Robinson, who succeeded Tilden as Governor, and was Comptroller under Tilden, received Fairchild's report on the Tweed affair and accepted it with no criticism. Perhaps Townsend was right: "Tweed and his friends recognized the combination, and were perfectly certain that Tilden's will would be Fairchild's law, and their judgment was not at fault." [48]

Dissatisfaction with the State's action in regard to Tweed led the Board of Aldermen to appoint a special committee to investigate the Ring frauds independently. The so-called Tweed Investigation ran from July 19 to December 29, 1877. Testifying were Tweed, Garvey, Ingersoll, Woodward, Creamer, George Miller, John Keyser, a reunion of the old gang with some conspicuous exceptions. Sweeny, about to leave for Europe, refused to testify, claiming the immunity Fairchild had given him. The investigation produced the most important document on the history of the Tweed Ring. The *New York Sunday News* in a headline called it: "What Tweed Was Ready to Testify to Before Attorney General Fairchild." [49] It disclosed, among other things, the methods of the Ring, some of its operations in the State legislature, the manipulation behind the Adjusted Claims Law of 1868, and the extent of the Ring's power.

Some of this information had been brought out in the 1871 crusade against the Ring, a good deal had not. But the testimony on Sweeny alone was enough to make the Attorney General's compromise look ridiculous.[50]

Most of the testimony, in fact, provided fuel for another crusade. But it was 1877, not 1871. Tilden had already capitalized as much as he could on the Ring scandals; Charles O'Conor was old and sick; reigning Democrats did not want the boat rocked, and there were still too many Republicans around who had done business with the Ring. Nothing was done about it.

Ironically, it was the *Times* which best expressed the change of mood. It said it was "totally at a loss" to find what good could be served by examining Tweed "or any one else on that subject."[51] The *Star*, often taken to task by the *Times* for its Democratic persuasion, could not resist a comment. "What change has come over the *Times* since that period to transform it into the apologist and defender of the old accomplices of the Ring, puzzles the uninitiated public at this hour."[52]

The Fairchild decision broke Tweed's spirit; the rigors of a year of hiding broke his health. At the end of the Aldermen's investigation, he was gray, listless, and down from 280 pounds to 160. "They will be preaching sermons about me," he told his secretary.[53] Four months later they were. On the morning of April 12, 1878, five days before his fifty-fifth birthday, he called William Eggleston, one of his many attorneys, to his bedside and said faintly, "I hope Tilden and Fairchild are satisfied now." These were his last words.[54] When the bell of the Essex Market clock tolled high noon, he died of pneumonia at Ludlow Street jail, which he as a member of the Board of Supervisors had authorized to be built in 1859. On the following Sunday, the Reverend De Witt Talmadge had a few words to say.

> Alas! alas! young men, look at the contrast—in an elegant compartment of a Wagner palace car, surrounded by wine, cards and obsequious attendants, going to his Senatorial place at

> Albany; then look again at the plain box . . . behold the low-studded room, looking out upon a mean little dingy court where, a prisoner, exhausted, forsaken, miserable, betrayed, sick, William M. Tweed lies a-dying. From how high up to how low down! [55]

"If he had died in 1870," said an old crony, Coroner Henry Woltman, "Broadway would have been festooned with black, and every military and civil organization in the City would have followed him to Greenwood." [56] In the next century, criminals who achieved the sobriquet of "notorious," like Frankie Yale, Dion O'Bannion, and Anthony D'Andrea, would get funerals worthy of a king. Not so for Tweed. It was a modest funeral attended by the family, a sprinkling of friends, and about twenty politicians, the most prominent of whom was the burly "Honest" John Kelly, who was to succeed Tweed as Boss of New York. A meager procession of eight carriages crossed by ferry to Brooklyn and Greenwood Cemetery. There Boss Tweed was buried in white lambskin—"the emblem of innocence." [57]

What, then, was the final reckoning of the Tweed Ring? Although Judges Barnard and McCunn were impeached, and removed from office, and Cardozo resigned but continued to practice law, none of the three were criminally prosecuted. With two exceptions, none of the Ring and its many partners in graft were ever caught or punished. Only Tweed and Ingersoll went to jail. From 1871 to 1878, Tweed spent less than half of that time in prison. Ingersoll who turned himself in, hoping for a light sentence, was sentenced to five years and seven months, but served only a few months of his term before he was pardoned by Tilden for turning State's evidence and promising to become a witness in any forthcoming Ring trials. At the time of Tweed's death sixteen suits were pending against various members of the Tweed Ring organization.[58] None came to trial. Garvey was granted immunity to appear as a witness at the Tweed and Hall trials. Although a millionaire, he never returned any of the money he made. Woodward was granted immunity for returning $155,000, although he had stolen over a million. John Keyser had the delightful gall to claim that it was the city who owed him, and he was almost successful in being awarded a $33,000 claim based on a fraudulent contract![59] Of the twenty to two hundred million dollars estimated to have been stolen by the Ring, it cost the city $257,848.34 to recover $894,525.44, most of which came from the estates of two dead men, James Watson and James Sweeny.

The ethos of reform, however, was essentially moralistic and conservative. For some the issue was a total commitment to punishing bad men, not the examination of the institutions and conditions that made it possible for bad men to exist and thrive. To them, the cause of corruption was the work of evil men. Their optimism blinded them to the realities of a rapidly growing society, the massive growth of a great city and the effects it would have on political life. For those who questioned institutions, the answer lay not in adaptation but in a return to the good old days of rule by gentry, suffrage restrictions, tight economy, and a tiny bureaucracy. In the months, years, and decades following the Ring's fall, the reformer, imprisoned by his own social philosophy, continued to alienate the immigrant newcomer. What could have been a source of power for the reformer remained the strength of later city bosses. As the city grew and its problems multiplied, the reformer continued to turn back to that Promised Land of the good old days for his solutions to corruption, patching the charter here, passing a resolution there, always haunted by his failure to restore the profession of politics to the nobility of the Old Republic. Exposure of the Tweed Ring had given him a glimpse into the hard realities of big-city politics. But he continued to be an innocent abroad in the strange land of the professional politician and practical politics, preferring the platitude to the free cigar. He never understood the politicians who made politics their business, their appeal to the masses, their attention to the plight of the immigrant, nor, indeed, the kind of world they were living in. Thus the rascals were routed, but their supreme achievement, the city machine itself, remained essentially intact, to become a model, a legacy, to be improved upon by succeeding monarchs of New York, the Kellys, the Crokers, and the Murphys.

After all was said and done, the crusade against the Tweed Ring won the battle but lost the war. In a real sense, William Marcy Tweed had the last word, when he asked, "Well, what are you going to do about it?"

NOTES

1. "THAT IMPUDENT AUTOCRAT"

1. Harold Zink, *City Bosses in the United States*, 1930, p. 96.
2. Eric F. Goldman, *Rendezvous With Destiny*, 1953, p. 30.
3. *New York Times*, May 19, 1871.
4. Charles Garrett, *The La Guardia Years*, 1961, p. 5.
5. Samuel J. Tilden, *The New York City Ring: Its Origin, Maturity and Fall*, 1873, p. 47.
6. Gustavus Myers, *History of Tammany Hall*, 1917, p. 285.
7. Charles Wingate, "Episode in Municipal Government," *North American Review*, Oct. 1874, p. 381, James Bryce, *American Commonwealth* (3rd ed.), Vol. 2, p. 400.
8. Francis G. Fairfield, *The Clubs of New York*, 1873, p. 243.
9. Ibid.
10. *New York Sun*, March 26, 1870.
11. April 14, 1870.
12. Denis Lynch, *Boss Tweed*, 1927, p. 417.
13. Wingate, "An Episode in Municipal Government," *North American Review*, Oct. 1874, p. 361.
14. M. R. Werner, *Tammany Hall*, 1928, p. 108.
15. Lynch, *Boss Tweed*, pp. 67-9, 73-9; Werner, *Tammany Hall*, pp. 107-8; Daniel Van Pelt, *Leslie's History of New York* (4 vols., 1898), Vol. 1, p. 435; Wingate, "Episode in Municipal Government," *North American Review*, Oct. 1874, pp. 365-6.
16. Lynch, *Boss Tweed*, p. 73.
17. Werner, *Tammany Hall*, p. 109.

2. THE TRIUMPH OF TWEED

1. *New York Herald Tribune*, Sept. 18, 1927.
2. *The Nation*, Nov. 7, 1878, p. 280.
3. Alexander C. Flick, *History of the State of New York*, Vol. 7, p. 144.
4. Werner, *Tammany Hall*, p. 85.
5. See *Sixteenth Annual Report*, 1911, American Scenic and Historic Preservation Society.
6. Robert B. Roosevelt (ed.), *The Poetical Works of Charles G. Halpine.*
7. *New York Herald*, May 20, 1871.
8. Lynch, *Boss Tweed*, p. 110.
9. *Proceedings of the Board of Supervisors of the City and County of New York:* July 1–Dec. 31, 1860, pp. 13, 207, 235, 275, 761; July 1–Dec. 31, 1862, pp. 25, 64.
10. Wingate, "Episode in Municipal Government," Jan. 1875, p. 130.
11. Board of Aldermen of New York City, *Report of the Special Committee of the Board of Aldermen Appointed to Investigate the "Ring" Frauds, Together with the Testimony Elicited During the Investigation*, Jan. 4, 1878, Document No. 8, pp. 20, 32. Hereafter cited as the *Tweed Investigation.*
12. Ibid. p. 29.
13. Ibid. pp. 19-22.
14. Lynch, *Boss Tweed*, p. 241.
15. *New York Times*, Aug. 22, 1871.
16. *Tammany Scrapbooks*, Vol. 1, no page listed.
17. *Tweed Investigation*, pp. 24-5. After the Voorhis affair, the State legislature in the following year adopted a law requiring seven votes instead of six to appoint Election Inspectors, "and we couldn't do it the next year; then we had to get a vote positively," Tweed explained. Ibid. p. 25. The following year, the legislature took the appointment of Election Inspectors away from the Supervisors.
18. Lynch, *Boss Tweed*, p. 236.
19. Myers, *Tammany Hall*, p. 255.
20. Ibid.
21. Lynch, *Boss Tweed*, p. 285.
22. Wingate, "Episode in Municipal Government," Oct. 1874, p. 386.
23. Ibid. p. 384.
24. Wingate, "Episode in Municipal Government," Oct. 1874, p. 387.
25. Cited in *New York Times*, Nov. 29, 1870.

3. "THOSE BEASTLY RASCALS"

1. Croswell Bowen, *The Elegant Oakey,* 1956, p. 4.
2. Ibid. p. 71.
3. Werner, *Tammany Hall,* pp. 120-21.
4. Bowen, *Elegant Oakey,* pp. 72-3.
5. Ibid. p. 72.
6. Ibid. p. 73.
7. *Hall Scrapbooks,* Vol. 3, p. 51, citing the *New York World,* no day or month cited.
8. Quoted in Werner, *Tammany Hall,* p. 120.
9. Bowen, *Elegant Oakey,* p. 83.
10. Ibid. p. 61.
11. Werner, *Tammany Hall,* p. 118.
12. Wingate, "Episode in Municipal Government," Oct. 1874, p. 373.
13. *New York Times,* Dec. 18, 1871.
14. Bowen, *Elegant Oakey,* p. 56.
15. Quoted in Lynch, *Boss Tweed,* p. 278.
16. *New York Telegram,* Apr. 14, 1870.
17. *Hall Scrapbooks,* Vol. 3, p. 51; *New York Sun,* 1868, no day or month cited.
18. Lynch, *Boss Tweed,* pp. 151-2.
19. *New York Herald,* Nov. 26, 1869.
20. *New York Sun,* Mar. 26, 1870.
21. Lynch, *Boss Tweed,* p. 151.
22. *Tweed Investigation,* p. 105.
23. John Savage, *Peter B. Sweeny on the 'Ring Frauds' and other Public Questions,* 1894, p. 12.
24. Quoted in ibid. pp. 13-14.
25. *New York Star,* Mar. 5, 1870.
26. *Elegant Oakey,* p. 40.
27. Wingate, "Episode in Municipal Government," Oct. 1874, p. 375-7.
28. Lynch, *Boss Tweed,* p. 282.
29. Wingate, "Episode in Municipal Government," Oct. 1874, p. 375; *New York Tribune,* July 29, 1871.
30. Lynch, *Boss Tweed,* pp. 150-51.

4. TWEED'S TOWN

1. Edward Crapsey, *The Nether Side of New York,* 1872, p. 128.
2. *New York World,* May 11, 1924.

3. J. F. Richmond, *New York and Its Institutions*, 1872, p. 109.
4. *New York Tribune*, June 22, 1924.
5. Richmond, *New York . . . Institutions*, pp. 108, 113.
6. For a general discussion of economic development, see R. G. Albion *Rise of New York Port 1815-1860*, 1939; Wilson, *Memorial History* Vol. III, 334ff., 413ff.
7. Oscar Handlin, *The Newcomers*, 1959, p. 9. By 1867, a total of 300,000 savings bank depositors registered $77,000,000 of capital; $100,000,000 of internal revenue was collected; warehouses held $200,000,000 of products from all over the world; New York exported goods at $224,000,000. "The Report of the Committee on Municipal Reform," 1867, p. 139.
8. Fifteenth United States Census, *Population*, Vol. I, pp. 18-19.
9. William Allen Butler, *Our Great Metropolis*, p. 21; Moses King, *King's Handbook of New York*, 1893, p. 257.
10. Richmond, *New York . . . Institutions*, pp. 104-5.
11. Quoted from *Valentine's Manual of Old New York*, no date or page in Richard O'Connor, *Hell's Kitchen*, 1948, p. 41.
12. *New York Times*, Dec. 5, 1869.
13. O'Connor, *Hell's Kitchen*, p. 12.
14. Herbert Asbury, *The Gangs of New York*, 1927, p. 177.
15. T. DeWitt Talmage, *The Masque Torn Off*, 1879, pp. 47, 194, 523.
16. Quoted in Lynch, *Boss Tweed*, no source cited.
17. Stephen Smith, "The City That Was," 1911, p. 43.
18. *New York Times*, Apr. 10, 1870.
19. O'Connor, *Hell's Kitchen*, p. 14.
20. Gustav Lening, *The Dark Side of New York*, 1873, p. 348.
21. O'Connor, *Hell's Kitchen*, p. 93.
22. *New York Times*, Feb. 5, 1871.
23. Ibid.
24. Lening, *Dark Side of New York*, pp. 394-5.
25. Crapsey, *Nether Side of New York*, p. 161.
26. Quoted in Asbury, *Gangs of New York*, p. 183, no source cited.
27. Crapsey, *Nether Side of New York*, p. 388.
28. Ibid. p. 611.
29. Eugene Post, "The Wig and the Jimmy," 1869, Appendix, p. 30.
30. Asbury, *Gangs of New York*, pp. 5, 43-4; Werner, *Tammany Hall*, p. 65.
31. Asbury, *Gangs of New York*, pp. 29-30, 51, 63-4, 255-6; O'Connor, *Hell's Kitchen*, pp. 74-5.
32. "The Downfall of Tammany Hall" (no author cited), p. 9.

5. THE NEWCOMER

1. For a general discussion of immigration, see Robert Ernst, *Immigrant Life in New York City, 1825-1863*, 1949; Kate H. Claghorn, "The Foreign Immigrant in New York City," United States Industrial Commission, *Reports on Immigration*, 1901, Vol. xv, 449ff.; Marcus L. Hansen, *The Atlantic Migration;* and Oscar Handlin's excellent *The Uprooted*, 1951.
2. Handlin, *The Newcomers*, p. 11.
3. Claghorn, "Foreign Immigrant," p. 462.
4. Handlin, *The Newcomers*, pp. 11-12.

   Population increase of New York City, 1820 to 1870:

1820	123,706	1850	515,547
1830	197,112	1860	813,669
1840	312,710	1870	942,292

   Fifteenth Census of the United States, *Population*, I, 18, 19.
5. John R. Commons, "Immigration and Its Economic Effects," U.S. Industrial Commission, *Reports on Immigration* (1901), Vol. xv, 324. For a good contemporary account of the immigrant poor, their way of life and the urban problems they faced, see Stephen Smith, "The City That Was," pp. 87-125, 133, 144-7.
6. Charles Loring Brace, *The Dangerous Classes* (1872 ed.), p. 35.
7. Ibid.
8. Handlin, *The Newcomers*, pp. 18-19.
9. *New York Times*, Dec. 30, 1870.
10. Roy Peel has argued that the Irish did not achieve dominance in New York until the later years of the 1890's (*Political Clubs of New York City*, 1935, p. 252). Joseph McGoldrick, on the other hand, dates Irish leadership from the Tweed Ring era ("The New Tammany," *American Mercury*, Sept. 1928, p. 8). See also Charles Garrett, *The La Guardia Years*, 1961, p. 338, *n.* 23.
11. Florence E. Gibson, *The Attitudes of the New York Irish Toward State, and National Affairs, 1848-1892*, 1951, pp. 240-41. Also see Bryce, *The American Commonwealth*, Vol. II (3rd ed.), pp. 380-81.
12. Louis S. Robbins, *The Royal Decrees of Scanderoon. To the Sachems of Tammany, and to the Other Grand Magnorums of Manhattan*, 1869, p. 43.
13. *The Nation*, Oct. 12, 1871, p. 237.
14. Wingate, "Episode in Municipal Government," Oct. 1874, p. 379.
15. James Parton, "The Government of New York," *North American Review*, Oct. 1866, pp. 459-60.

16. "The Judiciary in New York City," *North American Review*, July 1867, p. 173. No author cited.
17. Feb. 2, 1871; Jan. 23, 1871; Mar. 19, 1872; Jan. 9, 1870; Mar. 20, 1870; Dec. 14, 1870.
18. "Why Vote at all in 1872?" 1872, no author cited, pp. 28, 30.
19. Aug. 31, 1871.
20. Quoted in Handlin, *The Uprooted* (paperback edition, 1951), p. 219, with no citation.
21. William L. Riordon, *Plunkitt of Tammany Hall*, 1948, pp. 91-5.
22. Quoted in Richard J. Butler and Joseph Driscoll, *Dock Walloper*, 1933, p. 49.

6. CITY GOVERNMENT

1. James Parton, "The Government of New York," *North American Review*, Oct. 1866, p. 415.
2. Samuel P. Dinsmore, "Suggestions Touching the Municipal Government," 1860, p. 14.
3. William Allen Butler, *Our Great Metropolis*, pp. 8-9.
4. The English replaced the Dutch municipal system with one Mayor for two former Burgomasters, five Aldermen for five Schepens, and a Sheriff for the Schout. Aldermen did not represent wards; the Royal Governor appointed all officers.
5. Butler, *Our Great Metropolis*, p. 28.
6. The Montgomerie Charter of February 11, 1731, added another ward, so that one Alderman and one Assistant Alderman from each ward made a Common Council of fourteen members. A Chamberlain, with sixteen Assessors and seven Collectors under him, one High Constable, with sixteen Constables, one Marshal, and one Coroner were also added.

   Under the Constitution of 1777, all local officers were designated by and Council of Appointment, and this resulted in an "unseemly scramble" for offices, sometimes resulting in corruption. Alexander Flick, *Samuel Jones Tilden*, 1939, p. 192.
7. Such as Street Commissioner, a Commissioner of Repairs and Supplies, a Commissioner of Lamps and Gas. In 1849 this was increased to Police Inspector and City Inspector.
8. *New York Herald*, Nov. 26, 1869; *New York Times*, Dec. 28, 1871.
9. Bryce, *American Commonwealth* (1889 ed.), pp. 335-6.
10. For arguments for and against commission government, see George Noyes, "Argument in Favor of the Metropolitan Board of Public Works," 1867, and James Welsh, "The Root of the Municipal Evil," 1875; Union League, "Report on Municipal Reform," 1867, pp. 133ff.

11. Lynch, *Boss Tweed*, pp. 186-99.
12. Bryce, *American Commonwealth* (1889 ed.), p. 377.
13. "Report on Municipal Reform," p. 63.
14. Quoted with no citation in Bryce, *American Commonwealth* (1895 ed.), p. 381.
15. Breen, *Thirty Years of New York Politics*, p. 250.
16. "The Government of New York," *North American Review*, pp. 417-18, 419-21, 422, 427, 453.
17. *New York World-Telegram*, Dec. 4, 1937. This was a paraphrase of a jingle about George II.
18. "Government of New York," p. 421.

7. THE TIGER

1. R. G. Horton, *The History of Tammany Hall*, p. 98.
2. Quoted with no citation in O'Connor, *Hell's Kitchen*, p. 100.
3. William L. Riordon, *Plunkitt of Tammany Hall*, 1948, p. 75.
4. Edwin Kilroe, *Tammany Bibliography*, Vol. I, p. 102 (Manuscript, Columbia University).
5. Kilroe, "Saint Tammany: The Legends and Poetry," p. 190.
6. *New York Star*, Oct. 7, 1883.
7. Alexander Flick, *History of the State of New York*, Vol. VII, p. 141.
8. Edwin Kilroe, *The Story of Tammany*, pp. 63-7.
9. Gustavus Myers, "The Secrets of Tammany's Success," *Forum*, Vol. XXXI, June 1901, p. 495.
10. Ibid. p. 497.
11. Ibid. p. 494.
12. Ibid. p. 493.
13. Flick, *History of the State of New York*, Vol. VII, pp. 142-3.
14. *Literary Digest*, Dec. 31, 1927, p. 34.
15. *New York World*, Sept. 5, 1928.
16. Horton, *History of Tammany Hall*, p. 9.
17. Garrett, *The La Guardia Years*, 1961, p. 6.
18. Breen, *Thirty Years of New York Politics*, pp. 39-40.
19. *Tammany Scrapbooks*, Vol. I, no page number listed. Tammany had its own building from 1811 on. Prior to that time the members met in various taverns, most notable of which was Martling's Long Room, or as the wits of the time drolly named it, the Pigpen.
20. Fairfield, *Clubs of New York*, p. 7.
21. Jan. 25, 1871.
22. *New York Times*, Oct. 24, 1871.

23. Ibid. Apr. 22, 1871.
24. Fairfield, *Clubs of New York*, pp. 160-61. See also pp. 139-48.
25. Ibid. pp. 241-2.
26. March 15, 1870.
27. Fairfield, *Clubs of New York*, p. 220.
28. Shapley, *Solid for Mulhooly*, p. 94.
29. July 16, 1869.
30. Shapley, *Solid for Mulhooly*, p. 161.
31. Werner, *Tammany Hall*, p. 89.
32. *Tammany Scrapbooks*, Vol. 1, no page number listed.
33. Choate, *American Addresses*, pp. 65-6.
34. Twain, "Edmund Burke on Croker and Tammany," p. 2.
35. Myers, "The Secrets of Tammany's Success," p. 488.
36. "Tammany Past and Present," *Forum*, Vol. XXVI, Oct. 1898, pp. 201-2.

8. THE SHINY HAT BRIGADE

1. James Parton, "The Government of New York," p. 438.
2. Ibid. p. 439.
3. Leonard White, "The Spoils System," in *Encyclopaedia of the Social Sciences*, Vol. 14, p. 303.
4. *The Nation*, Oct. 12, 1871, p. 236; *New York Times*, Oct. 3, 1871.
5. Roosevelt, *The Poetical Works of Charles G. Halpine*. Halpine, a popular satirist of the time, also wrote under the name of Miles O'Reilly.
6. *New York Times*, Dec. 6, 1870; July 27, 1871.
7. Ibid. Oct. 4, 1871.
8. Ibid.
9. Ibid. Oct. 2, 1871.
10. Union League, 1873, "The Street Railroads of the City of New York" pp. 21-2.
11. Lynch, *Boss Tweed*, p. 340; *New York Times*, Aug. 10, 1871.
12. *Tweed Investigation*, pp. 564-5.
13. *New York Times*, Aug. 12, 1871; Oct. 4, 1871.
14. Andrew Green, "A Year's Record of a Reformer as Comptroller of New York City," 1872, pp. 22-3.
15. *New York Times*, Oct. 4, 1871.
16. *Ibid.* Feb. 10, 1871.
17. Breen, *Thirty Years of New York Politics*, pp. 256-7.
18. *New York Times*, Aug. 26, 1923.

19. *New York Times*, Oct. 4, 1871.
20. Ibid.
21. Ibid. Oct. 5, 1871.
22. *New York Tribune*, Apr. 16, 1875; *New York Times*, Oct. 3, 1871.
23. *New York Times*, Oct. 4, 1871.
24. Ibid. Oct. 5, 1871.
25. Vol. I, pp. 107-10.
26. *Tweed Investigation*, pp. 222-3.
27. *New York Times*, Aug. 10, 1871.
28. Kilroe, *Saint Tammany: The Legends and Poetry*.
29. *New York Times*, Aug. 10, 1871.
30. Wingate, "Episode in Municipal Government," July 1875, p. 123. See also Frederick Law Olmsted, *Spoils of the Park*, 1882, p. 29ff.
31. Sept. 27, 1871.
32. Wingate, "Episode in Municipal Government," July 1875, p. 122.
33. *New York Times*, Sept. 29, 1871. See also, Dec. 6, 1870, and Oct. 2, 1871.
34. Shapley, *Solid for Mulhooly*, p. 48.
35. *Tweed Investigation*, pp. 208-9.
36. *New York Times*, Oct. 11, 1870.
37. Ibid. Aug. 3, 1871.

9. CRIME AND PUNISHMENT

1. *Democracy in America*, Henry Reeve text, 1945 (as revised and corrected by Francis Bowen and Phillips Bradley), Vol. I, p. 279.
2. "The Judiciary of New York," *North American Review*, July 1867, p. 150. No author cited.
3. *New York Times*, Feb. 18, 1871, July 21, 1871.
4. Ibid. Aug. 10, 1871.
5. Ibid. Oct. 4, 1871.
6. Ibid. Feb. 14, 1872.
7. Ibid. Nov. 28, 1870.
8. *Tweed Investigation*, p. 147.
9. Werner, *Tammany Hall*, p. 125.
10. New York State Assembly, *Charges of the Bar Association of New York against George G. Barnard and Albert Cardozo*, Vol. III, 1872, p. 1857. See also Vol. II, pp. 872-4.
11. *New York Herald*, Apr. 13, 1878.
12. Wingate, "Episode in Municipal Government," Oct. 1874, p. 394.

13. Matthew Breen, *Thirty Years of New York Politics*, p. 159. It was Roy Peel who described Breen as one of the earliest and best of those who exposed city bosses. I can only second the motion. (See Riordon, *Plunkitt of Tammany Hall*, p. xlvi.)
14. See C. F. and Henry Adams, *Chapters of Erie*, 1871, *passim*.
15. Lynch, *Boss Tweed*, p. 220.
16. Wingate, "Episode in Municipal Government," Oct. 1874, pp. 395-6. See *Memorial History of New York*, p. 543. His son, Benjamin Cardozo, became one of the most distinguished jurists in the history of the United States Supreme Court.
17. Myers, *History of Tammany Hall*, p. 263.
18. Wingate, "Episode in Municipal Government," Oct. 1874, p. 396.
19. Ibid.
20. Wilson, *Memorial History of New York*, p. 543.
21. "Record of John K. Hackett, as Recorder, Founded upon Official Documents" (Kilroe Collection; no author cited), 1875, p. 4.
22. Ibid. pp. 4-5. See also pp. 22-4, and *New York Herald*, Sept. 8, 1875.
23. "Record of John K. Hackett," p. 8.
24. Ibid. pp. 10-11.
25. Citizens' Association, "How the Money Goes," 1867, p. 1.
26. Ibid. pp. 4-5, 10, 15.
27. Nov. 19, 1867.
28. "How the Money Goes," p. 2; *New York Herald*, Nov. 19, 1867.
29. See New York State Assembly, "Report of the Select Committee to Investigate the Causes of the Increase of Crime in the City of New York," 1875. In 1863 there was an investigation made of the Police Commissioners (see H. K. Blauvelt, "Charges against the Commissioners of the Metropolitan Police," 1863), and much publicity was given to the police riot of 1857, but neither was investigated on the scale or with the thoroughness of the one in 1875. Like later and more well-known investigations, it came to naught.
30. Crapsey, *The Nether Side of New York*, p. 11.
31. Myers, *History of Tammany Hall*, p. 269.
32. O'Connor, *Hell's Kitchen*, pp. 24-5. See also Crapsey, "Why Thieves Prosper," *The Galaxy*, Oct. 1869, p. 521.
33. *New York Times*, Sept. 4, 1871, no source cited.
34. "The Spider and the Fly," no author cited, p. 9.
35. *New York Times*, June 26, 1875.
36. Lening, *The Dark Side of New York*, pp. 352-3, 385.
37. New York State Assembly, *Charges of the Bar Association against George Barnard and Albert Cardozo*, pp. 142-3.

38 "The Judiciary of New York" (no author cited), *North American Review*, July 1867, p. 157. See also, New York State Assembly, "Report of the Select Committee to Investigate the Causes of the Increase of Crime," pp. 19-20, and the *New York World*, May 15, 1925.

39 *New York Tribune*, Apr. 27, 1872.

40 O'Connor, *Hell's Kitchen*, p. 61. See also *New York Tribune*, Mar. 25, 1870.

41 May 13, 1872.

42 O'Connor, *Hell's Kitchen*, p. 131.

43 Crapsey, "Why Thieves Prosper," p. 521. See also Lening, *The Dark Side of New York*, pp. 706-7.

44 *New York Times*, Apr. 27, 1871.

45 *New York Times*, Dec. 12, 1869.

46 Ibid.

47 New York State Assembly, "Report of the Select Committee on Crime," p. 87.

48 Dec. 12, 1869.

49 Richard Rovere, *Howe and Hummel*, 1947, p. 28.

50 Ibid. p. 145.

51 Ibid. p. 80.

52 Ibid. p. 114.

53 Ibid. pp. 31-2.

10. THE OPEN DOOR POLICY

1 Myers, *History of Tammany Hall*, p. 276.

2 *New York Telegram*, Mar. 20, 1921.

3 "Boss Tweed's Public Welfare Program," *The New York Historical Society Quarterly*, Oct. 1961, p. 411.

4 F. J. Zwierlein, *Life and Letters of Bishop McQuaid*, Vol. III, p. 314.

5 *New York Times*, Apr. 7, 1871.

6 Pratt, "Tweed's Welfare Program," p. 409.

7 Ibid. pp. 409-10; David M. Schneider and Albert Deutsch, *The History of Public Welfare in New York State*, Vol. II, p. 20; Zwierlein, *Bishop McQuaid*, Vol. III, pp. 313-14; *Christian Advocate*, May 27, 1869; and the *New York Times*, May 12, 1869.

8 Pratt, "Tweed's Welfare Program," pp. 403-4; see also *New York Times*, May 10, 11, 13, 1869; New York State *Laws*, 1869, Chap. 876, sec. 10; see also, Senate *Journal*, 1869, pp. 701-4, 1126-37, 1176-80; New York State Assembly *Journal*, 1869, pp. 2053-64, 2165.

9 *Christian Advocate*, June 3 and Oct. 14, 1869.

10. "Statement and Plea," pp. 18-19.
11. Pratt, "Tweed's Welfare Program," p. 407.
12. New York Senate, *Journal*, 1868, pp. 513, 287, 292, 359.
13. New York Senate, *Journal*, 1869, p. 61; 1870, p. 349; 1868, p. 320; 1870, p. 327.
14. Personal (Misc.) Papers of William M. Tweed, Box 13, New York Public Library.
15. Senate *Journal*, 1870, p. 394.
16. Ibid. pp. 78, 363.
17. Senate *Journal*, 1869, p. 5; 1868, pp. 512, 244.
18. Ibid. 1870, p. 645; 1868, p. 424.
19. Mark Hirsch, "More Light on Boss Tweed," *Political Science Quarterly*, June 1945, p. 273.
20. These sums were as follows:

1866	$16,725.00
1868	944.10
1869	3,100.00
1870	163,591.97
1871	98,678.16
1872	5,553.60
1873	162.17

(From Hirsch, "More Light on Boss Tweed," p. 273.)

21. Citizens' Association, "Report of the Executive Council of the Citizens' Association," p. 16.
22. Dec. 29, 1870.
23. Jan. 3, 1871.
24. *New York Times*, Jan. 3, 1871.
25. "The Misgovernment of New York," *North American Review*, Oct. 1871, pp. 323-4.
26. Pratt, "Tweed's Welfare Program," pp. 410-11.
27. Garrett, *The La Guardia Years*, p. 16.
28. "Tammany Past and Present," *The Forum*, Oct. 1898, p. 210.

11. "HONEST GRAFT"

1. "The New York City 'Ring,' " p. 11.
2. Nov. 6, 1871; Nov. 7, 1871.
3. Werner, *Tammany Hall*, p. 160.
4. Myers, *History of Tammany Hall*, pp. 297-8.
5. *Tweed Investigation*, pp. 852-71.
6. Ibid. p. 397.

7 Flick, *Samuel Tilden*, p. 211.
8 Werner, *Tammany Hall*, pp. 193-4.
9 Ibid. p. 161.
10 *Tweed Investigation*, p. 716.
11 *New York Times*, July 20, 1871; Willoughby Jones, *The Life of James Fisk, Jr., Including the Great Frauds of the Tammany Ring*, 1872, p. 212.
12 *New York Times*, July 20, 1871.
13 *Tweed Investigation*, pp. 28-9.
14 Dec. 9, 1870.
15 Jones, *The Life of Fisk*, p. 213.
16. "Official Document on Extravagance of the Tammany Ring," 1871, p. 6.
17. Genung, *The Frauds of New York*, pp. 37-8.
18. *The Nation*, Jan. 4, 1872, p. 5.
19. Parton, "Government of New York," p. 431.
20. Ibid. pp. 432-3.
21. *New York Times*, Dec. 13, 1870.
22. Ibid.
23. Ibid.
24. *Tweed Investigation*, pp. 191-9.
25. *New York Times*, Dec. 10, 1870.
26. Otto Kempner, "Boss Croker's Career," p. 10.
27. *Tweed Investigation*, p. 257.
28. Genung, *The Frauds of New York*, pp. 24-5.
29. Lynch, *Boss Tweed*, p. 339. According to another source, however, the figure over a two-year period (1870-71) was $286,495.61, *Tweed Investigation*, p. 257.
30. Lynch, *Boss Tweed*, p. 340.
31. "The Government of New York," p. 452.
32. Shapley, *Solid for Mulhooly*, p. 49.
33. Wingate, "Episode in Municipal Government," *North American Review*, Jan. 1875, p. 136.
34. Ibid.
35. *Tweed Investigation*, pp. 257-8.
36. *New York Times*, Dec. 19, 1870.
37. Ibid. Aug. 31, 1871. Lynch, *Boss Tweed*, p. 302, provides a different figure. He argues that from Jan. 1, 1869 to "the first half of the year 1871," $2,703,308.48 was paid for city advertising.
38. Shapley, *Solid for Mulhooly*, p. 49.
39. New York City Council of Political Reform, "Report of the New York City Council of Political Reform," p. 30; Wingate, "Episode in Munic-

ipal Government," *North American Review*, Jan. 1875, p. 123; Lynch, *Boss Tweed*, p. 301; *New York Times*, Oct. 28, 1871. There were conflicting opinions on the amounts paid in advertising to newspapers during the Ring's rule. The New York City Council of Political Reform argued that for the five years ending with 1871 it was $5,180,995.35. The Booth Committee thought it was $2,703,308.48. The *Times* tallied it at $181,420.78 for just the year 1869.

The newspapers included some of the most influential ones in New York City; for example, between 1867 and 1871 the following: the *Daily News* ($489,980.67), the *World* ($120,775.60), the *Herald* ($91,491.88), the *Sun* ($82,850.59), the *Tribune* ($54,847.94), the *Times* ($75,160.08), the *Commercial Advertiser* ($101,050.90), the *Express* ($157,239.17), the *Star* ($241,711.01), Pomeroy's *Democrat* ($130,881.90). There were others, some well known, some obscure, like the *New York Official Railroad News*, the *Real Estate Record*, *Era*, the *Stockholder*, the *Wall Street Journal*, the *Gazette*, the *Weekly Inquirer*, and the *Sunburst*. Immigrant or foreign organs, like the *Jewish Messenger*, the *German News*, the *Irish People*, and the *Irish World*, also participated, as did upstate journals in Albany, Troy, Hudson, Syracuse, Rochester, Buffalo, and other towns.

40. *Tweed Investigation*, pp. 213-15. Tweed sent on to prove his contentions by offering as evidence letters from both of these journals, Ibid. pp. 231-9. The Ring also used loans to cement friendship. Both M. M. "Brick" Pomeroy of the *New York Democrat* and Joseph Howard, Jr., owner and editor of the *New York Star*, either owed Tweed money or begged for loans. Howard once wrote him pleading for a loan of $1000. Tweed, a generous man, gave it to him. Mark Hirsch, "More Light on Boss Tweed," *Political Science Quarterly*, p. 277.
41. The Papers of George Jones, New York Public Library. See also miscellaneous Papers of A. O. Hall, New York Public Library and *New York Herald*, Oct. 4, 1869.
42. *New York Times*, Oct. 4, and May 23, 1871.
43. Ibid. Sept. 4, 1871.
44. Wingate, "Episode in Municipal Government," *North American Review*, Jan. 1875, p. 134. Gratz Nathan, a relative of Judge Cardozo, acted as Commissioner in five different street openings and widenings; Edward Connolly, kin to Slippery Dick, in five others.
45. Parton, "Government of New York," pp. 441-2.
46. Ibid. p. 442.
47. Ibid. p. 131. For a detailed account of the properties the Ring accumulated, see *New York Times*, Feb. 15, 16, Mar. 17, 18, 21, 23, 1871.

48. See *New York Times*, March 4, Feb. 27, Sept. 19, 1871; George Noyes, "Arguments in Favor of the Metropolitan Board of Public Works," pp. 17-18.
49. Shapley, *Solid for Mulhooly*, p. 35.

12. "PECULATION TRIUMPHANT"

1. *New York Times*, July 8, 1871.
2. Ibid.
3. Ibid. Sept. 22, 1871.
4. Lynch, *Boss Tweed*, p. 362; *New York Times*, July 8, 1871; Jones, *Life of James Fisk, Jr.*, p. 203.
5. Dec. 31, 1871.
6. *New York Times*, July 20, 1871.
7. Ibid. July 29, 1871.
8. Parton, "Government of New York," p. 451.
9. Robert Daly, "Alfred Ely Beach and His Wonderful Pneumatic Underground Railway," *American Heritage*, June 1961, p. 54. See also Robert Daly, *The World Beneath the City*, 1959, pp. 66-90.
10. Gustavus Myers, "History of Public Franchises in New York City," *Municipal Affairs*, Mar. 1900, p. 164; New York Senate *Journal*, 1871, pp. 482-3; Myers, *Tammany Hall*, p. 276; *New York Times*, Mar. 18, 1870.
11. *New York Times*, Feb. 16, 18, 1871.
12. Ibid. June 14, 1871; Genung, *The Frauds of New York Exposed*, p. 28; Lening, *The Dark Side of New York*, p. 692.
13. "History of Public Franchises," p. 135.
14. Wingate, "Episode in Municipal Government," Jan. 1875, p. 148.
15. Thomas De Voe, "Report upon the Present Condition of the Public Markets," p. 6.
16. Wingate, "Episode in Municipal Government," Jan. 1875, p. 148.
17. De Voe, "Report on Public Markets," p. 24.
18. Sept. 8, 1871.
19. Brace, *The Dangerous Classes* (1872 ed.), p. 73.
20. *New York Times*, Mar. 10, 1871.
21. *The Nation*, Nov. 4, 1875, p. 288.
22. *Tweed Investigation*, pp. 765-6.
23. Ibid. pp. 552, 578.
24. *New York Times*, Sept. 18, 1871.
25. Ibid. Feb. 1, 1872.

26. *New York Times*, Dec. 9, 1870.
27. Ibid. Mar. 21, 1872.
28. *New York Times*, Mar. 21, 1872; Wingate, "Episode in Municipal Government," July 1875, p. 125.
29. *Tweed Investigation*, p. 82.
30. Quoted in Werner, *Tammany Hall*, p. 194.

13. "THE HOUSE THAT TWEED BUILT"

1. "The House That Tweed Built" (no author cited), 1871, p. 23; *New York Times*, Jan. 6, 1871; Werner, *Tammany Hall*, p. 167.
2. *New York Times*, Aug. 2, 1871.
3. Citizens' Association, "Report of the Executive Council to the Honorary Council of the Citizens' Association," 1866, pp. 11-13.
4. *New York Times*, Aug. 2, 1871.
5. Ibid. May 11, 1871.
6. *Tweed Investigation*, pp. 580-81.
7. "Political Corruption in New York," 1871, p. 13.
8. Lynch, *Boss Tweed*, p. 365.
9. "National and State Politics of 1871 Reviewed," 1871, p. 9.
10. July 29, 1871. For a detailed breakdown but not a complete tabulation, see *New York Times*, "How New York Is Governed," (pamphlet), 1871.
11. Roscoe Conkling, "National and State Politics of 1871 Reviewed," p 9.
12. Lynch, *Boss Tweed*, p. 365.
13. *New York Times*, Mar. 1, 1871.
14. Ibid. July 26, 29, 1871.
15. Ibid. Oct. 7, 1871.
16. Werner, *Tammany Hall*, p. 167.
17. *New York Times*, July 26, 1871.
18. Werner, *Tammany Hall*, p. 167. There is a difference of opinion of the correct spelling of Fillippo Donaruma. See Lynch, *Boss Tweed*, p. 347.
19. Ibid. p. 166.
20. *New York Times*, July 23, 1871.
21. Ibid. Sept. 8, 1871.
22. Hirsch, "More Light on Boss Tweed," p. 268ff.; *New York Times*, June 18, 1872.
23. Werner, *Tammany Hall*, p. 166; *New York Times*, July 26, 29, Sept. 8, 1871.
24. *New York Times*, July 26, 1871.
25. Ibid.

26. Ibid. April 7, 1871.
27. Werner, *Tammany Hall*, p. 241.

14. THE BLACK HORSE CAVALRY

1. Butler, *The Dock Walloper*, pp. 65, 68.
2. Wingate, "Episode in Municipal Government," Oct. 1874, p. 403.
3. Myers, *Tammany Hall*, p. 260 N.
4. House of Representatives, *House Report No. 31 on Election Frauds in New York*, p. 632.
5. John Davenport, *The Election and Naturalization Frauds in New York City* (2nd ed.), 1894, pp. 95-6.
6. Werner, *Tammany Hall*, pp. 436-7.
7. Ibid. p. 439. Quoted in *Harper's Weekly*, Oct. 18, 1913.
8. Werner, *Tammany Hall*, p. 508.
9. Cited in Bowen, *The Elegant Oakey*, pp. 50-51. See also Hirsch, *Whitney*, p. 55 N.
10. *The Nation*, Oct. 29, 1868. See also Gibson, *The Attitudes of the New York Irish*, pp. 222-30.
11. Post, "The Wig and the Jimmy," p. 30.
12. Lynch, *Boss Tweed*, p. 293. See also Gibson, *Attitudes of Irish*, p. 228.
13. Wingate, "Episode in Municipal Government," Oct. 1874, p. 404; Lynch, *Boss Tweed*, pp. 292-3; *Tweed Investigation*, p. 226.
14. *Tweed Investigation*, pp. 133-7.
15. Ibid. p. 225.
16. Wingate, "Episode in Municipal Government," Oct. 1874, pp. 403-4.
17. *New York Times*, Jan. 26, 1871.
18. *Other Essays from the Easy Chair*, p. 49.
19. Breen, *Thirty Years of New York Politics*, p. 89.
20. *Ibid.* p. 84.
21. Tilden, *The New York City "Ring,"* pp. 28-9.
22. H. H. Boone and Theodore P. Cook, *Life Sketches of Executive Officers and Members of the Legislature*, 1870, p. 215.
23. Ibid. p. 149.
24. Quoted with no citation in Breen, *Thirty Years of New York Politics*, p. 120.
25. Lynch, *Boss Tweed*, p. 287.
26. *New York Times*, Dec. 19, 1871; Andrew Green, "A Year's Record of a Reformer as Comptroller," p. 21. See also Miscellaneous MSS. of Tweed Papers, New York Historical Society, for a letter of May 28,

1869, where Hoffman asks Tweed for "firm suggestions" on legislative matters.

27. *New York Times*, Apr. 6, 1870.
28. Bowen, *The Elegant Oakey*, p. 91.
29. Lynch, *Boss Tweed*, p. 288.
30. Parton, "Government of New York," p. 457.
31. *Tweed Investigation*, pp. 179-80.
32. Ibid. p. 156.
33. Flick, *Tilden*, p. 198; see also, Charles and Henry Adams, *Chapters on the Erie.*
34. Lynch, *Boss Tweed*, pp. 300-301; *New York Times*, Apr. 27, 1873.
35. *Tweed Investigation*, p. 147.
36. Flick, *Tilden*, p. 198.
37. *New York Times*, Apr. 2, 1873.
38. Myers, *Tammany Hall*, p. 264; *Tweed Investigation*, pp. 434-9.
39. Breen, *Thirty Years of New York Politics*, pp. 126-7.
40. Ibid. pp. 127-8.
41. *Tweed Investigation*, p. 851.
42. *New York Times*, Nov. 2, 3, 1869.
43. Wingate, "Episode in Municipal Government," Jan. 1875, p. 128.

15. THE WAR OF THE RINGS

1. Henry Clinton, "Letters of Henry L. Clinton," 1878, p. 8.
2. *New York Times*, Mar. 24, 1870.
3. *La Guardia*, Vol. I, p. 129.
4. Van Pelt, *Leslie's History of New York*, Vol. II, p. 512.
5. *New York Star*, Mar. 5, 1870. For a detailed description of the Tweed charter, see Citizens' Association, "Address to the People of the City of New York by the Citizens' Association," pp. 3-13; Bryce, *American Commonwealth* (1889 ed.), pp. 343-4; *New York Times*, May 5, 1870.
6. *New York Sun*, Mar. 26, 1870.
7. See *New York Times*, Mar. 11, 1870, for a full discussion of its parts.
8. See Citizens' Association, "Memorial of the Citizens' Association of New York, and Petition of Tax-payers in Favor of the New Charter," *New York Times*, May 5, 1870. Croswell Bowen was not correct when he said that reformers paid little attention to it (*The Elegant Oakey*, p. 60), and Alexander Flick has overestimated the reformers' opposition to it (*Tilden*, pp. 206-8).
9. Lynch, *Boss Tweed*, p. 331.

10. *New York Times*, Apr. 5, 1870.
11. See Union League Club, "The Report of the Committee on Municipal Reform," 1867; "Report on Cities," 1867.
12. Apr. 8, 1870. See also Apr. 6, 13.
13. Bryce, *American Commonwealth* (1889 ed.), pp. 342, 352-3.
14. See Van Pelt, *Leslie's History of New York*, Vol. II, p. 512; Wilson, *The Memorial History of New York*, pp. 550-52.
15. *New York Times*, Mar. 10, 1870.
16. The *Leader*, Mar. 12, 1870.
17. Norris Winslow, V. Harpending, Theodore L. Minier, George Bowen, and William H. Brand.
18. Boone and Cook, *Life Sketches*, 1870, p. 142.
19. *Tweed Investigation*, pp. 89, 11-20.
20. Ibid. p. 89.
21. Ibid. pp. 94-5.
22. *Tweed Investigation*, p. 551.
23. Mar. 23, 1870.
24. *New York Sun*, Mar. 27, 1870.
25. Mar. 29, 1870.
26. Lynch, *Boss Tweed*, p. 330; *New York Times*, Mar. 30, 1870.
27. (Anon.) "History of a Moral Journalist," p. 50.
28. Apr. 12, 1870.
29. Werner, *Tammany Hall*, p. 185.
30. Flick, *Tilden*, p. 207; *New York Times*, Apr. 5, 1870.
31. *Tweed Investigation*, p. 565.
32. (Anon.) "History of a Moral Journalist," p. 47.
33. Myers, *Tammany Hall*, p. 272.
34. *New York Times*, Apr. 10, 1870.

16. HALCYON DAYS

1. Apr. 13, 1870.
2. *New York Herald*, Apr. 13, 1870.
3. *New York Sun*, Apr. 13, 1870.
4. Edward Sears, "The Central Park Under Ring-Leader Rule," *National Quarterly Review*, Mar. 1871, p. 21. See also Frederick Law Olmsted, *The Spoils of the Park*.
5. Miscellaneous MSS. of Tweed Papers, New York Historical Society.
6. Tilden, *The New York City "Ring,"* p. 24; Lynch, *Boss Tweed*, p. 338. Tweed later testified that the Board never met in formal session on this

day. Watson had prepared the paper work for the steal in advance, and Hall forged minutes to the meeting which the Ring members signed—as a precaution in the event of trouble. *Tweed Investigation*, pp. 140-1.

7. *New York Times*, Sept. 23, 1870. See also Mark Hirsch's excellent "Samuel J. Tilden: The Story of a Lost Opportunity," *American Historical Review*, LVI (July 1951), pp. 794-5, *passim*.
8. Wingate, "Episode in Municipal Government," July 1875, pp. 131-2.
9. Quoted in ibid. As Matthew Sloan remembers Tilden fifty years later:

   > He certainly could talk. Why, I remember one night that he lit into the Republicans and called them more different kinds of blackguards than you could ever remember, but he didn't use a single hard word. No sir, just told the truth about them in a nice way and said nothing mean.

   New York Times Magazine, Oct. 17, 1926.
10. *New York Times*, Oct. 14, 1870.
11. Ibid. Nov. 26, 1870.
12. Lynch, *Boss Tweed*, p. 347.
13. Nov. 22, 1870. See also Bowen, *The Elegant Oakey*, p. 79.
14. Nevins and Thomas, *The Diary of George Templeton Strong*, Vol. IV, p. 317.
15. *New York Times*, Nov. 6, 1870.
16. Ibid. Oct. 19, 1870; Nov. 9, 1870.
17. Ibid. Nov. 14, 1870; Lynch, *Boss Tweed*, pp. 347-8.
18. Myers, *Tammany Hall*, pp. 276-7; *New York Times*, Apr. 19, 1871.
19. The *New York Times*, Apr. 19, 1871, lists more than a dozen newspapers which played up the story.
20. Apr. 17, 1871, quoted in Lynch, *Boss Tweed*, p. 358.
21. Everett P. Wheeler, *Sixty Years of American Life*, 1917, p. 320.
22. Mar. 27, 1871.
23. Ibid. May 8, 1871.
24. Ibid. May 1, 1871.
25. *Thirty Years of New York Politics*, pp. 154-5.
26. *New York Times*, Aug. 6, 1873.
27. Wingate, "Episode in Municipal Government," Jan. 1875, pp. 127-8.
28. Sept. 28, 1870.
29. Fairfield, *The Clubs of New York*, p. 206.
30. Ibid. p. 206; *New York Times*, Aug. 6, 1873.
31. "Alderman Rooney at the Cable Banquet: An Improvised Epic by Himself," Kilroe Collection, Columbia University.
32. *Tammany Newspaper Clippings*, Vol. I, p. 171, Kilroe Collection, Columbia University.

33 Newspaper quotes were quoted in Werner, *Tammany Hall*, pp. 190-93.
34 Ibid. pp. 192-3.
35 Dec. 12, 1870.
36 Myers, *Tammany Hall*, p. 279; *New York Times*, Mar. 17, 1871.
37 Quoted in Werner, *Tammany Hall*, pp. 201-2.

17. THE CRUSADE AGAINST THE TWEED RING

1. Wingate, "Episode in Municipal Government," July 1875, p. 150.
2. See Citizens' Association, "An Appeal by the Citizens' Association of New York against the Abuses in the Local Government to the Legislature of the State of New York, and to the Public" (New York, 1866); "Items of Abuse in the Government of the City of New York" (New York, 1866); "Report of the Executive Council to the Honorary Council of the Citizens' Association" (New York, 1866); "Wholesale Corruption! Sale of Situations in Fourth Ward Schools" (New York, 1864); Union League Club, "Report on Cities" (New York, 1867); "The Report of the Committee on Municipal Reform" (New York, 1867).
3. Jan. 24-25, Feb. 15, 1870. The *Times* also reported on Mar. 9, 1870, that Richard Connolly was fighting the Ring.
4. Apr. 8, 13, 1870. See also Apr. 6, 12, and May 1, 1870.
5. July 13, 1871, quoted in the *Times*, July 14, 1871.
6. Apr. 3, 1872.
7. J. D. Townsend, *New York in Bondage* (1901), p. 73.
8. Nov. 3, 1870.
9. Ibid.
10. Ibid.; Sept. 16, 1871.
11. Dec. 4, 1870. When the celebrated Henry Ward Beecher said he pitied wicked men because their consciences would surely suffer, the *Times* replied in a blistering attack, saying Beecher's pity was "morbid, unwholesome, sentimental." Oct. 24, 1871.
12. Oct. 3, 1870.
13. Sept. 24, 1870.
14. Feb. 26, May 1, 1871; Oct. 3, 1870.
15. "The great strength of General Grant's Administration . . . lies in the fact that he is believed to be honest himself, and disposed to enforce honesty and fidelity in all departments of the Government under his control." *New York Times*, Sept. 21, 1871.
16. Unidentified newspaper, *Scrapbooks of Clippings Relating to the Career of A. Oakey Hall* (New York Public Library), Vol. IV, p. 113.

17. *New York Times*, Jan. 25, 1873.
18. July 28, 31, 1871. See also *New York World*, Aug. 2, 7, 10, 1871. The *New York Sun* and *New York Evening Post* also criticized the *Times*. Bowen, *The Elegant Oakey*, p. 99. Moreover, Charles Nordhoff, the managing editor of the *Evening Post*, was fired for attacking Tweed. Lynch, *Boss Tweed*, p. 355.
19. Bowen, *The Elegant Oakey*, p. 106. See also Allan Nevins and Thomas Milton Halsey, *The Diary of George Templeton Strong*, III (4 vols.), pp. 376, 383, 385-6.
20. Genung, *Frauds of New York*, pp. 9-13.
21. *Tweed Investigation*, pp. 50-55; Hirsch, "More Light on Boss Tweed," p. 272.
22. For a compilation of the *Times*'s evidence, see *New York Times*, "How New York is Governed. Frauds of the Tammany Democrats," 1871.
23. Breen, *Thirty Years of New York Politics*, p. 337.
24. *New York Times*, Sept. 5, 1871.
25. Oct. 2, 1871.
26. *New York Times*, Oct. 10, 1870; Jan. 20, Mar. 6, 1871.
27. *New York Times*, July 12, 1871.
28. Ibid. July 16, 1871.
29. "Report of the Executive Council to the Honorary Council of the Citizens' Association" (New York, 1866), p. 21. See also "Civil Rights: A History of the New York Riot of 1871" (1871), p. 20; Nevins and Halsey, *Diary of Strong*, IV, p. 352; Thomas Nast, *Miss Columbia's School, or Will It Blow Over?*, 1871, p. 71, *passim*; *Harper's Weekly*, July 29, 1871. For other examples of the nativist impulse, see *The Nation*, July 20, 1871, p. 36; *New York Times*, Mar. 18, Apr. 7, July 17-18, 21, 24, Aug. 17, 1871; Wingate, "Episode in Municipal Government," Oct. 1874, pp. 378-9; Townsend, *New York in Bondage*, p. 186; Nevins, *Diary of Strong*, IV, p. 317.

    While nativism was widespread in the reformers' camp, some were anti-nativist. See A. R. Lawrence, "The Government of Cities" (New York, 1868), pp. 4-5, 11.
30. *New York Times*, Sept. 17, 1869; Jan. 7, Nov. 30, 1870; Mar. 19, 26, July 16, Sept. 17, 1871. Otto Kempner, "Boss Croker's Career," p. 6.
31. July 16, 1871. See also Sept. 17, 1869; Oct. 17, 1870; Feb. 2, Mar. 19, 1871.
32. *The Nation*, Nov. 16, 1871, p. 316.
33. Jan. 25, 1871. See also *New York Times*, Jan. 24, 1870; *New York Star*, Mar. 25, 1870; Wingate, "Episode in Municipal Government," CXIX (Oct. 1874), p. 379.

34. "Statement and Plea of the New York City Council of Political Reform," p. 34.
35. *American Addresses*, pp. 61-2, 72; *New York Times*, Sept. 18, 1871; (Anon.) "Why Vote at All in '72," p. 37. Robert Roosevelt declared that the Ring "pulled away the very keystone of the arch of liberty." If the public money is stolen, wrote another reformer, "why not the public liberties too?"
36. Feb. 8, April 3, Oct. 12, 17, Nov. 3-4, 1870; Jan. 24, Feb. 24-25, Apr. 7, May 1, July 16, Sept. 5, 26-27, Oct. 27, Nov. 3, 1871.
37. Jones, *Fisk*, p. 226; *New York Times*, Sept. 4, Nov. 3, 1871. See also Abram Genung, *The Frauds of the New York City Government Exposed*, p. 41; Gustav Lening, *The Dark Side of New York*, p. 694; James Welsh, "The Root of the Municipal Evil," p. 7; Nast, *Miss Columbia's School*, pp. 39, 71; New York Council of Political Reform, "Statement and Plea," p. 40.
38. Sept. 29, 1871.
39. "Report on Municipal Reform," pp. 17-18; see also, "Why Vote at All in '72," p. 72; Welsh, "Root of the Municipal Evil," p. 5.
40. *New York Times*, Jan. 23, 1871.
41. New York City Council of Political Reform, "Report of the New York City Council of Political Reform," p. 3.
42. "Statement and Plea," p. 28. See also "Report of the New York City Council of Political Reform," pp. 4-11; The Citizens' Association, "Report of the Executive Council to the Honorary Council," p. 22; Wilson, *Memorial History*, III, p. 562; Bryce, *American Commonwealth* (1889 ed.), II, p. 353, (1895 ed.), II, pp. 391, 403.

For an interesting criticism of the "best people" theory, see *The Nation*, Aug. 24, 1871, p. 125.
43. "The Government of New York," p. 451.
44. "The Commonwealth Reconstructed," p. 26.
45. *The Nation*, Apr. 18, 1878, p. 257; Nov. 9, 1871, p. 300; Nov. 27, 1873, p. 350.
46. Ibid. Nov. 4, 1875, p. 288; Oct. 18, 1877, p. 238; Nov. 27, 1873, p. 350; Apr. 18, 1878, p. 257; Oct. 12, 1871, p. 237; Nov. 4, 1875, p. 289. See also Union League, "Report on Municipal Reform," pp. 19-20, 76-7, 88; Parton, "Government of New York," p. 463.

For an attack on this position, see Charles Nordhoff, "The Mis-Government of New York, a Remedy Suggested," *North American Review*, CCXXXIII (Oct. 1871), pp. 321-43, *passim*.
47. Francis Lieber, "Reflections on the Changes Which May Seem Necessary in the Present Constitution of the State of New York," p. 4; Parton,

"Government of New York," p. 460; *Rochester Union and Advertiser*, Oct. 3, 1871.

48. "Root of Municipal Evil," p. 19.
49. *New York Times*, Sept. 11, 1869.
50. Parton, "Government of New York," p. 457.
51. (Anon.), "Why Vote at All in '72," p. 29.
52. Werner, *Tammany Hall*, p. 210.
53. Albert Paine, *Thomas Nast*, 1904, p. 182.
54. *New York Times*, Aug. 24, 1871.
55. Nevins and Thomas, *Diary of Strong*, Vol. IV, p. 394.
56. For Hall's excuses, see *New York Times*, July 12, 29, Aug. 12, Sept. 11, Oct. 10, 13; *The Leader*, Aug. 19, 1871.
57. Flick, *Tilden*, p. 213; see also *New York Times*, Aug. 29, 1871.
58. *New York Times*, Sept. 22, 1871.
59. Ibid. Sept. 17, 1871.
60. Green had served thirteen years on the Park Commission, helped to plan Central Park, suggested Riverside Drive and many of the smaller parks, established the American Scenic and Historic Preservation Society, and did much to effect the merger of the Tilden, Astor, and Lenox foundation in the New York Public Library.
61. Wingate, "Episode in Municipal Government," Oct. 1876, p. 379.
62. Lynch, *Boss Tweed*, p. 375.
63. Sept. 27, 1871.
64. Flick, *Tilden*, p. 219.
65. *New York Times*, Nov. 5, 1871.
66. Ibid. Nov. 6, 1871.
67. Nevins and Thomas, *Diary of Strong*, Vol. IV, p. 382.
68. Wingate, "Episode in Municipal Government," Oct. 1876, p. 389.
69. Nov. 11, 1871.
70. O'Connor, *Hell's Kitchen*, p. 50; Lynch, *Boss Tweed*, pp. 383-4.
71. Nov. 8, 1871.
72. Ibid.
73. Cited with no date in *New York Times*, July 12, 1872.
74. *The Nation*, Nov. 9, 1871, p. 300.

18. "WHAT ARE YOU GOING TO DO ABOUT IT?"

1. See *Proceedings of the Joint Investigating Committee of Supervisors, Aldermen, and Associated Citizens, Appointed to Examine the Public Accounts of the City and County of New York*, 1872; *Tweed Investigation*, pp. 405-22; 427-31; 434-40.

2. *New York Times*, Oct. 30, 1871.
3. Ibid. Nov. 4, 1871.
4. Ibid. Feb. 22, 1872.
5. Nevins and Thomas, *Diary of Strong*, Vol. IV, p. 506.
6. *New York Times*, Oct. 4, 1871.
7. Ibid. Dec. 23, 25, 1873.
8. *New York Times*, Nov. 10.
9. Wingate, "Episode in Municipal Government," Oct. 1876, p. 390. The day after the 1871 election, his late associates in the Board of Education rescinded the resolution proposed by him, barring Harper textbooks from the public schools.
10. New York City Council of Political Reform, "Report of the New York City Council of Political Reform, for the Years 1872, 1873, and 1874," p. 31.
11. Dec. 30, 1871.
12. Dec. 22, 1871.
13. Townsend, *New York in Bondage*, p. 96.
14. Wingate, "Episode in Municipal Government," Oct. 1876, p. 416.
15. *New York Times*, Nov. 30, 1871.
16. Bowen, *The Elegant Oakey*, p. 125.
17. *New York Times*, Nov. 30, 1871.
18. Bowen, *The Elegant Oakey*, p. 124.
19. *New York Times*, Dec. 1, 1871.
20. Bowen, *The Elegant Oakey*, p. 132.
21. *Tweed Investigation*, pp. 76-9; 140-41; 555-6; 692, 696.
22. "Summing up of John Graham to the Jury, on the Part of the Defense, on the Trial of William M. Tweed," p. 16.
23. Dec. 31, 1871.
24. For a detailed, but prejudiced account, replete to the last technicality, see Charles O'Conor, *Peculation Triumphant*, 1875.
25. *New York Times*, Feb. 1, 1873; Lynch, *Boss Tweed*, p. 394.
26. Breen, *Thirty Years of New York Politics*, p. 467.
27. *New York Times*, Nov. 23, 1873.
28. Nov. 23, 1873.
29. Nevins and Thomas, *Diary of Strong*, Vol. IV, p. 502.
30. Wilson, *The Memorial History of the City of New York*, Vol. III, p. 561; Wheeler, *Sixty Years of American Life*, p. 328; Myers, *Tammany Hall*, p. 293.
31. Lynch, *Boss Tweed*, p. 397; Werner, *Tammany Hall*, p. 244.
32. Werner, *Tammany Hall*, p. 247, *Harper's Weekly*, Apr. 14, 1877.
33. Ibid. p. 250.

34. Ibid. p. 252.
35. Hirsch, *Whitney*, pp. 122-3; Townsend, *New York in Bondage*, pp. 134-6.
36. Townsend, *New York in Bondage*, p. 117.
37. Ibid. pp. 138-41.
38. *Attorney General Charles S. Fairchild's Report to Governor Robinson on the Tweed Suits*. See *Report* in *Albany Argus*, June 28, and *New York Tribune*, *Herald*, June 29, 1877.
39. Dec. 15, 1875.
40. June 14, 1877; see also, Breen, *Thirty Years of New York Politics*, p. 566; Hirsch, *Whitney*, p. 125; Townsend, *New York in Bondage*, Chap. XXII, *passim*.
41. Hirsch, "More Light on Boss Tweed," pp. 274-6. See also the *New York Daily Register*, Feb. 29, 1876.
42. Miscellaneous Papers of W. E. P. Stokes, New York Public Library.
43. Fairchild Papers, July 20, 1877. New York Historical Society.
44. Ibid. July 20, 1877, Whitney to Fairchild.
45. Ibid. May 25, 1877.
46. Ibid. May 3, 1877.
47. Ibid.
48. Townsend, *New York in Bondage*, p. 121.
49. Sept. 30, 1877.
50. *Tweed Investigation*, pp. 206, 208, 399-400, 418, 552-4.
51. Sept. 12, 1877.
52. Sept. 21, 1877.
53. Werner, *Tammany Hall*, p. 258.
54. Breen, *Thirty Years of New York Politics*, p. 569. There are many versions of Tweed's dying words. Breen's account in my judgment was the most accurate.
55. Werner, *Tammany Hall*, pp. 258-60, quoted from the *World*.
56. Breen, *Thirty Years of New York Politics*, p. 569.
57. Lynch, *Boss Tweed*, p. 418.
58. *Tweed Investigation*, pp. 841-5.
59. Ibid. pp. 601-85.

BIBLIOGRAPHY

MANUSCRIPTS

Board of Aldermen of New York City. *Documents*, XIX, 1852.

———. Proceedings of the Joint Investigating Committee of Supervisors, Aldermen, and Associated Citizens, Appointed To Examine the Public Accounts of the City and County of New York. 1872.

Fairchild, Charles Stebbins. Papers. New York Historical Society.

Hall, A. O. Scrapbooks of Clippings Relating to the Career of A. Oakey Hall. 14 vols. New York Public Library.

———. Miscellaneous Papers of Abraham Oakey Hall. Manuscript Room, New York Public Library.

Jones, George. Jones Papers. New York Public Library.

Kilroe, Edwin Patrick. A Complete Bibliography of Saint Tammany, Tammany Hall, and the Tammany Societies in the United States. 2 vols. New York Public Library.

———. *Kilroe Collection.* Carbon copy of volume of material relating to Michael Norton, New York State Senator. Columbia University.

———. Legends and Poetry of Saint Tammany. 2 vols. Columbia University, 1927.

———. Saint Tammany: The legends and poetry of the patron and guiding spirit of the Tammanial movement in the United States, including a brief history of the early Tammany societies. Columbia University, 1928.

———. Tammany Newspaper Clippings; Tammany Obituaries. 4 vols. Columbia University, 1936.

Nast, Thomas. Nast's Tammany Scrap Book, with original drawings. 1900.

New York Herald. Scrapbook of clippings on the trial of Mayor Hall, March 2-9, 1872. New York Public Library.

Stokes, W.E.D. Miscellaneous Papers. New York Public Library.

Tilden, Samuel. Tilden Papers. New York Public Library.

Tweed, William M. Miscellaneous Manuscripts. New York Historical Society Library.

———. Personal (Miscellaneous) Papers of William Marcy Tweed. New York Public Library.

———. Scrapbooks on the Tweed Scandals (1877-78). 5 vols. New York Historical Society.

PRINTED DOCUMENTS

New York State Assembly. "Charges of the Bar Association of New York against Hon. George G. Barnard and Hon. Albert Cardozo, Justices of the Supreme Court, and Hon. John H. McCunn, A Justice of the Superior Court of the City of New York, and testimony thereunder taken before the Judiciary Committee of the Assembly of the State of New York, 1872." 3 vols. New York, 1872.

———. Report of the Special Committee of the Board of Aldermen Appointed to Investigate the "Ring" Frauds, Together with the Testimony Elicited during the Investigation (Board of Aldermen, January 4, 1878, Document No. 8; 1878).

New York State Senate. Proceedings of a Select Committee of the Senate of the State of New York, Appointed to Investigate Various Departments of the Government of the City of New York. Senate Document No. 38, 88th Sess., 1865.

———. Report of the Select Committee of the Senate, Appointed April 10, 1868, in Relation to Members Receiving Money from Railway Companies. Senate Document No. 52, 1869.

———. Documents. New York Historical Society.

———. Journals.

U.S. House of Representatives. New York Election Frauds. Reports of Committees of the House of Representatives, Vol. II. Report No. 31. 40th Cong., 3d Sess., 1869.

PERIODICALS

"Alderman Rooney at the Cable Banquet; An Improvised Epic by Himself," edited by D. O'C. T. New York, 1866.

Buel, C. "Blackmail as a Heritage, or New York's Legacy from Colonial Days," *Century Magazine*, XLIX, No. 5 (March 1895), pp. 769-79.

Cary, Edward. "Tammany Past and Present," *The Forum*, xxvi (Oct. 1898), pp. 200-210.

Daly, Robert. "Robert Ely Beach and His Wonderful Pneumatic Underground Railway," *American Heritage*, June 1961.

Dickens, Charles. "The Dying Tiger," *All the Year Round*, Nov. 23, 1872, pp. 36-42.

Edwards, E. J. "The Rise and Overthrow of the Tweed Ring," *McClure's*, v (July 1895), pp. 132-43.

———. "Tammany," *McClure's*, iv (April 1894), v (May 1895).

Ellis, David. "Upstate Hicks versus 'City Slickers,'" *The New York Historical Society Quarterly*, (April 1959), pp. 202-19.

Godkin, E. L. "The Boss's Rule," *The Nation*, Oct. 12, 1871.

———. "Christmas and Thieves," *The Nation*, Nov. 2, 1871.

———. "Moral Career of Tweed," *The Nation*, April 18, 1878.

———. "Overthrow of Tweed," *The Nation*, Nov. 27, 1873.

———. "Rising against the Ring," *The Nation*, Nov. 9, 1871.

Hawley, Walter. "The Strength and Weakness of Tammany Hall," *North American Review*, Oct. 1901, pp. 481-6.

———. "What New York Owes to Tweed," *Munsey's Magazine*, April 1907, pp. 616-20.

Hirsch, Mark. "More Light on Boss Tweed," *Political Science Quarterly*, June 1945, pp. 267-78.

———. "Samuel J. Tilden: The Story of a Lost Opportunity," *American Historical Review*, lvi (July 1951), pp. 788-802.

"The Judiciary of New York City," *North American Review*, July 1867, pp. 148-76.

Livingston, Ford Duane. "The History of Tammany Hall," *The Editorial Review*, Aug. 1909, pp. 4-23.

Merwin, Henry Childs. "Tammany Hall," *Atlantic Monthly*, Feb. 1894, pp. 240-51.

Myers, Gustavus. "The History of Public Franchises in New York City," *Municipal Affairs*, March 1900.

———. "The Secrets of Tammany's Success," *The Forum*, June 1901, pp. 488-500.

Nadal, E. "The New York Alderman," *The Forum*, Sept. 1886, pp. 49-59.

———. "Those Broken Rings," *The Nation*, July 4, 1872.

———. "What Has Been Done to Punish the Ring?" *The Nation*, May 2, 1872.

Nordhoff, Charles. "The Misgovernment of New York," *North American Review*, Oct. 1871.

Parsons, George Frederic. "The Saloon in Politics," *Atlantic Monthly*, Sept. 1886, pp. 404-14.

Parsons, Herbert. "The System of Fraudulent Voting," *The Editorial Review*, Nov. 1909, pp. 372-9.

Parton, James. "The Government of New York City," *North American Review*, Oct. 1866.

"The Police of New York," *Scribner's Magazine*, July 1878, pp. 342-56.

Pratt, John W. "Boss Tweed's Public Welfare Program," *New York Historical Society Quarterly*, XLV (Oct. 1961), pp. 396-411.

"The Right of Tweed and Other Convicts," *Old and New*, April 1874, pp. 495-504.

Roosevelt, Theodore. "Machine Politics in New York City," *Century Magazine*, Nov. 1886.

———. "Taking the New York Police out of Politics," *Cosmopolitan Magazine*, Nov. 1895, pp. 40-52.

Sears, Edward I. "The Central Park under Ring-Leader Rule," *National Quarterly Review*, March 1871.

Sedgwick, A. G. "Decision in the Case of William Tweed," *The Nation*, July 29, 1875.

Sterne, S. "What are you going to do about it?" *The Nation*, Aug. 24, 1871.

"Tammany and Election Frauds," *The Editorial Review*, Nov. 1909, pp. 380-81.

Waring, George Edwin, Jr. "New York Drink Problem in City Politics," *Outlook*, LX (Oct. 15, 1898), pp. 436-40.

Wingate, Charles. "An Episode in Municipal Government," *North American Review*, Oct. 1874; Jan., July 1875; Oct. 1876.

PAMPHLETS

Abbott's Practice Report. "The People Against Tweed." New Ser., Vol. XIII New York, 1872.

"Address of the Liquor Dealers and Brewers of the Metropolitan Police District to the People of the State of New York." New York, 1868.

Assembly of the State of New York. "Report of the Select Committee Appointed by the Assembly of 1875 to Investigate the Causes of the Increase of Crime in the City of New York." New York, 1876.

"The Attempt of the Anti-Tammany Democrats (so-called) to Disfranchise Three-fourths of the Democratic Voters in the Cities of New York and Brooklyn, and Other Democratic Cities in this State, Exposed and Denounced." New York, 1877.

Blauvelt, H. K. "Charges against the Commissioners of the Metropolitan Police." Albany, 1863.

Budlong, Pharaoh. "President Greeley, President Hoffman, and the Resurrection of the Ring. A History of the Next Four Years." New York, 1872.

Butler, William Allen. "Our Great Metropolis: Its Growth, Misgovernment and Needs." New York, 1880.

Calkins, Hiram, and De Witt Van Buren. "Biographical Sketches of John T. Hoffman and Allen C. Beach." New York, 1868.

"The Chronicles of Gotham." New York, 1871.

Citizens' Association. "Address of the Citizens' Association of New York to the Public: History of Its Work—The Department of Docks—The Department of Health—The Fire Department." New York, 1871.

———. "Address to the People of the City of New York by the Citizens' Association of New York." May 6, 1870.

———. "An Appeal by the Citizens' Association of New York against the Abuses in the Local Government, to the Legislature of the State of New York, and to the Public." New York, 1866.

———. "City Finances, Items of Expenditure for Stationery, Printing, etc." New York, 1864.

———. "The Constitutional Convention. The Metropolitan Commissions; Letter from the Citizens' Association." New York, 1867.

———. "How the Money Goes. Letter from the Citizens' Association to Richard O'Gorman Relative to His Office." New York, Nov. 12, 1867.

———. "Important Reform Measures Passed by the Legislature of 1866."

———. "Items of Abuse in the Government of the City of New York: Tax-Payers, Citizens, Read! Read! Read!" New York, 1866.

———. "Memorial of the Citizens' Association of New York, and Petition of Taxpayers in favor of the New Charter for that City as Passed by the Assembly." New York, 1870.

———. "Report of the Citizens' Association of New York under the Condition, etc., of the Institutions under the Charge of the Commissioners of Public Charities and Correction." New York, 1868.

———. "Report of the Executive Council to the Honorary Council of the Citizens' Association." New York, Nov. 17, 1866.

———. "Wholesale Corruption! Sale of Situations in Fourth Ward Schools (subtitle, Report of the Commission Appointed by the Board of Education)." New York, 1864.

The Citizens' Committee. "Appeal to the People of the State of New York Adopted by the Executive Committee of Citizens and Taxpayers for the Financial Reform of the City and County of New York." New York, 1871.

"Civil Rights: A History of the New York Riot of 1871." New York, 1871.

Clark, C.C.P. "The Commonwealth Reconstructed." Oswego, N.Y., 1872.

Clinton, Henry. "Argument of Henry L. Clinton against the So-Called Omnibus Bill, Relating to the City of New York, before Governor Lucius Robinson." New York, May 15, 1877.

———. "Letters of Henry L. Clinton." New York, 1878.

———. "Tammany Ring Exposed and Denounced." New York, 1872.

"The Committee of Seventy-five." New York, 1872.

Conkling, Roscoe. "National and State Politics of 1871 Reviewed." Speech of Conkling, Tweedle Hall, Albany, Oct. 11, 1871.

Crapsey, Edward. "Why Thieves Prosper." Reprinted from the *Galaxy*, VIII (New York, 1869), pp. 519-27.

De Voe, Thomas F. "Report upon the Present Condition of the Public Markets of the City and County of New York." New York, 1873.

Dinsmore, Samuel P. "Suggestions Touching the Municipal Government." New York, 1860.

Disbecker, Abraham. "Answer of Abraham Disbecker to the 'Personal' Communication of the Mayor and the Charges and Specifications against the Board of Police." New York, Oct. 14, 1875.

Eaton, Dorman B. "The Great City Problem. The Evil and the Remedy of New York City Government." New York, 1871.

———. "The Report of the Committee on Municipal Reform, especially in the City of New York." New York, 1867.

Evarts, William M. "Address of the Association of the Bar of the City of New York, on an Elective Judiciary." New York, Oct. 24, 1872.

Gover, William C. "The Tammany Hall Democracy." New York, 1875.

Graham, John. "Summing up of John Graham to the Jury, on the part of the defense, on the Trial of William M. Tweed, in the Court of Oyer and Terminer of the County of New York." Jan. 30, 1873.

Green, Andrew H. "A Three Years' Struggle with Municipal Misrule." New York, Feb. 18, 1875.

———. "A Year's Record of a Reformer as Comptroller of New York City, being a brief review of the Financial Administration of Hon. Andrew H. Green." New York, 1872.

"The Growth of New York." New York, 1865.

Hartwell, Rev. Joseph. "Romanism and Politics. Tammany Hall and the Stronghold of Rome." New York, 1887.

Hawkins, Dexter A. "New York City Council of Political Reform. Five Reports." New York, 1873.

Hawkins, Rush C. "Statements of Rush C. Hawkins, Late a Member of the Legislature of the State of New York, from the Eleventh Assembly District of New York City." New York, 1872.

"History of a Moral Journalist." New York, 1870.

"The House that Tweed Built." New York, 1871.

"Judge Davis and Six Gentlemen of the New York Bar, by a Member of the Profession." New York, 1874.

Kempner, Otto. "Boss Croker's Career. A Review of the Pugilistic and Political Activity of Bill Tweed's Pupil and Successor (with an appendix comparing the Croker Ring with the Tweed Ring and Urging a Union of all Factions against Tammany Hall)." New York, 1894.

Kilroe, Edwin P., Abraham Kaplan, and Joseph Johnson. "The Story of Tammany." New York, 1924.

Lawrence, A. R. "The Government of Cities. Remarks of A. R. Lawrence, Jr., of New York in the New York Constitutional Convention, January 28, 1868, upon the Report of the Committee on Cities." New York, 1868.

Lieber, Francis. "Reflections on the Changes which may seem Necessary in the Present Constitution of the State of New York." New York, 1867.

Matsell, George W. "Answer and Protest of George W. Matsell to Charges Made against the Commissioners of Police by the Mayor." New York, 1875.

The New York City Council of Political Reform. "Official Document on Extravagance of the Tammany Ring." New York, 1871.

———. "Report of the New York City Council of Political Reform for the Years 1872, '73, and '74." New York, 1875.

———. "Statement and Plea of the New York City Council of Political Reform." New York, 1870.

New York Daily Tribune. "An Anti-Tammany Candidate for a County Office." Reprinted from the *Tribune* issue of April 16, 1875.

"New York Governed," *The New York Quarterly*, IV (April 1855), No. 1, pp. 1-20.

New York Herald. "The Political Situation, Resulting from the Late State Election." Interview with Peter B. Sweeny. Nov. 1869.

New York State. "From Henry W. Genet to the Senate of the State of New York, in Relation to the Report of the Committee Appointed to Investigate the Alleged Frauds in the Building of the Ninth District Court House in the City of New York." State of New York, Senate Document No. 88, May 29, 1873.

New York Times. "How New York Is Governed. Frauds of the Tammany Democrats." 1871.

Noyes, George F. "Argument in Favor of the Metropolitan Board of Public Works, before Senate and Assembly Committees." Albany, 1867.

O'Conor, Charles. "The Court of Appeals and Its Relation to the Methods by which Public Peculations Have Evaded Justice." New York, 1876.

Olin, Stephen H. "Argument upon the Charter of the Committee of Seventy." New York, 1872.

Olmsted, Frederick Law. "The Spoils of the Park." New York, 1882.

Post, Eugene J. "The Wig and the Jimmy: or, A Leaf in the Political History of New York." New York, 1869.

"The Record of John K. Hackett, as Recorder, Founded upon Official Documents." New York, 1875.

Roosevelt, R. B. "Political Corruption in New York." New York, Sept. 4, 1871.

St. John and Coffin. "The Downfall of Tammany Hall, No Fall at All, Not by A. Oakey Hall." New York, 1871.

Smith, Stephen. "The City That Was." New York, 1911.

"Speech of T. N. Carr, in Support of Charges against Francis I. A. Boole, City Inspector, before His Excellency Horatio Seymour." New York, June 3, 1864.

Tammany Society, or Columbian Order. "Celebration of the Ninety-fourth Anniversary of American Independence, at Tammany Hall, Monday July 4, 1870." New York, 1870.

———. "Celebration at Tammany Hall, on Saturday, July 4, 1863."

———. "Proceedings of the Tammany Society on Laying the Corner-Stone of their New Hall in Fourteenth Street, and Celebrating the Ninety-first Anniversary of the Declaration of American Independence, July 4, 1867." New York, 1867.

Twain, Mark. "Edmund Burke on Croker and Tammany," 1901. An address before the Organization Committee of the Acorns. New York, Oct. 17, 1901.

"Tweedle Hall or, New York City Politics in 1870." New York, 1870.

Twohey, David J. "Address to the Assembly of the State of New York," May 19, 1875.

Union League Club. "Report on Cities." New York, 1867.

———. "The Report of the Committee on Municipal Reform." New York, 1867.

———. "The Street Railroads of the City of New York." New York, Jan. 9, 1873.

"A Vindication of Tammany Hall and Its Policy, as the Regular Democratic Republican Organization in the City and County of New York." New York, 1876.

Welsh, James. "The Root of the Municipal Evil." New York, 1875.

"Why Vote at all in '72?" New York, 1872.

BOOKS

Academy of Political Science in the City of New York. *The Government of the City of New York.* New York, 1915.

Adams, Charles F., Jr., and Henry Adams. *Chapters of Erie and Other Essays.* Boston, 1871.

Albion, R. G. *Rise of New York Port, 1815-1860.* New York, 1939.

Alexander, De Alva Stanwood. *A Political History of the State of New York.* 3 vols. New York, 1909.

Asbury, Herbert. *The Gangs of New York.* New York, 1927.

Atkins, George. *Health, Housing and Poverty in New York City, 1865-1898.* New York, 1947.

Barnes, David. *The Draft Riots in New York.* New York, 1863.

Bigelow, John. *Letters and Literary Memorials of Samuel J. Tilden.* New York, 1908.

———. *The Life of Samuel J. Tilden.* New York, 1895.

———. *The Writings and Speeches of Samuel J. Tilden.* 2 vols. New York, 1885.

Blake, E. Vale. *History of the Tammany Society.* New York, 1901.

Boone, H. H., and Theodore P. Cook. *Life Sketches of the Executive Officers and Members of the Legislature of the State of New York.* New York, 1870.

Bowen, Croswell. *The Elegant Oakey.* New York, 1956.

Brace, Charles Loring. *The Dangerous Classes of New York.* New York, 1872.

Breen, Matthew P. *Thirty Years of New York Politics.* New York, 1899.

Browne, Julius Henri. *The Great Metropolis: a Mirror of New York. A Complete History of Metropolitan Life and Society, with Sketches of Prominent Places, Persons and Things in the City as they Actually Exist.* New York, 1869.

Bryce, James, *The American Commonwealth.* New York, 1895 ed.

Butler, J. Richard, and Joseph Driscoll. *Dock Walloper, The Story of "Big Dick" Butler.* New York, 1933.

Caldwell, L. K. *The Government and Administration of New York.* New York, 1954.

Carman, J. H. *The Street Surface Railway Franchises of New York City.* New York, 1919.

Chadbourne, Paul A., and Walter Burritt Moore. *The Public Service of the State of New York.* 3 vols. Boston, 1882.

Choate, Joseph H. *American Addresses.* New York, 1911.

Clinton, H. L. *Celebrated Trials.* New York, 1897.

Coleman, Charles H. *The Election of 1868: The Democratic Effort to Regain Control.* New York, 1933.

Costello, Augustine E. *Our Firemen: A History of the New York Fire Department*. New York, 1885.

———. *Our Police Protectors: History of the New York Police from the Earliest Period to the Present Time*. New York, 1885.

Daly, Robert. *The World Beneath the City*. New York, 1959.

Davenport, John Isaacs. *The Election and Naturalization Frauds in New York City, 1860-1870*. 2nd ed. New York, 1894.

Depew, Chauncey. *My Memories of Eighty Years*. New York, 1922.

Dictionary of American Biography. Vol. VIII.

Ellis, David M., James A. Frost, Harold C. Syrett, Harry J. Carman. *A Short History of New York State*. New York, 1957.

Encyclopaedia of the Social Sciences. 1951 edition.

Ernst, Robert. *Immigrant Life in New York City*. New York, 1949.

Fairfield, Francis Gerry. *The Clubs of New York*. New York, 1873.

Flick, Alexander C. (ed.). *History of the State of New York*. 10 vols. New York, 1937.

Flick, Alexander Clarence. *Samuel Jones Tilden*. New York, 1939.

Foord, John. *The Life and Public Services of Andrew Haswell Green*. New York, 1913.

Franklin, Allan, and Thomas Nast (illustrator). *The Trail of the Tiger, being an account of Tammany from 1789; The Organization and Sway of the Bosses*. New York, 1928.

Garrett, Charles. *The La Guardia Years, Machine and Reform Politics in New York City*. New Jersey, 1961.

Genung, Abram Polhemus. *The Frauds of the New York City Government Exposed. Sketches of the Members of the Ring and Their Confederates*. New York, 1871.

Gibson, Florence E. *The Attitudes of the New York Irish Toward State, and National Affairs, 1848-1892*. New York, 1951.

Hale, William Harlan. *Horace Greeley, Voice of the People*. New York, 1950.

Handlin, Oscar. *The Uprooted*. New York, 1952.

Harlow, S. R., and H. H. Boone. *Life Sketches of the State Officers, Senators and Members of the Assembly of the State of New York in 1867*. Albany, 1867.

Haswell, Charles H. *Reminiscences of an Octogenarian of the City of New York*. New York, 1896.

Hertford, Joseph. *Personals; or, Perils of the Period in New York*. New York 1870.

Hirsch, Mark. *William C. Whitney*. New York, 1948.

Hudson, W. C. *Random Recollections of an Old Political Reporter*. New York, 1911.

Ingraham, Abijah. *A Biography of Fernando Wood. A History of the Forgeries, Perjuries and Other Crimes of Our Model Mayor*. New York, 1856.

Jones, Willoughby. *The Life of James Fisk, Jr., Including the Great Frauds of the Tammany Ring*. Chicago, 1872.

Josephson, Matthew. *The Politicos, 1865-1896*. New York, 1938.

Kilroe, Edwin P. *Saint Tammany and the Origin of the Society of Tammany or Columbian Order in the City of New York*. New York, 1913.

King, Moses. *King's Handbook of New York City*. 2nd ed. Boston, 1893.

Kofoed, Jack. *Brandy for Heroes; A Biography of the Honorable John Morrissey*. New York, 1938.

Lening, Gustav. *The Dark Side of New York, and Its Criminal Classes from Fifth Avenue down to the Five Points. A Complete Narrative of the Mysteries of New York*. New York, 1873.

Lynch, Denis Tilden. *Boss Tweed, The Story of a Grim Generation*. New York, 1927.

McElroy, William H., and Alex McBride. *Life Sketches of Executive Officers and Members of the Legislature of the State of New York for 1873*. Albany, 1873.

———. *Life Sketches of Government Officers and Members of the Legislature of the State of New York for 1874*. Albany, 1874.

McGuire, James K. (ed.). *The Democratic Party of the State of New York*. 3 vols. New York, 1905.

Mack, Edward C. *Peter Cooper, Citizen of New York*. New York, 1949.

Mandelbaum, Seymour. *Boss Tweed's New York*. New York, 1965.

Maverick, Augustus. *Henry J. Raymond and the New York Press for Thirty Years*. Hartford, 1870.

Morris, Lloyd. *Incredible New York*. New York, 1951.

Myers, Gustavus. *The History of Tammany Hall*. New York, 1917.

Nast, Thomas. *Miss Columbia's Public School, or Will It Blow Over?* New York, 1871.

Nevins, Allan. *The Emergence of Modern America: 1865-1878*. New York, 1927.

———. *Hamilton Fish*. New York, 1937.

Nevins, Allan, and Thomas Milton Halsey. *The Diary of George Templeton Strong*. 4 vols. New York, 1952.

O'Connor, Richard. *Hell's Kitchen*. New York, 1958.

O'Conor, Charles. *Peculation Triumphant*. New York, 1875.

Olmsted, Frederick Law. *Spoils of the Park*. New York, 1882.

Paine, Albert Bigelow. *Thomas Nast: His Period and His Pictures*. New York, 1904.

Patton, Clifford W. *The Battle for Municipal Reform: Mobilization and Attack, 1875-1900*. New York, 1940.

Pleasants, Samuel Augustus. *Fernando Wood of New York*. New York, 1948.

Reynolds, James Bronson (ed.). *Civic Bibliography for Greater New York*. New York, 1911.

Riordon, William L. *Plunkitt of Tammany Hall*. New York, 1948.

Richmond, Rev. J. F. *New York and Its Institutions, 1609-1873*. New York, 1873.

Robbins, Louis S. *The Royal Decrees of Scanderoon*. "To the Sachems of Tammany, and to the Other Grand Magnorums of Manhattan." New York, 1869.

Roosevelt, Robert B. (ed.). *The Poetical Works of Charles G. Halpine*. New York, 1869.

Rovere, Richard. *Howe and Hummel*. New York, 1947.

Scisco, Louis Dow. *Political Nativism in New York State*. New York, 1901.

Shapley, Rufus E. *Solid for Mulhooly: A Sketch of Municipal Politics under the Leaders, the Ring, and the Boss*. New York, 1881.

Shaw, Frederick. *The History of the New York City Legislature*. New York, 1957.

Smith, Matthew Gale. *Sunshine and Shadow in New York*. New York, 1869.

The Spider and the Fly, or Tricks, Traps, and Pitfalls of City Life, by One Who Knows. New York, 1873.

Stoddard, Theodore Lothrop. *Master of Manhattan, the Life of Richard Croker*. New York, 1931.

Stone, William L. *History of New York City*. New York, 1872.

Sullivan, James. *History of the State of New York*. 6 vols. New York, 1927.

Talmage, T. De Witt. *The Masque Torn Off*. Chicago, 1879.

Tammany Society. *Celebration at Tammany Hall of the Ninety-Fourth Anniversary of the Declaration of American Independence by the Tammany Society, July 4, 1870*. New York, 1870.

Tilden, Samuel J. *The New York City "Ring," Its Origin, Maturity and Fall*. New York, 1873.

Townsend, J. D. *New York in Bondage*. New York, 1901.

Van Deusen, Glyndon. *Horace Greeley, Nineteenth-Century Crusader*. New York, 1953.

Van Pelt, Daniel. *Leslie's History of the Greater New York*. 4 vols. New York, 1898.

Walling, George Washington. *Recollections of a New York Chief of Police*. New York, 1887.

Werner, M. R. *Tammany Hall.* New York, 1928.

Wheeler, Everett P. *Sixty Years of American Life.* New York, 1917.

White, Bourck. *The Book of Daniel Drew.* New York, 1910.

Wilson, James Grant. *The Memorial History of the City of New York.* 4 vols. New York, 1893.

Zink, Harold. *City Bosses in the United States: A Study of Twenty Municipal Bosses.* Durham, N.C., 1930.

NEWSPAPERS

New York City:

Commercial Advertiser
Daily Morning News
Evening Post
Herald
Independent
Mail and Express
Star
Sun
Telegram
Times
Tribune
World

Albany:

Argus
Atlas
Evening Journal
Times

INDEX